Christian Menkens

Web-Telecom Converged Application Delivery

Christian Menkens

Web-Telecom Converged Application Delivery

From Service Delivery to a SOA-based Middleware for Web-Telecom Converged Applications in the Telecommunication Industry

Südwestdeutscher Verlag für Hochschulschriften

Impressum / Imprint
Bibliografische Information der Deutschen Nationalbibliothek: Die Deutsche Nationalbibliothek verzeichnet diese Publikation in der Deutschen Nationalbibliografie; detaillierte bibliografische Daten sind im Internet über http://dnb.d-nb.de abrufbar.
Alle in diesem Buch genannten Marken und Produktnamen unterliegen warenzeichen-, marken- oder patentrechtlichem Schutz bzw. sind Warenzeichen oder eingetragene Warenzeichen der jeweiligen Inhaber. Die Wiedergabe von Marken, Produktnamen, Gebrauchsnamen, Handelsnamen, Warenbezeichnungen u.s.w. in diesem Werk berechtigt auch ohne besondere Kennzeichnung nicht zu der Annahme, dass solche Namen im Sinne der Warenzeichen- und Markenschutzgesetzgebung als frei zu betrachten wären und daher von jedermann benutzt werden dürften.

Bibliographic information published by the Deutsche Nationalbibliothek: The Deutsche Nationalbibliothek lists this publication in the Deutsche Nationalbibliografie; detailed bibliographic data are available in the Internet at http://dnb.d-nb.de.
Any brand names and product names mentioned in this book are subject to trademark, brand or patent protection and are trademarks or registered trademarks of their respective holders. The use of brand names, product names, common names, trade names, product descriptions etc. even without a particular marking in this works is in no way to be construed to mean that such names may be regarded as unrestricted in respect of trademark and brand protection legislation and could thus be used by anyone.

Coverbild / Cover image: www.ingimage.com

Verlag / Publisher:
Südwestdeutscher Verlag für Hochschulschriften
ist ein Imprint der / is a trademark of
AV Akademikerverlag GmbH & Co. KG
Heinrich-Böcking-Str. 6-8, 66121 Saarbrücken, Deutschland / Germany
Email: info@svh-verlag.de

Herstellung: siehe letzte Seite /
Printed at: see last page
ISBN: 978-3-8381-3600-4

Zugl. / Approved by: München, TU, Diss., 2012

Copyright © 2012 AV Akademikerverlag GmbH & Co. KG
Alle Rechte vorbehalten. / All rights reserved. Saarbrücken 2012

Abstract

The Web/Internet's tremendous success at providing multimedia-communication services and applications puts the traditional fixed and mobile Telecommunications industry at a crossroads. Since most innovation in this area has come from Application Service Providers (ASP) on the Web/Internet, Communication Service Providers (CSP) have been pushed into being a mere "Bit Pipe" for the Web/Internet's innovative and successful services and applications.

The Telecommunications industry has started to acknowledge the disadvantages of this transformation. To regain flexibility and competitiveness, Telecommunication standardization bodies have started to shift their focus towards adopting Web/Internet, Service Oriented Architecture (SOA) and Service Delivery Platform (SDP) technologies and concepts. That shift has led to a compatibility of Web/Internet and Telecommunication systems, which has enabled the concept of Web-Telecom Convergence. This allows developers to implement future innovative services and applications by combining Telecommunication services, provided by CSPs, with Web/Internet services, provided by ASPs.

The goal of the research work is to define and evaluate the concept and reference architecture of a Web-Telecom Convergence Application Delivery Platform (ADP) that supports developers at the development and delivery of Web-Telecom Converged applications. The work identifies CSPs, ASPs, Device/Platform Manufacturers, Developers and End-Users as the most relevant stakeholders, and illustrates their major Web-Telecom Convergence related goals. It compares and analyzes common Telecommunication SDP proposals and Web-Telecom Convergence concepts, and identifies that most of them are heavily Telecommunication and limited Web/Internet focused. It identifies that all of them cover certain limited aspects of Web-Telecom Converged applications, but none covers their whole spectrum end-to-end, ranging from the underlying access networks over the Web/Internet and Telecommunication services to the clients on the end-users' devices.

The work defines a generic architecture for a distributed Web-Telecom Converged application that covers this whole spectrum end-to-end and fosters a clear separation of a collection of reusable and a collection of application-specific services. Based on that, it applies SOA concepts to extend existing Telecommunication SDP proposals and Web-Telecom Convergence concepts to define the logical reference architecture of the ADP. The ADP enables an end-to-end development and delivery of such distributed Web-Telecom Converged applications by supporting the import and management of reusable Web/Internet and Telecommunication services, the convergence of those services in separated application-specific services and the delivery of the applications via cross-platform compatible end-user clients.

The work evaluates the defined ADP concept and reference architecture through the design of an exemplary technical architecture, the development of two platform prototype iterations and the implementation of two Web-Telecom Convergence case-study application prototypes on top.

Acknowledgments

I conducted this research work as a research assistant at the Chair for Software and Systems Engineering as well as a management team member at the Center for Digital Technology and Management (CDTM) at the Technische Universität München (TUM). The underlying CDTM project Telecom Service Enabler Architecture (TeSEA) was supported by Deutsche Telekom Laboratories.

As part of the CDTM management team, I experienced how many great things a small and dedicated group of highly motivated people can achieve. It was a tremendous pleasure to work with everyone at the CDTM and TUM, and therefore, my special thanks go out to my wonderful colleagues Rebecca Ermecke, Fabian Dany, Andreas Schmid, Isabel Dörfler, Philip Mayrhofer, Bernhard Kirchmair, Benedikt Römer, Julian Sussmann, Marie-Luise Lorenz, Nikolaus Konrad, Uta Weber, Mark Bilandzic, Patrick Nepper, Florian Gall, Maximilian Engelken, Kilian Moser and Claudius Jablonka for their support and feedback, especially in the tough final months when writing my thesis.

I would like to thank my thesis advisors Prof. Dr. Dr. h.c. Manfred Broy and Prof. Dr. Jörg Eberspächer, who always engaged me in fruitful discussions and who provided invaluable feedback for guiding me towards my research goals.

Apart from my colleagues and advisors, my students Michael Würtinger, Irina Todoran, Alexander Friedl, Tianyi Li and Chi Cuong Le have provided invaluable contributions to the success of the TeSEA project, and I would like to thank them for that.

My friends in Austria and Germany have always supported and encouraged me throughout the highs and lows of my research project work. I thank you all for that.

I would like to especially thank my partner, Angela Schöllig, for her tireless encouragement and strength over the four years of research work and long-distance relationship between Munich and Zurich.

To conclude, I would like to thank my parents Hannelore and Manfred Menkens for their continuous support throughout the many years of my education, studies and research, for their wisdom and for their generosity. To them I owe it all.

Contents

Abstract   iii

Acknowledgments   v

Acronyms   xiii

1   **Introduction**   1
    1.1   Problems and Motivation 3
        1.1.1   Competition by Web/Internet Application Service Providers 3
        1.1.2   Web-Telecom Service and Application Convergence 5
        1.1.3   Third Party Developer Platforms 6
        1.1.4   Developer Communities 7
        1.1.5   Application Stores 7
        1.1.6   Cross-Platform Compatible Applications 9
        1.1.7   Towards Proprietary Monopolies for Communication Services 9
        1.1.8   Conclusion 10
    1.2   Contributions 10
    1.3   Methodology and Approach 11
        1.3.1   Design Science 11
        1.3.2   Research Approach 13
    1.4   Structure of Thesis 15

2   **Terminology, Definitions and Concepts**   17
    2.1   Distinction between Service and Application 17
    2.2   Service Oriented Architectures 18
        2.2.1   SOA Manifesto 20
        2.2.2   Web Service 20
        2.2.3   SOA Triangular Model 20
        2.2.4   Service Lifecycle 21

		2.2.5	Service Layers	23
	2.3	Enterprise Service Bus		25
	2.4	SOA Reference Architecture		28
	2.5	Service Delivery Platform		29
	2.6	Device Centric vs. Service Delivery Platform Centric		31
	2.7	Application Lifecycle		32
	2.8	Convergence		33
		2.8.1	Fixed-Mobile Convergence	33
		2.8.2	Media-Telecom Convergence	36
		2.8.3	Web-Telecom Convergence	36

3 Web-Telecom Convergence Stakeholder Goals   **39**

   3.1   Communication Service Providers 40
   3.2   Application Service Providers 43
   3.3   Device and Platform Manufacturers 45
   3.4   Developers 49
   3.5   End-Users 57
   3.6   Technology Providers, Content Providers, Advertisers 62

4 Analysis   **63**

   4.1   The Evolution of Telecommunication Service and Application Development 63
       4.1.1   Intelligent Networks 64
       4.1.2   Customized Applications for Mobile Enhanced Logic 65
       4.1.3   Telecommunication Information Networking Architecture 66
       4.1.4   Open Application Programming Interface 66
            4.1.4.1   Parlay 66
            4.1.4.2   Java API for Intelligent Networks 67
            4.1.4.3   Conclusion 68
       4.1.5   Adoption of Web/Internet Servlet Development Concepts 69
       4.1.6   Web Service-Based Concepts 69
       4.1.7   Telecommunication Service Orchestration 70
   4.2   Evaluation of Web-Telecom Convergence Concepts and Platforms 71
       4.2.1   Comparing Established Web-Telecom Convergence Platform Concepts . . . 71
            4.2.1.1   Comparison Methodology 71
            4.2.1.2   Defining Comparison Methodology Parameters 73
            4.2.1.3   Comparison of Web-Telecom Convergence Platform Proposals . . 76
       4.2.2   Discussing Web-Telecom Convergence Research Results 77

Contents vii

		4.2.3	Evaluation Conclusions	78
	4.3	Evaluation of Mobile Application Development Technologies		79
		4.3.1	Mobile Platforms	80
		4.3.2	Mobile Development Frameworks	83

5 Design of Web-Telecom Converged Applications   87

	5.1	Web-Telecom Convergence Application Scenarios		87
		5.1.1	Unified Address Book	87
		5.1.2	Social Notification Application	88
		5.1.3	Postal Service Notification	89
		5.1.4	Dynamic Voice Mail Message	89
		5.1.5	Automated Telephone Conference	90
		5.1.6	Click-to-Call Supplement to Business Software	90
	5.2	Logical Reference Architecture of a Web-Telecom Converged Application		90
	5.3	Technical Architecture of a Web-Telecom Converged Application		92

6 Requirements for a Web-Telecom Convergence Platform   95

	6.1	Deriving Requirements from Stakeholder Goals	95
	6.2	Deriving Requirements from Analysis and Applications Design	101

7 Design of the Application Delivery Platform   103

	7.1	Core Concepts of the Application Delivery Platform			103
		7.1.1	C1 - Extending the Concepts of Service Delivery Platform to an Application Delivery Platform		103
		7.1.2	C2 - Separation of Networks and Applications		105
		7.1.3	C3 - Layered Architecture		107
			7.1.3.1	C3.1 - Web-Telecom Convergence on Lowest Platform Layer	107
			7.1.3.2	C3.2 - Separation of Shared and Application Services Layers	108
			7.1.3.3	C3.3 - The Introduction of the ISO/OSI Application Layer in Telecommunications	109
			7.1.3.4	C3.4 - Quality of Service (QoS), Authentication, Authorization, Accounting (AAA), SCIM and PEEM Layers	110
		7.1.4	C4 - Layered Telecommunication Standardization		112
		7.1.5	C5 - Scopes and Types of ADP Services		113
		7.1.6	C6 - SOA Concepts-based Application Delivery Platform		115
		7.1.7	C7 - Inside-Out through Telecommunication Service Exposure		118
		7.1.8	C8 - Outside-In through Semi-Automatic Service Import		119
		7.1.9	C9 - Internet of Services through a Collaboration of Platforms across Domains		120

        7.1.10   C10 - Application Distribution 120
        7.1.11   C11 - Services and Applications Monitoring 121
    7.2 Logical Reference Architecture of the Application Delivery Platform 122
        7.2.1   Network Layer 123
        7.2.2   Telecommunication Services Layer 123
        7.2.3   Web/Internet Services Layer 123
        7.2.4   Shared Services Layer 123
        7.2.5   Application Services Layer 125
        7.2.6   Client Proxy Layer 127
        7.2.7   Thin Client Layer 127
    7.3 Technical Architecture of the Application Delivery Platform 127
        7.3.1   Device Platforms and APIs Layer 129
        7.3.2   Network Layer 129
        7.3.3   Telecommunication Services Layer 129
        7.3.4   Web/Internet Services Layer 130
        7.3.5   Shared Services Layer 130
        7.3.6   Application Services Layer 131
        7.3.7   Client Proxy Layer 132

8 Validation and Evaluation of the Application Delivery Platform Concept   133
    8.1 Requirements Assessment 133
    8.2 Proof of Concept Prototypes 135
        8.2.1   First Iteration Application Delivery Platform Prototype 136
        8.2.2   Unified Address Book Application Prototype 137
        8.2.3   Second Iteration Application Delivery Platform Prototype 138
            8.2.3.1   Semi-Automatic Service Import 139
            8.2.3.2   Application Delivery Platform 141
        8.2.4   Social Notification Application Prototype 142
            8.2.4.1   Motivation and Goals 142
            8.2.4.2   Component Architecture 143
    8.3 Core Concepts Assessment 144

9 Conclusion and Future Work   147

Appendix   149

A Web-Telecom Convergence Concepts and Platforms Evaluation Details   149

A.1	Business Requirements	149
A.2	Architectural Services	150
A.3	Quality Subfactors	152

B Service Description Languages Evaluation — 155

C Mobile Application Development Technologies Evaluation Details — 157

C.1	Mobile Platforms	157
C.2	Cross-Platform Mobile Development Frameworks	158

D Semi-Automatic Service Integration Prototype Template — 161

E SNApp Exemplary Message Sequence of Facebook Support — 163

F Related Technologies, Standards and Specifications — 165

F.1	Internet and Telecommunication Protocols	165
F.2	Multimedia Streaming Protocols	177
F.3	Voice-over-IP (VoIP)	182
F.4	Mobile Web/Internet Access Network Technologies	185
F.5	Mobile IP Core Network Technologies	190
F.6	Open Services Gateway Initiative (OSGi)	210
F.7	Representational State Transfer (REST)	211

List of Figures — 215

List of Tables — 219

Listings — 221

Bibliography — 223

Acronyms

3GPP	Third Generation Partnership Project [217]
A4C	Authentication, Authorization, Accounting, Auditing and Charging
AAA	Authentication, Authorization, Accounting
AADM	Asset-Based Architecture Design Methodology for Rapid Telecom Service Delivery Platform Development
ADP	Application Delivery Platform
AJAX	Asynchronous JavaScript and XML [75]
ALM	Application Lifecycle Management
API	Application Programming Interface
ASP	Web/Internet Application Service Provider
BIS	Business Information System
BPEL	Business Process Execution Language [157]
BSS	Business Support System
CAB	Converged Address Book [169]
CAMEL	Customized Applications for Mobile Enhanced Logic
CAPEX	Capital Expenditure
CEP	Complex Event Processing [131, 137]
CRM	Customer Relationship Management
CSCF	Call Session Control Function
CSP	Communication Service Provider
DoSAM	Domain Specific Software Architecture Comparison Model
DPE	Distributed Processing Environment
DSL	Digital Subscriber Line [100]
EAI	Enterprise Application Integration
EDA	Event Driven Architecture
EDGE	Enhanced Data Rates for GSM Evolution
EPC	Evolved Packet Core [160] [6] [65]
EPS	Evolved Packet System [124]
ERP	Enterprise Resource Planning
ESB	Enterprise Service Bus
ETSI	European Telecommunications Standards Institute
FMC	Fixed Mobile Convergence
GGSN	Gateway GPRS Support Node
GPRS	General Packet Radio Service
GSM	Global System for Mobile Communication
GUI	Graphical User Interface
HLR	Home Location Register
HSDPA	High Speed Downlink Packet Access
HSOPA	High Speed OFDM Packet Access

HSPA	High Speed Packet Access [78] [33]
HSS	Home Subscriber Server
HSUPA	High Speed Uplink Packet Access
HTML	Hypertext Markup Language [240]
HTML5	Hypertext Markup Language Version 5 [247]
HTTP	Hypertext Transfer Protocol [71]
IaaS	Infrastructure-as-a-Service
ICT	Information and Communication Technology
IDE	Integrated Development Environment
IDM	Identity Management
IETF	Internet Engineering Task Force
IMS	IP Multimedia Subsystem [213]
IN	Intelligent Network
INAP	IN Application Protocol
ISDN	Integrated Services Digital Network
ISP	Internet Service Provider
IT	Information Technology
ITU	International Telecommunication Union
JAIN	Java API for Intelligent Networks
JCA	JAIN Coordination and Transaction
JCC	JAIN Call Control
JCP	Java Community Process
JNI	Java Native Interface
JSLEE	JAIN Service Logic Execution Environment
JSON	JavaScript Object Notation
JSR	Java Specification Request
LTE	Long Term Evolution [36] [147] [89] [186]
MDA	Model Driven Architecture
MGCP	Media Gateway Control Protocol
MIMO	Multiple Input Multiple Output
MOM	Message Oriented Middleware
MSC	Mobile Services Switching Center
MVC	Model View Controller [201]
MVNO	Mobile Virtual Network Operator
NDK	Native Development Kit
NFC	Near Field Communication
NGN	Next Generation Network
OEM	Original Equipment Manufacturer
OFDM	Orthogonal Frequency Division Multiplexing
OFDMA	Orthogonal Frequency Division Multiple Access
OIPF	Open IPTV Forum
OMA	Open Mobile Alliance
OMG	Object Management Group
OPEX	Operational Expenditure
OS	Operating System
OSA	Open Service Access
OSAG	Open Service Access Gateway
OSE	OMA Service Environment [163]
OSGi	Open Services Gateway Initiative [177]
OSI	Open Systems Interconnection
OSPE	OMA Service Provider Environment [168]

OSS	Operations Support System
OTT	Over-the-Top
PaaS	Platform-as-a-Service
PBX	Personal Branch Exchange
PDF	Policy Decision Function
PEEM	Policy Evaluation Enforcement and Management [165]
POTS	Plain Old Telephone System
PSTN	Public Switched Telephone Network
QoE	Quality of Experience
QoS	Quality of Service
RAN	Radio Access Network
RCS	Rich Communication Suite
REST	Representational State Transfer [70]
RFC	Request for Comment
RNC	Radio Network Controller
RPC	Remote Procedure Call
RSVP	Resource Reservation Protocol [252]
RTCP	Real Time Control Protocol
RTP	Real Time Transport Protocol
RTSP	Real Time Streaming Protocol
SaaS	Software-as-a-Service [202]
SAE	System Architecture Evolution [160]
SCE	Service Creation Environment
SCIM	Service Capability Interaction Manager [225, 107, 146]
SCP	Service Control Point
SCXML	State Chart XML [146]
SDE	Service Delivery Environment [7]
SDF	Service Delivery Framework [222]
SDK	Software Development Kit
SDL	Service Description Language
SDLC	Software Development Lifecycle
SDP	Service Delivery Platform [168] [163] [7] [222] [158] [132] [2] [148]
SE	Service Environment [163]
SGCP	Simple Gateway Control Protocol
SGSN	Service GPRS Support Node
SIB	Service Independent Building Block
SIP	Session Initiation Protocol
SLA	Service Level Agreement
SLF	Subscriber Location Function
SOA	Service Oriented Architecture [66]
SOAP	Simple Object Access Protocol [241]
SOARA	Service Oriented Architecture Reference Architecture [251]
SPICE	Service Platform for Innovative Communication Environment
SQMM	Software Quality Metrics Methodology
SS7	Signaling System 7
TCP/IP	Transmission Control Protocol / Internet Protocol [228]
TINA	Telecommunications Information Networking Architecture
TISPAN	Telecoms and Internet converged Services and Protocols for Advanced Networks
TMForum	Tele Management Forum
UDP	User Datagram Protocol

UML	Unified Modeling Language
UMTS	Universal Mobile Telecommunication System
URI	Uniform Resource Identification
UTRAN	UMTS Terrestrial Radio Access Network
VOD	Video-on-Demand
VoIP	Voice-over-IP
W3C	World Wide Web Consortium
WAC	Wholesale Applications Community [235]
WADL	Web Application Description Language [180]
WAP	Wireless Access Protocol
WCDMA	Wideband Code Division Multiple Access
WLAN	Wireless Local Area Network
WSCI	Web Service Choreography Interface [243]
WSDL	Web Service Description Language [244]
XCAP	XML Configuration Access Protocol [189]
XDMS	XML Document Management Server
XML	Extensible Markup Language

Chapter 1

Introduction

Over recent decades, modern Information and Communication Technologies (ICTs) have transformed the way in which we live, work and play. Fixed and mobile Telecommunications and the Web/Internet have evolved to an integral component of our society and are steadily advancing technologically to provide an ever increasing number of innovative services and applications.

The currently used business model of Communication Service Provider (CSP) has been optimized from the invention of the telephone in 1876 through the mass adoption of the mobile telephone. This Voice-Driven Circuit-Switched paradigm is based on vertical integration, charging based on time, duration and distance as well as on the intelligence and control being located within the CSPs network. This forms a one-sided market revenue model where the CSPs buy equipment and content from vendors and suppliers, integrate those to Telecommunication services and applications on their fully owned and controlled networks, and bill their customers for the use of these services and applications [148, 50].

With the Web/Internet research and developments starting in the 1950s a data-driven and packet-switched paradigm has emerged. This is characterized by a decoupling of services and applications such as voice, data, video, images from the underlying data transfer networks. It is based on a horizontal integration, flat-rate charges based on data rate or data volume, and the intelligence being located in the terminals connected at the edge of the networks [110, 128].

The Web/Internet becoming accessible to the general public at the beginning of the 1990s forms the start of several transformations in the Telecommunications industry. At first the boundaries were well-defined, CSPs were still offering simple communication services and applications to consumers and more complex communication and connectivity services and applications to businesses. Internet Service Providers (ISPs) were offering data connectivity for simple data driven applications like E-Mail, Web Sites, Text Chat, etc. that were provided by Web/Internet Application Service Providers (ASPs) [123].

The wide availability of high-speed Web/Internet access enabled by xDSL, Fiber and Cable blurred these boundaries and provided a platform for enormous innovation in Web/Internet communication, media and entertainment services and applications such as online chat, instant messaging, web 2.0, social networking, advertising, search, music/video downloads, audio/video streaming, Voice-over-IP, IPTV, and many more. Innovative ASPs applied a two-sided market revenue model where they acquire customers using either cheap or free content and where advertising, for brand owners and merchants, is their primary revenue source. Figure 1.1 illustrates the shift in traffic and revenue from CSPs traditional voice traffic to ASPs services and applications data traffic. It can clearly be seen that through that speed of innovation on the Web/Internet data traffic has been growing rapidly while traffic and revenue from traditional services and applications of CSPs like voice has declined from roughly 80% around the year 2000 to less than 50% today [148, 123].

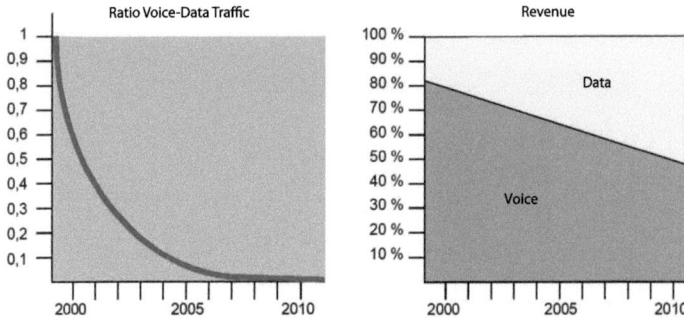

Figure 1.1: Ratio of Voice and Data Traffic and Revenue [38]

Many ASPs such as AOL, Yahoo, Google, Microsoft, Skype, Facebook etc. have played major roles in the growth and spread of innovative Web/Internet communication, media and entertainment services and applications. As a reaction to the growth of data traffic and the prospects of business opportunities in this area, most CSPs expanded their service offerings to data traffic/volume revenue models on their networks. Nevertheless, most CSPs were too slow to innovate new services and applications around new business models within their Telecommunication networks and/or on the Web/Internet. Hence, in most cases, CSPs have not been the source of service and application innovation but have only provided the data transfer network ("bit pipe") for these new over-the-top services and applications of ASPs. [193, 86, 23].

In parallel to the developments in the Fixed Telecommunication and the Web/Internet industry, in the Mobile Telecommunication industry a large penetration of mobile devices, in particular smart phones, and the development of mobile broadband have been important factors for the increasing emergence of innovative mobile applications and services [99, 50, 206].

Already at the end of 2008 close to half of the world's population had a mobile phone and about 54% of the CSPs revenues came from mobile services and applications. The smart phone penetration is with approximately 8% still low, which means that these devices and the mobile services and applications they can access are still a niche, but they expand fast. The advanced capabilities of smart phones bring many of the already established and successful Web/Internet services and applications of ASPs as well as new and innovative services and applications to mobile devices. Through 3G (High Speed Packet Access [78] [33] (HSPA)), 4G (Long Term Evolution [36] [147] [89] [186] (LTE)) and 5G (IMT Advanced) technologies as well as the handover to Wi-Fi and WiMax networks, as can be seen in figure 1.2, the available bandwidth in mobile networks for these mobile applications is increasing as fast as on fixed networks.

As in the Fixed Telecommunication industry, also in Mobile Telecommunication industry, CSPs have not been the drivers of innovation. On the contrary, they have been focusing on providing traditional Telecommunication services such as voice, video and messaging as well as the data transfer network for the mobile services and applications offered by ASPs [153].

1.1. Problems and Motivation

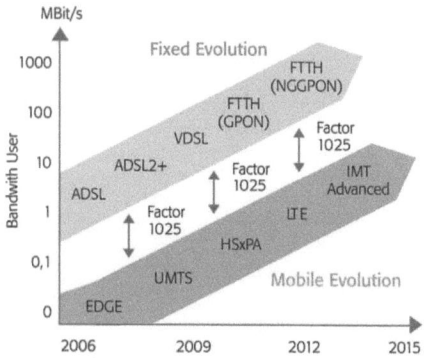

Figure 1.2: Fixed and Mobile Bandwidth Evolution [150]

In contrast to ASPs on the Web/Internet and CSPs on their Fixed and Mobile Telecommunication networks, mobile phone, especially smart phone, Original Equipment Manufacturers (OEMs) invented a device-centric revenue business model. This is characterized by building a large community of mobile service and application developers around a smart phone software platform, implementing a revenue share model with those developers and, through OEM owned platform-specific application stores, realizing a direct distribution and sales channel for these new services and applications from the developers over the store right to the smart phones [148, 153].

1.1 Problems and Motivation

This section discusses the increasing competition between CSPs and ASPs at end-user multimedia communication services and applications. It outlines the CSPs plans to succeed in this competition through the increase of services and applications innovation. It discusses their ideas of deploying Web-Telecom Convergence platforms, launching application stores and building developer communities and highlights their major challenges, which also motivate this research work.

1.1.1 Competition by Web/Internet Application Service Providers

Today, high-speed Web/Internet access with speeds of up to tens or even hundreds of megabits per second are typically available to end-user at home and work. This enables ASPs to deliver high-quality real-time audio/video multimedia services and applications over the Web/Internet per, so called, best-effort meaning without the need to control parameters or features of the underlying data transfer network. By that, the services and applications, and the network, that is mostly provided by CSPs, are completely separated. The former major advantages and business proposition of CSPs, to deliver higher quality Telecommunication services and applications by having full control over the services and applications, the network and its end-to-end connection parameters (e.g. QoS) is rapidly diminishing. Nowadays, end-users often receive a similar QoS and Quality of Experience (QoE) from ASPs multimedia services and applications at a much lower price or even for free [236, 128].

This increasing success of ASPs at providing real-time multimedia services and applications over the Web/Internet poses an increasing threat and competition to the CSPs business models. Figure 1.3 illustrates the projected development of voice traffic in percent of total voice traffic in Europe. The bottom two segments show the CSPs traditional and enhanced voice traffic and the top two segments the ASPs voice traffic over dedicated as well as in other Web/Internet services and applications embedded communication services and applications. It illustrates clearly that ASPs have already taken over a large amount of voice traffic from CSPs and that this trend is continuing and even accelerating. This, combined with large infrastructure investment in fixed (Digital Subscriber Line [100] (DSL), cable and fiber) and mobile (HSPA, LTE) access networks, the fact that voice and data services are increasingly seen as commodity by customers, the strong competition between CSPs and the resulting decline in prices for voice minutes, messaging and data volume puts a heavy burden on CSPs business prospects.

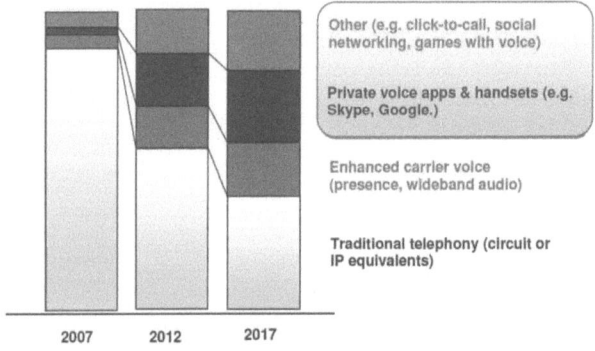

Figure 1.3: Development of Voice Traffic [208]

CSPs realize that, in order to grow revenue and their business, they need to extend their Telecommunication centric service portfolios and business models as well as move up in the value chain. They need to expand towards developing, managing and delivering innovative value-added services and applications across their Telecommunication networks and the Web/Internet all the way to customers. Figure 1.4 illustrates a simplified value chain for Web/Internet services and applications. So far, CSPs were mainly active in the segments "Network Provisioning and Operation" to provide a high-quality voice, video and data transmission network as well as "Standard Services" providing network controlled voice/video call, SMS/MMS messaging and data transport services [123].

In order to grow business even when traditional Telecommunication services will be low priced commodities, CSPs need to find means to become active in "Services and Applications Enabling" [57, 135, 119] meaning to support developing and delivering innovative services and applications that combine their core Telecommunication assets with assets from the Web/Internet. Hence, they need to become increasingly active in the value chain segments of developer platforms, service and application development as well as service and application distribution to customers.

1.1. Problems and Motivation

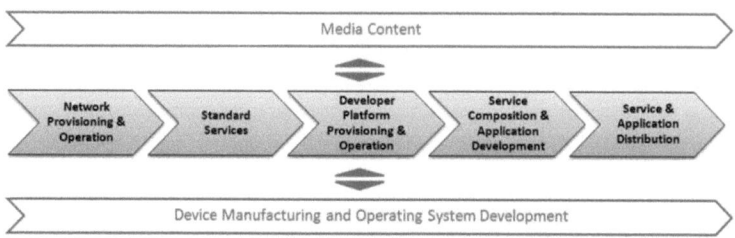

Figure 1.4: Web/Internet Service and Application Value Chain [128]

1.1.2 Web-Telecom Service and Application Convergence

For CSPs, this move towards Web-Telecom Convergence (see section 2.8.3) leads to challenges and major changes in their networks and technologies. It makes many industry standards and specifications as well as currently in the networks deployed service delivery systems and technologies obsolete. New standards and specification are being developed and new Telecommunication architectures and platforms are being deployed. The Telecommunication industry focuses on service oriented infrastructures based on Transmission Control Protocol / Internet Protocol [228] (TCP/IP) (also called "All-IP" [64]), IP Multimedia Subsystem [213] (IMS), Service Oriented Architecture [66] (SOA) using for example ParlayX [214] and Service Delivery Platform [168] [163] [7] [222] [158] [132] [2] [148] (SDP).

Telecommunication industry research and specification efforts are focused on Enablers [170], Telecommunication Service Environments and SDPs around new Telecommunication core infrastructures such as System Architecture Evolution [160] (SAE), Evolved Packet System [124] (EPS) and Evolved Packet Core [160] [6] [65] (EPC) for high bandwidth mobile technologies like LTE. The most widely used and referenced specifications in this area are the Open Mobile Alliance (OMA) Service Environment [163] (SE) and OMA Service Provider Environment [168] (OSPE). These specifications define some first basics about how Telecommunication functionalities and features can be encapsulated into services and exposed to Telecommunication external developers.

Nevertheless, these research concepts and specifications stop at the exposure of basic Telecommunication services. They do not provide any SDP centric concepts for composing Telecommunication services with Web/Internet services on a Web-Telecom Service and Application Convergence platform deployed distributed or centralizes in the CSPs networks. Service exposure specifications such as ParlayX [214] focus only on Business Information System (BIS) technologies for service exposure such as Simple Object Access Protocol [241] (SOAP) and are incompatible with today's common Web/Internet technologies such as Hypertext Transfer Protocol [71] (HTTP), Hypertext Markup Language [240] (HTML), Asynchronous JavaScript and XML [75] (AJAX), Representational State Transfer [70] (REST).

Current Telecommunication core network specifications such as SAE, EPS and EPC still mix specifications for Telecommunication services such as voice, video and messaging with specifications for the underlying data network. There is no decoupling of the services and applications and the network, which would be very important to enable faster service and application innovation while keeping the slower and standardization-based Telecommunication network innovation and update cycles.

1.1.3 Third Party Developer Platforms

Telecommunication industry specifications and standards related to client devices like computers, (IP)TVs and mobile devices such as OMA Mobile Application Environment [173], OMA Client Provisioning [167], OMA Device Management [162], OMA Software Component Management [166], OMA Software and Application Control Management [172] or OMA Browsing [174] are limited to provisioning, configuration and in parts delivery of applications or components to client devices. They do not include any solutions or concepts for application development support or application lifecycle management [11]. To support developers and CSPs at Web-Telecom Converged service and application development, management and distribution it is necessary to focus on the whole Open Systems Interconnection (OSI) Application Layer [97]. This spans from basic Web/Internet and Telecommunication services deployed and running on SDPs to managing third party developer applications running on end-user devices and platforms.

Telecommunication industry specifications and standards related to Telecommunication services and applications do not discuss or specify any concepts or solutions for how developers could be supported at integrating exposed Telecommunication services into their innovative new Web-Telecom Converged services and applications. Hence, CSPs cannot provide any standardized tools, environments or support that would help developers to overcome the barriers of integrating exposed Telecommunication services into their applications. Popular mobile application development platforms such as Apple iPhoneOS [14], Google Android [79], Symbian [220], MeeGo [219] and Windows Phone 7 [143] do not support Telecommunication industry specifications such as IMS and/or Session Initiation Protocol (SIP) by default. Mobile application developers need to use external libraries such as PJSIP [181] or MJSIP [145] to develop applications that use services from the Telecommunication industry.

Since Telecommunication standards and mobile application development platforms do not provide any solutions, the mobile application development industry and so, most new and innovative mobile applications are oriented at Web/Internet instead of Telecommunication technologies, standards, specifications and protocols. Based on these, mobile application developers and ASPs develop over-the-top applications that use the Telecommunication networks only as bit pipes for data transmission. This leads to a re-implementation and re-invention of existing Telecommunication services based on Web/Internet technologies. This is problematic since existing Telecommunication services have typically a higher-level of quality and reliability [184] than the Web/Internet technologies-based re-implementations. Hence, ideally, in innovative Web-Telecom Converged applications, the high-quality services should be reused from CSPs and re-implementations should be avoided. Mostly, these re-implemented and re-invented services are proprietary/incompatible solutions (e.g. Voice Call over Skype [21]) that limit the possibilities developers have for new applications and so prevent the forthcoming of innovative Web-Telecom Converged Applications.

CSPs need to shift the developers' orientation towards their Telecommunication services and applications they are going to offer on SDPs. This can be done by adopting wide spread Web/Internet technologies, standards and protocols and by promoting them in the mobile applications development industry. Therefore, some CSPs such as British Telecom [50, 42], Orange [72, 49] and Deutsche Telekom [56, 60] have already been developing own proprietary developer platform solutions for exposing some of their Telecommunication functionalities to Web/Internet developers. These solutions are incompatible due to differing architecture concepts and technologies and do not constitute SDPs for the development and deployment of innovative Web-Telecom Converged services. Unfortunately, these platforms foster the convergence of Web/Internet and Telecommunication services to be distributed and encapsulated within each single application running on a client device instead of central and shared on an SDP. This leads to applications that are hard to maintain and for example need to be updated on all client devices when any of the Telecommunication or Web/Internet services that are being converged in the applications

1.1. Problems and Motivation

change or are updated. Innovation through Web-Telecom Convergence only happens within the application on the client device and so, Web-Telecom Converged services cannot easily be leveraged, reused and built upon by a community of third party developers. This leads to slower service and application innovation and, since developers need to redevelop Web-Telecom Converged services for every application, to fewer features and capabilities within new Web-Telecom Converged applications.

1.1.4 Developer Communities

ASPs have seen third party integration as a chance rather than a threat much earlier than CSPs. They have established developer platforms around their successful services and applications and have leveraged their large existing user base to attract many developers and build large communities.

Developer communities of ASPs built around Web/Internet technologies oriented platforms are successful. Communities such as Apple's with around 28.000 developers developed around 134.000 mobile applications for the iPhone [77] and Google's with around 100.000 developers [55] develop thousands of applications on the Web/Internet (Google Apps Marketplace [80]) as well as mobile applications for the Android platform [231, 128].

As mentioned in the previous section, CSPs started their own proprietary developer platforms around their exposed Telecommunication services. These platforms have active communities that are smaller, less successful and some of them like British Telecom's Web21C [153, 29, 42] were even stopped already. Orange's Orange Partner [72, 49] community has around 600 developers registered and Deutsche Telekom's Developer Garden [56, 60] reports 1500 registered developers. Ribbit, a platform including a developer community that was bought by British Telecom after Web21C has around 21.000 developers that use the platform's services in their applications. Vodafone's Betavine [234, 239] is with around 20.000 developers and 7.000 applications the biggest and most successful CSP developer community [128].

Due to their mostly geographical focus on one or a couple of countries they operate Telecommunication networks in, it is challenging for CSPs to build large scale or worldwide developer communities. The only options to succeed are to cooperate with the large Web/Internet technologies oriented communities of ASPs or to build a worldwide alliance of CSPs and build a community in cooperation. The latter is what the 2010 initiated and currently growing Wholesale Applications Community [235] (WAC) represents. WAC has been assembled by 24 globally active and large CSPs such as AT&T, Vodafone, Deutsche Telekom, Docomo, China Mobile, Orange, Telefonica. So far it is not clear if this initiative can really draw developers' orientation more towards Web-Telecom Convergence and application development and distribution in cooperation with CSPs [231, 114, 23].

1.1.5 Application Stores

With first versions of stores in Danger OS or online through Handango and GetJar, the worldwide application stores market was very immature and experimental through most of the 90s and beginning of the 2000s [114, 232]. Nevertheless, it matured quickly by the launch of Apple's App Store [13] in 2007. By growing over thirteen thousand Apps per month the App Store has now exceeded 200.000 applications and remains the undisputed leader of this market [231].

The Google Android Market [22] was started in 2008 and has, with over 25.000 Apps and 1.7 million downloads per day, quickly been rising to the second most successful market. Since Android OS and the Android Market are supported by several leading smart phone vendors such as Motorola, HTC, Samsung, they are growing faster than the Apple App store and so, have the biggest potential to compete with Apple. Unlike Apple, Google allows for multiple application stores to exist for Android. Independent stores such as AndSpot, SlideMe and AndAppStore attract developers and users with better search and recommendation features [114, 23].

Far behind the two leaders, Nokia OVI Store is followed by Blackberry App World, Samsung, LG App Stores, Windows Marketplace for Mobile, Sony Ericsson PlayNow and Palm App Catalog offering a few thousand applications each.

For CSPs this quick development of this market puts an additional burden on their business expectations. They were to slow in developing own business in this market and now, are not the ones that control the ecosystem and benefit from the unique differentiation and the brand loyalty an application store generates. Most applications distributed through application stores are over-the-top applications such as re-implementations of Telecommunication services that use the CSPs networks only as bit pipe. In the future, this makes it even harder for CSPs to fully monetize their hundreds of millions of investments in 3G and 4G mobile broadband technologies and networks [231, 148].

After Apple's and Google's success, several CSPs have picked up the opportunity to offer own application stores and Vodafone, Orange, China Mobile, Telefonica and several others have already launched their stores. Figure 1.5 shows an overview about the time line of some of the store openings. Generally CSPs would have the resources necessary to drive a successful application store business and the experience in working with application developers but the successful application store providers will be those capable of creating attractive business models for third party developers and providing them with marketing, sales and payment solutions [114, 23, 148].

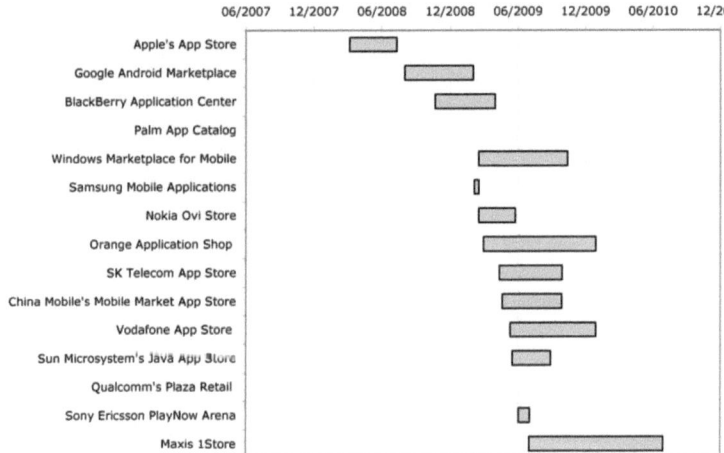

Figure 1.5: Launch Dates of Application Stores [148]

After CSPs own application stores have not been too successful so far, as mentioned in the previous section, 24 major CSPs founded the WAC initiative in 2010 to reduce the fragmentation of CSPs application stores and simplify application development and distribution. Besides building an active developer community WAC is also supposed to provide a centralized white label application store solution that all partners can launch under their brands in their Telecommunication networks. For application developers WAC will provide means to deploy their applications centrally once and to monetize applications sold through all associated partner application stores.

1.1.6 Cross-Platform Compatible Applications

The success of OEM owned application stores and the OEMs control of the whole ecosystems allows them to promote their devices, software platforms and preferred development technologies. This generates a proprietary and closed technology platform for applications on their devices [91, 232].

Mobile application developers want to offer their innovative applications to an, as broad as possible, base of end-users, independent of what client devices or software platforms they are using. Since the OEMs' platforms are incompatible and applications cannot easily be moved from one to another, they need to focus and learn every single platform's technology and development tools to port their applications. This requires a large amount of time and investments for every single application. It increases the time-to-market of applications and slows down application innovation drastically [48, 47, 84].

CSPs want to offer their customers an, as broad as possible, selection of client devices and platforms that those can use on their Telecommunication networks. They do not want to be drawn into the rising competition of smart phone OEMs, their application stores and software platforms but want to offer their customers the most innovative devices with access to the most innovative applications. CSPs want to offer their customers applications that they can use across all devices, platforms and screens such as IPTV, smart phone, PC, laptop, tablet they own. The incompatibility of the different OEMs' platforms, their application stores and their device centric concepts do not allow that. Hence, CSPs favored SDP centric concepts that would allow the development of cross-platform compatible Web-Telecom Converged applications.

As mentioned earlier, in 2010 24 major CSPs initiated the WAC. One of its goals is to encourage open standardized technologies and to provide commercial models complimentary to the ones of the OEMs. It should allow developers to deploy applications across multiple devices and multiple network operators without the need to negotiate with each of them [114, 23, 47]. WAC does not promote an SDP centric development concept and focuses heavily on the client centric mobile application development based on technologies adopted from Web/Internet development. Nevertheless, CSP might be able to combine it with their future SDP centric concepts to build an environment for cross-platform compatible Web-Telecom Convergence for services and applications.

1.1.7 Towards Proprietary Monopolies for Communication Services

Over the last decades, it took a lot of effort to turn the Telecommunication monopolies worldwide into an open Telecommunications market that allows competition and innovation. Nevertheless, even when exploiting their monopolies, CSPs have always seen the need of worldwide compatibility of their technologies and systems. Even though it has slowed down innovation and time-to-market, standardization of technologies and systems that enable modern fixed and mobile Telecommunication services has always been a priority. Due to that, today, end-users can use a single mobile device or computer to connect to communication and mobile Web/Internet services of almost all CSPs worldwide.

Since the Web/Internet has been separated from the Telecommunication networks technologically and conceptually over the last decades, at Web/Internet ASPs a different, mostly market and users driven, mindset has developed. As mentioned in the previous sections, they built some innovative (communication) applications and services and re-invented existing Telecommunication services based on their own proprietary technologies and protocols on the Internet. This has resulted in a collection of incompatible applications and services that implement similar services and that compete for end-users worldwide. Success is often measured by the number of users that are registered or that are using a service regularly. In addition, business models are often based on advertisement targeted at those users and so, ASPs running these services are not interested in collaborating with others since they need to lock their users to their service in order to generate revenue. Typical examples of such proprietary and incompatible services on the Web/Internet and mobile Web/Internet are Skype, Google Talk, Facebook, Google+, StudiVZ, ICQ, MSN, Xing, LinkedIn, WhatsApp.

ASPs providing such services and applications are aiming to build new types of monopolies they fully control. Even worse than CSPs in the past, by technology and business model design, they are not planning to build cooperations, define worldwide standards together or enable compatibility between each other. Further, they do not plan to open their systems so others can use them as "defacto standards" on the Web/Internet for innovative applications and services. Their goals are to compete on the Web/Internet services and applications market and succeed by maximizing the market-share/user-base of their fully closed and controlled service or application.

Through that, ASPs build even stronger monopolies than CSPs ever did and end-users are locked into these services and applications much tighter than into the CSPs worldwide compatible mobile and fixed Telecommunication networks. For end-users, this development has been very disadvantageous, but since it conflicts with their business and success strategies, ASPs don't seem to care too much about their users' needs in this respect. For example, for end-users, this development induces very high switching costs and made moving from one service to another almost impossible. The end-user would not only have to move his/her account to the new service, but would also need to convince all his/her communication partners to move their accounts, or to create new accounts as well.

1.1.8 Conclusion

Once, means to solve most of these major problems for CSPs are found, these current transformations in the Telecommunication industry and on the Web/Internet combined with the rise of these powerful programmable platforms for computers, (IP)TVs [98] and mobile devices such as Linux [218], iOS [14], Android [79], Symbian [220], MeeGo [219], Windows Phone 7 [143] provide the opportunities to form an environment for application developers and innovative visionaries that has never been available before. Such an environment can lead to unprecedented possibilities for the development of innovative distributed, ubiquitous and mobile services/applications across Telecommunication networks and the Web/Internet and can put the CSPs in a central position of the technology as well as business opportunities around them.

1.2 Contributions

The goal of this research is to bring Telecommunication service development closer together with Web/Internet and mobile application development. It applies the Web-Telecom Convergence concept to conceptualize and design an Application Delivery Platform (ADP) that extends current Telecommunication ADP concepts and solutions with SOA and Web/Internet services and technology concepts.

The work is based on a specification of common and new terminology, definitions and concepts, and on a thorough analysis of the current challenges of stakeholders in the Telecommunications industry, of SDP and Web-Telecom Convergence concepts and platforms, of Telecommunication service and application development concepts and technologies, and of mobile application development concepts and technologies.

It develops the design of a logical and exemplary technical architecture of a generic Web-Telecom Converged application. It derives requirements and develops the design of core concepts, a reference architecture and an exemplary technical architecture of the ADP. Thereby, this work focuses on the development of Telecommunication network and application separation concepts, the design of a SOA-based layered ADP reference architecture and the development of a semi-automatic outside-in service import concept. For supplementary components of the ADP it identifies, summarizes and integrates existing proposals and solutions.

The work evaluates the ADP by assessing the requirements and core concepts, and implementing and deploying two iterations of ADP prototypes combined with the development of two exemplary case-study prototypes on top of the platform prototypes.

1.3 Methodology and Approach

This section provides a theoretical summary of the Design Science/Design Research methodology and illustrates how its central aspects were applied in the approach to conceptualize and prototype a Web-Telecom Convergence Application Delivery Platform.

1.3.1 Design Science

Within Design Science/ Design Research, "knowledge and understanding of a problem domain and its solution are achieved in the building and application of the designed artifact" [87, p. 77]. So the goal of the Design Science paradigm is the development of useful solutions based on information technology. Within Design Research these solutions should be examined through the building and the evaluation of artifacts using models, methods or systems [238, p. 281]. "Design, [...], is concerned with how things ought to be, with devising artifacts to attain goals" [200, p. 114].

Behavioral science and Design Science complement one another. Behavioral science tries to predict why an artifact works and Design Science's aim is to determine how well an artifact works. Therefore Hevner et al. state that the goal of behavioral science is truth and the goal of Design Science is utility [87, p. 80]. However there is an exchange between the two disciplines as it is important to understand why an artifact does solve a certain problem in order to be able to design new artifacts that tackle the problem even more effectively. And vice versa, the Design Science can have an impact on the behavioral science as "utility informs theory" [87, p. 80] as well.

Design Research can be seen as a process and as an artifact, and product respectively, at the same time. During the design process the researcher builds an innovative product, i.e. the artifact. Afterwards the designed artifact will be evaluated. This evaluation "provides feedback information and a better understanding of the problem in order to improve both the quality of the product and the design process" [87, p. 78]. Similarly Collins et al. refer to Design Research as an "approach of progressive refinement" [46, p. 18]. A first version of a design is put into the world. The researcher then sees how the design works and constantly revises it based on evaluation and experience. Thus the focus on progressive refinements enables the researcher to build more robust designs over time.

According to Hevner et al. there are seven guidelines that enable the researchers to conduct Design Research in an effective way [87, pp. 82].

- The Design Science researcher has to build a viable artifact. This could either be a construct, a model, a method or an instantiation.

- The research effort should tackle important and relevant problems by developing technology-based solutions.

- In the evaluation phase, the researcher has to demonstrate the utility, quality, and efficacy of the designed artifact using well executed evaluation methods. The goal of this phase is to provide feedback to the design and construction phase and thus to facilitate a higher quality of the design process and the artifact.

- Hevner et al. identify three areas of potential contributions of effective Design Research: (i) The artifact itself as it might help other researchers to build good artifacts, (ii) design foundations, i.e. knowledge about how to build good artifacts, and (iii) design methodologies, i.e. knowledge and methods that help to evaluate the artifact.

- The researcher must apply rigorous methods when it comes to building as well as evaluating the designed artifact.

- Design Research is seen as an iterative search process.

- The researcher has to present the results to technology oriented as well as management oriented audiences.

Design Research has several distinct advantages. Within a short period of time the user will have an actual hands-on experience [103, p. 305]. Hence, the researcher will have no difficulties explaining a theoretical application or a specification. The user will not have to be able to explicitly articulate his or her needs but will experience a real-world artifact instead. The Design Research approach generates immediate feedback and so has the potential to fail fast and to quickly incorporate improvements on the way to a better artifact [1]. Therefore it is a powerful tool as "it is both imaginative and empirical" [106, p. 39] at the same time.

Nevertheless, Design Research is a very complex and time consuming approach. There might be much iteration, as for example several ones for the building and for the evaluation phase, needed before an appropriate artifact is built. From a researcher's perspective, Design Science is very demanding as theoretical knowledge as well as practical skills are required.

Certainly there are limitations to the application of Design Research. Hence, in some cases Design Science needs to be complemented with other methods such as Action Research, Quantitative Research and Qualitative Research [26]. In various phases of the design process the researcher has to use well-proven methods that ensure the building and construction of good artifacts. Empirical and qualitative methods should be adopted when it comes to phases like problem identification and also the evaluation of an artifact [87, p. 77].

Summing up, the scientific paradigm of Design Research is focused on the development of useful IT solutions following an iterative process of gathering knowledge, building artifacts and evaluating these artifacts. Abowd et al. wrap it up in their claim: "Do not spend too much time predicting the future; aim to invent it" [1].

1.3.2 Research Approach

This research work's approach applies the major Design Science research methodology concepts previously explained. It combines Telecommunication industry and state of the art analysis with an iterative artifacts designing and prototyping cycle that is completed twice with two different case study prototypes. Figure 1.6 illustrates the approach's main steps and their connections.

- **Introductory Research** - In this phase current problems of CSPs, trends and developments in the Telecommunication industry are identified and analyzed. This is achieved through a structured literature review and analysis of industry reports, vendor publications, industry/business studies and Telecommunication projects in cooperation between industry and academia.

- **Analysis** - In this phase the requirements for a Web-Telecom Convergence Platform and Applications are identified and structured. First, Telecommunication industry stakeholders are identified and their technical and business goals in relation to Web-Telecom Convergence are analyzed. Second, research results from EU projects, university research labs and vendors are reviewed in order to analyze existing concepts and solutions for Web-Telecom Convergence and to identify drawbacks and open problems. Third, the mobile application development industry is analyzed and mobile application development technologies, platforms and frameworks are evaluated based on Telecommunication industry stakeholder goals and Web-Telecom Convergence concept compatibility.

- **Requirements** - In this phase, based on the results from Introductory Research and Analysis, requirements for a Web-Telecom Converged Platform and Applications are elaborated, structured and illustrated.

- **Design** - In this phase, the concepts and logical architectures for Web-Telecom Converged Applications as well as a Web-Telecom Convergence Platform are developed. The resulting logical architecture for the platform constitutes a reference architecture for future implementations and based on this architecture an exemplified technical architecture for a Web-Telecom Platform deployment is created.

- **Prototype and Case Studies Implementations** - In this phase, software artifacts of a Web-Telecom Platform prototype as well as of two case study prototype Web-Telecom Converged applications are developed, analyzed and evaluated. First, an initial Web-Telecom Platform prototype based on the major concepts of the technical architecture is deployed. Second, this prototype is used to implement a Web-Telecom Converged Address Book application on top of it. Third, as first iteration, the development process and software artifacts of the Address Book application are evaluated and learnings for improvements are fed back into the Web-Telecom Convergence Platform prototype and from there to its technical architecture. Fourth, all improvements are implemented on the platform prototype and a Web-Telecom Converged Social Network application is implemented on top of it. Finally, as second iteration, the development process and software artifacts of the Social Network application are evaluated and learnings for improvements are fed back to the Web-Telecom Convergence Platform prototype and the technical architecture.

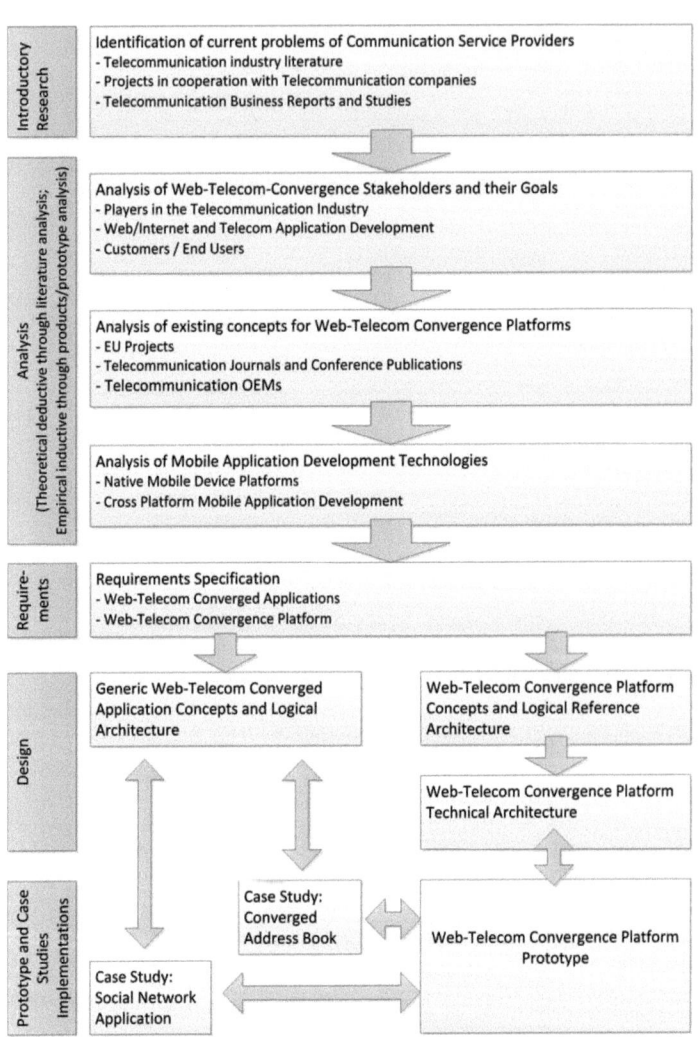

Figure 1.6: Thesis Research Approach

1.4 Structure of Thesis

This section provides an overview about the structure of this thesis document and illustrates, in figure 1.7, how the different chapters build upon each other's results.

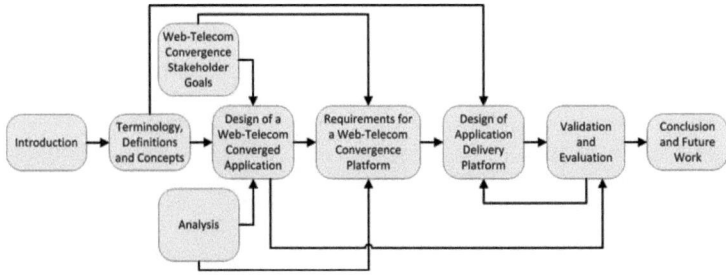

Figure 1.7: Relations between Chapters

Chapter 1 - Introduction motivates this thesis by discussing the major problems the Telecommunication industry faces today, presents an overview about this thesis' contributions and presents this work's Design Science-based research methodology and applied research approach.

Chapter 2 - Terminology, Definitions and Concepts defines important terms and their disjunction for this research work, discusses existing SOA-related concepts that are an essential foundation for this research work's contributions, and illustrates existing as well as introduces new concepts for application architectures, application lifecycles and convergence.

Chapter 3 - Web-Telecom Convergence Stakeholder Goals presents an overview about all stakeholders that are relevant for future Web-Telecom Convergence Applications or a Web-Telecom Convergence Platform. It structures the stakeholders, summarizes their main characteristics and identifies their major Web-Telecom Convergence related goals.

Chapter 4 - Analysis presents an overview about the evolution of Telecommunication services and applications development and evaluates Web-Telecom Convergence concepts and platforms as well as mobile application development technologies.

The overview introduces the evolution from early purely Telecommunication specific service and application development concepts, over software engineering and business information system development inspired concepts, to Web/Internet service and application development-based concepts.

The evaluation of Web-Telecom Convergence concepts compares the most widely referenced and recognized SDP proposals using an architecture comparison methodology composed from three popular methodology proposals. This comparison is a fully self-contained process within the chapter and provides an overview about the level of fulfillment and completeness of major SDP requirements and components. In addition to the SDPs, the evaluation discusses widely referenced and recognized Web-Telecom Convergence research results qualitatively. From both, it draws Web-Telecom Convergence focused evaluation conclusions.

The evaluation of mobile application development technologies identifies the major platform-specific development technologies as well as cross-platform development frameworks. It defines structured evaluation and comparison criteria for both categories and evaluates the technologies and frameworks independently. From there, it draws Web-Telecom Convergence focused evaluation conclusions.

Chapter 5 - Design of a Web-Telecom Converged Application introduces some new and innovative exemplary Web-Telecom Converged application scenarios and defines a new generic Web-Telecom Converged applications architecture. It leverages selected concepts and results from chapters 2, 3 and 4 to define a new logical reference architecture as well as a new exemplary technical architecture for future Web-Telecom Converged applications.

Chapter 6 - Requirements for a Web-Telecom Convergence Platform derives the requirements for a new Web-Telecom Convergence platform that can host and deliver Web-Telecom Converged applications according to chapter 5. It leverages the stakeholders' goals from chapter 3, the state-of-the-art analysis results from chapter 4 and the applications architecture concepts from chapter 5.

Chapter 7 - Design of Application Delivery Platform introduces the new ADP concept and defines a logical reference architecture as well as an exemplary technical architecture for it. It leverages concepts from chapter 2 as well as first iteration prototype results from chapter 8 to fulfill the ADP requirements defined in chapter 6. The chapter presents the core concepts for the ADP design and architecture in detail and applies those to define the logical reference architecture. From there, it discusses implementation, deployment and system components decisions to derive an exemplary technical architecture.

Chapter 8 - Validation and Evaluation assesses the level of fulfillment of the requirements from chapter 6 in the core concept from chapter 7. To validate the ADP concepts from chapter 7, it illustrates two iterations of development and deployment of an ADP prototype. For every iteration, a certain Web-Telecom Converged application scenario is selected from chapter 5, implemented, and deployed on top of the ADP prototype. For the first iteration, a Web-Telecom Converged Unified Address Book scenario is selected. For the second iteration, a Web-Telecom Converged Social Notification Application scenario is selected. Finally, it assesses the level of fulfillment and implementation of the core concepts from chapter 7 in the two iterations of ADP prototypes.

Chapter 9 - Conclusion and Future Work illustrates an overview about the learnings and results from this research work, illustrates areas and ideas for future research projects and discusses how a commercial ADP product could be deployed, managed and operated by a CSP, ASP or independent provider in the future.

Chapter 2

Terminology, Definitions and Concepts

2.1 Distinction between Service and Application

This section provides a distinction between the terms service and application for this research work and compares them to the typical usage of the term service in the Telecommunication industry.

Service

In this work, adapted from [242] [246] [245], a service is defined as "an abstract resource that represents a capability of performing tasks that form a coherent functionality from the point of view of providers entities and requesters entities". It is a software artifact designed to support interoperable machine-to-machine interaction over a network. It has a clearly defined interface described in a machine-processable format and is designed to be reused by other services or applications. Services interact in a manner defined by its interface descriptions using messages over defined protocols and related standards. A service can be deployed and managed by a service lifecycle management system such as an SDP.

Application

In this work, an application is defined as a software artifact designed to support interoperable human-to-machine interaction through an end-user client device or software. It is not designed to be reused by other services or applications but it reuses none to many services. End-users have universal access to an application through their clients and interact with an application through one to many (graphical) user-interfaces on different types of end-user clients and platforms.

Telecommunication Service

As illustrated in [133], [110] and [140], in the Telecommunication industry, a service describes and controls a capability/functionality that is offered by a CSP through the combination of worldwide standardized protocols, hardware/software systems deployed in Telecommunication core networks and service specific user-interfaces on end-user devices or software clients. A Telecommunication service fulfills the special purpose of abstracting from the pure system capabilities and realizing the end-to-end exchange of information in a standardized way. Hence, a Telecommunication service is delivered to and meant to be used by an end-user though its user-interface and is typically not reused by other Telecommunication services. Moreover, it is rather clearly separated from other services in a so called "Service Silo" [83] as depicted in figure 2.1.

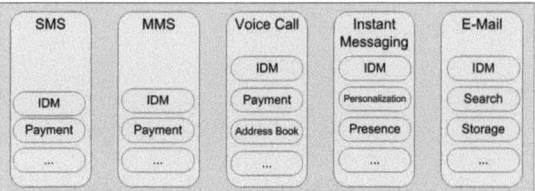

Figure 2.1: Telecommunication Service Silos

Every service implements all common functionalities such as Identity Management (IDM), Payment and Presence completely independent of other services. This ensures that one service does not interfere with other services that are delivered in parallel. Examples for Telecommunication services are voice/video call, call routing in Personal Branch Exchanges (PBXs), voice/video conferencing, SMS and MMS.

As a conclusion, by this research works definition, a Telecommunication service can represent a service if only the deployment at the Telecommunication core network is considered and the provided functionality can be reused by other applications. In the traditional sense, in that a Telecommunication service is used by an end-user through a user-interface on a specific device, a Telecommunication service represents an applications by this works definition.

Mobile Telecommunication Service

Mobile Telecommunication services use mobile Telecommunication hardware/software systems for the standardized end-to-end exchange of information. For a mobile service at least one hop of the data transmission path is supported by a wireless link such as Global System for Mobile Communication (GSM), General Packet Radio Service (GPRS), Enhanced Data Rates for GSM Evolution (EDGE), Universal Mobile Telecommunication System (UMTS), LTE or Wireless Local Area Network (WLAN).

The conclusion in terms of service and application definitions of this research work is similar to the one of traditional Telecommunication services.

2.2 Service Oriented Architectures

The term SOA is not clearly or often slightly differently defined in the literature, in research reports and on the web [66, 154, 205, 178]. The main differences are in the context they apply the term, the level of abstraction from the technical system as well as formulations of definitions. Nevertheless, the common understanding in all definitions is that SOA is a paradigm to increase flexibility of large-scale information systems [67].

In [66] the following common characteristics of contemporary SOA are defined:

- Contemporary SOA is at the core of service-oriented computing platforms.
- Contemporary SOA increases quality of service.
- Contemporary SOA is fundamentally autonomous.
- Contemporary SOA is based on open standards.
- Contemporary SOA supports vendor diversity.

2.2. Service Oriented Architectures

- Contemporary SOA fosters intrinsic interoperability.
- Contemporary SOA promotes discovery.
- Contemporary SOA promotes federation.
- Contemporary SOA promotes architectural composability.
- Contemporary SOA fosters inherent reusability.
- Contemporary SOA emphasizes extensibility.
- Contemporary SOA supports a service-oriented business modeling paradigm.
- Contemporary SOA implements layers of abstraction.
- Contemporary SOA promotes loose coupling throughout the enterprise.
- Contemporary SOA promotes organizational agility.
- Contemporary SOA is a building block.
- Contemporary SOA is an evolution.
- Contemporary SOA is still maturing.
- Contemporary SOA is an achievable ideal.

SOA does not define a concrete software architecture or reference but a set of guiding principles and methodologies that promote the design and development of applications based on interoperable and loosely coupled services [115]. The services implement self-contained and well-defined business functionalities and can be reused for different purposes by other services and applications. The basis for the interoperability of SOA services is their formally defined services interfaces (Contracts) that are independent of the underlying protocols, programming technologies or platforms [68].

In [66] the following widely regarded guiding principles for development, maintenance and usage of SOA, common to all SOA platforms, are defined.

- **Standardized Service Contract** - Services express their purpose and capabilities via a service contract. The contract expresses service functionality, data types and data models as well as specific usage policies.

- **Loose Coupling** - Services maintain a relationship that minimizes dependencies and are only required to keep an awareness of each other. The principle promotes the independent design and evolution of a service's logic and implementation while still guaranteeing baseline interoperability with consumers that have come to rely on the service's capabilities.

- **Service Abstraction** - Derived from the software design principle of information hiding, services are required to hide as many internal details as possible from external entities. Service contracts only contain essential information and information about services is limited to what is published in service contracts. This directly enables and preserves the previously described principle of loose coupling.

- **Service Reusability** - Services contain and express agnostic logic and can be positioned as reusable enterprise resources.

- **Service Autonomy** - The underlying logic of any service needs to have a significant degree of control over its environment and resources in order to ensure its ability to consistently and reliably perform their capabilities.

- **Service Statelessness** - Services minimize resource consumption by deferring the management of state information when necessary.

- **Service Discoverability** - Services are supplemented with communicative meta-data by which they can be effectively discovered and interpreted.

- **Service Composability** - Services are effective composition participants, regardless of the size and complexity of the composition.

2.2.1 SOA Manifesto

The SOA Manifesto [17] is a collection of 6 value statements and 14 principles that were defined by 17 leaders of the SOA industry in 2009 and that has been signed by over 800 supporters from the software industry so far. At that time, when SOA suffered a lack of clarity and direction those specialists combined their efforts to define a common understanding and direction for the whole industry.

The following value statements were defined:

- **Business Value** over Technical Strategy
- **Strategic Goals** over Project Specific Benefits
- **Intrinsic Interoperability** over Custom Integration
- **Shared Services** over Specific Purpose Implementations
- **Flexibility** over Optimization
- **Evolutionary Refinement** over Pursuit of Initial Perfection

2.2.2 Web Service

In this context, a Web Service is a technical concept to realize a SOA. It is a software artifact designed to support interoperable machine-to-machine interaction over a network using standardized communication protocols. It can be implemented in any programming technology but has an interface precisely described in a standardized machine-processable format (specifically Web Service Description Language [244] (WSDL)). Other systems interact with the Web Service in a manner prescribed by its interface description using SOAP-messages, typically conveyed using HTTP with an Extensible Markup Language (XML) serialization in conjunction with other Web-related standards [242, 246, 245].

In contrast, a RESTful Web Service [180] uses the increasingly spreading REST architectural principles instead of WSDL and SOAP. It is designed to focus on a system's resources, including how resource states are addressed and transferred over HTTP by a wide range of clients written in different languages.

2.2.3 SOA Triangular Model

Traditionally, the simple end-to-end Requestor - Provider model [66] illustrated on the top of figure 2.2 was used to define the information exchange for services. In this model, the Provider notifies all connected Requestors about the specifics of the service interface and those use this information to invoke the service.

Through the evolution of SOA concepts this model has evolved to the triangular model [61, 251, 205] illustrated on the bottom of figure 2.2. This model builds the basis for distributed service creation, registration, discovery and composition and defines three roles based on their behavior and responsibilities: Service Provider, Service Registry and Service Requestor.

- **Service Provider** - Hosts the implementations of services, publishes services at a Service Registry and provides the service to Requestors that invoke it.

2.2. Service Oriented Architectures

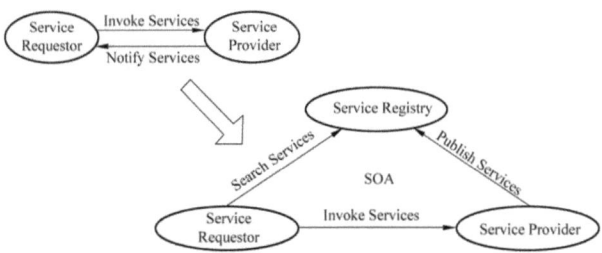

Figure 2.2: SOA Triangular Model [61]

- **Service Registry** - Provides a Publishing Interface where Service Providers can register their services. It registers and organizes published services and provides a Query Interface for Service Requestor that implements search functionalities so they can find services that they are interested in, based on meta-data descriptions. Once the service was found, the Query Interface returns the location information of the corresponding Service Provider.

- **Service Requestor** - Uses the Service Registry to find Service Providers for required services and binds to the Service Provider to invoke the service. For Service Requestors, the SOA triangular model provides a generic way to search, discover and invoke an appropriate service from a repository of published services.

2.2.4 Service Lifecycle

The Service Lifecycle [250] constitutes a concept for the design and development of SOA-based business solutions. It starts when a service is needed and ends when the service is no longer used. As illustrated in figure 2.3 it consists of nine phases: Modeling, Development, Deployment, Publishing, Monitoring/Management, Discovery, Invocation, Composition and Collaboration. These phases may overlap or be performed iteratively.

In the Lifecycle, multiple parties may be involved dynamically in one or more phases and all phases can be mapped to the three roles: Creator, Host/Broker, and Consumer. One party can also take several roles simultaneously or consecutively.

- **Modeling** - In this phase the service is designed using conceptual modeling techniques such as the, to date dominant, Web Services modeling approach of platform-independent WSDL-based top-down decomposition method. A field growing in importance is the modeling of the semantics of a service in order to enable dynamic Web Service invocations. In contrast to a single service, Object Management Group (OMG) Unified Modeling Language (UML)-based Model Driven Architecture (MDA) is a modeling approach that can be used to specify the complexities of whole SOA and Web Services-based business solutions.

- **Development** - In this phase, after the interface of the service has been specified, the implementation of the service can be done using any software development technology (e.g. C/C++, Java, .Net). During the service development a typical software development process for design, development and testing such as Rational Unified Process (RUP) [117], Waterfall [204] or Agile [138] can be applied.

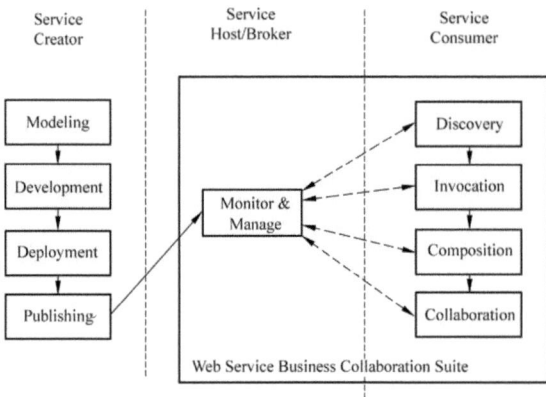

Figure 2.3: Service Lifecycle [251]

- **Deployment** - In this phase, the service is deployed onto a platform/container that hosts, executes and provides the service to consumers. The deployment typically binds the abstract service to certain technologies for communication protocols such as SOAP over HTTP and message formats such as XML.
- **Publishing** - In this phase, the service information for interfacing, binding and using/consuming a service is published onto Web Service registries on the Web/Internet and in Intranets.
- **Monitoring and Management** - When services are invoked by requesters their execution is monitored and controlled. Typical aspects are Access Control, Performance/QoS Monitoring, Service Level Agreement (SLA) Monitoring and Exception Handling. In addition to real-time monitoring also long-term data and information analysis features need to be applied.
- **Discovery** - In this phase, based on the SOA Triangular Model, requesters find their appropriate Web Services dynamically from heterogeneous registries.
- **Invocation** - In this phase, after discovering/searching for an appropriate service, a Service Requestor uses the service interface technology and binding information obtained from the Service Registry to invoke it. Optionally, before an invocation, a SLA can be negotiated dynamically between the Service Requestor and the Service Provider that hosts and executes the service.
- **Composition** - In this phase, based on predefined business requirements, comprehensive business processes are adaptively composed from several available and appropriate Web Services into executable business process flows. Standardized solutions for describing such process flows are Business Process Execution Language [157] (BPEL) and Web Service Choreography Interface [243] (WSCI).
- **Collaboration** - In this phase, multiple services that need to collaborate towards a common goal in a comprehensive business process are managed. Such services are typically

provided and invoked by different Service Providers and so coordination needs to span across a distributed network of services. In such a network, the information exchange and interactions between services needs to be coordinated based on semantic information and requirements of business processes.

2.2.5 Service Layers

An enterprise constitutes an ever-evolving entity that adapts to external and internal influences. An enterprise IT system aims to provide an Enterprise Logic that can be divided into Business Logic and Application Logic where each realizes a part of the organizational structure. [61]

- **Business Logic** - Is a specified and documented realization of an enterprise's business requirements combined from all its business areas. In today's enterprises, a business logic is typically expressed as Business Processes that fulfill all requirements and constraints and cope with dependencies and outside influences.

- **Application Logic** - Is an implementation of the Business Logic structured into several technology solutions mostly spread out through the entire enterprise. Business Process workflows are expressed through purchased or custom-developed software systems within the confines of an enterprise's IT infrastructure, security constraints, technical capabilities and vendor dependencies.

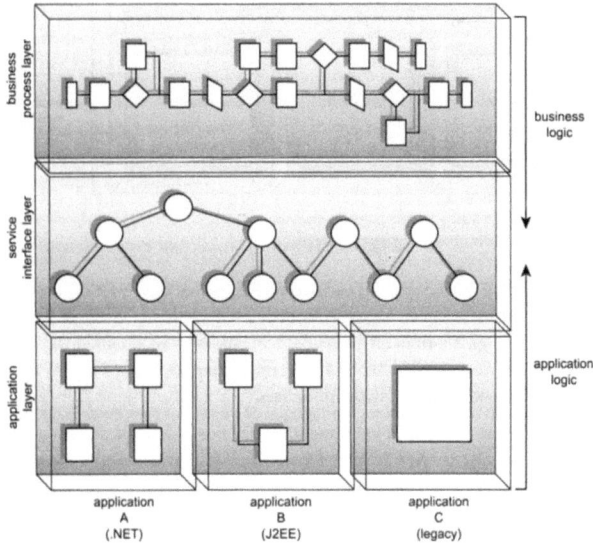

Figure 2.4: Service Interface Layer positioned between Business Process Layer and Application Layer [66]

SOA introduces the concept of services to the Enterprise Logic and changes the way how the logic is represented, viewed, modeled and shared. As figure 2.4 illustrates, services realize an abstraction between traditional Business Process and Application Layers and can encapsulate physical Application Logic as well as Business Process Logic. The Application Layer is fragmented into individual applications that are dependent on their respective proprietary platform they are implemented on. Services are implemented on a single continuous Service Interface Layer that provides open connectivity and communication via open protocols that frees services from proprietary ties and that spans across all application platforms.

Service can be layered so that parent services can encapsulate child services and so that services can be separated to accommodate business, application and orchestration considerations independently. This structures the Service Interface Layer further into the abstraction layers Application Service Layer, Business Service Layer and Orchestration Service Layer as illustrated in figure 2.5.

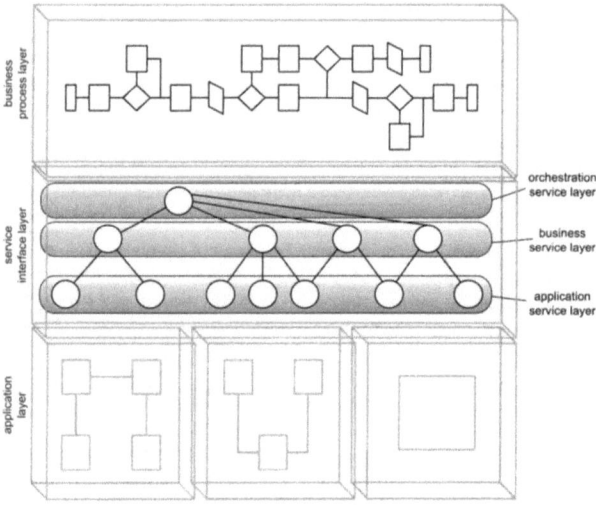

Figure 2.5: The three Service Layers [66]

- **Application Service Layer** - It abstracts logic that is not derived from business models into a collection of Application/Utility Services that provide reusable functionalities that represent common resources and capabilities across the whole enterprise. Services on this layer (also called Utility Service Layer or Infrastructure Service Layer) are defined as generic Application/Utility services providing reusable operations and are implemented SOA-application-independent. They are composed to Business Services to realize business process requirements.

  Special kinds of services that are typically deployed on this layer are Wrapper Services. On the one hand, they are used for legacy integration and encapsulate functionalities of legacy systems, platforms and environments to expose them to Service Requestors. On the other, they are used to bind protocol and technology independent service to protocols such as SOAP or REST to enable them to participate in communication with other services.

- **Business Service Layer** - It provides a collection of services from which each is assigned to a functional context that is derived from one or more existing enterprise business models and specifications. Analyst, architects and IT professionals conduct a detailed Service Oriented Analysis process through which these services are identified and specified. There are two common types of Business Services, Task Centric and Entity Centric that compose Application Services to realize their required business logic for a SOA application.

    – Task Centric Business Service - Encapsulate business logic that is specific to certain tasks or business processes that typically involves several business entities (e.g. invoice, time sheet). Since they are mostly very specialized, they generally have a limited potential of being reused.

    – Entity Centric Business Service - Encapsulate business logic that is responsible for processing data associated with some business entity. These services typically are generalized, business process independent and so, reusable in several SOA applications.

- **Orchestration Service Layer** - Orchestration allows to directly link business process logic with service interaction within a standardized workflow logic (specified in e.g. BPEL) and combines business process modeling with service oriented modeling and design. On this layer, Process Services compose Business and Application Services to execute business process logic and so, free all those services from managing interaction details required to ensure that services are executed in a specific sequence according to the business process specifications.

2.3 Enterprise Service Bus

An Enterprise Service Bus (ESB) [136, 108, 139, 118] is a new approach for an architectural middleware concept that provides a set of infrastructure capabilities for the integration of a heterogeneous environment of platforms, systems and services. It can provide the foundations for a loosely coupled, reusable, reliable, secure, managed, highly distributed and highly interoperable integration system that can scale beyond the limits of previous Enterprise Application Integration (EAI) brokers and solutions.

"An ESB is a standards-based integration platform that combines messaging, web services, data transformation and intelligent routing to reliably connect and coordinate the interaction of significant numbers of diverse applications across extended enterprises with transaction integrity." [43]

An ESB is event driven, so applications and services are defined as abstract service endpoints that can readily respond to asynchronous events. A SOA provides an abstraction from the details of the underlying connectivity and the service implementations do not need to understand the communication protocols or how messages are routed to other services. Services receive a message from the ESB as an event, they process the message and the ESB is responsible to deliver the message to all services that need to receive it.

In an ESB, the network of virtual channels to route messages throughout an extended enterprise and beyond is based on the architectural concept of a Message Oriented Middleware (MOM). In a MOM oriented system messages are exchanged asynchronously and communicating services or applications are abstractly decoupled. Senders and receivers are not aware of each other but send and receive messages to and from the MOM system. This system is fully responsible for routing all messages to their intended destinations. In theory there are two different messaging models for MOM systems, Publish-Subscribe and Point-to-Point. In a Publish-Subscribe model service consumers subscribe to topics they are interested in getting updates about. Producers publish these updates by sending messages on the different channels that are related on these topics and each subscriber receives a copy. In case there are no consumers subscribed for a channel when a message is published, messages that are not specifically flagged as reliable or important can be discarded by the MOM system. In a Point-to-Point model only one consumer may receive a message published by a producer. For load-balancing or hot-backup concept realizations several consumers might be connected to the MOM system as consumers, but only one receives and processes the message. In case there are no consumers connected to the MOM system, the message stays in the system until a consumer connects and consumes the message.

There is no official technical specification for an ESB implementation, but it is commonly accepted that an ESB is usually realized through a service container distributed across a networked environment and that it must at least provide integration, message routing, transformation and management services. Figure 2.6 illustrates a simplified view on an ESB with these core services.

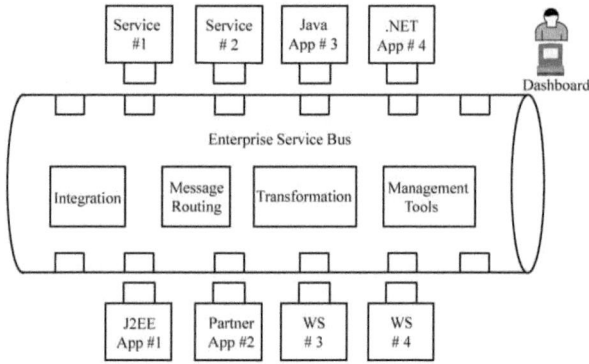

Figure 2.6: Enterprise Service Bus [251]

An ESB provides a common platform that allows different Legacy Services, Applications and Web Services to plug in and communicate with each other. This integration is typically realized through adapters that allow external components developed in any technologies (e.g., Java/J2EE, .Net, Web Service (WS), legacy services) to be easily integrated into the ESB.

The following provides an overview about the commonly accepted core services of an ESB:

- **Integration** - This service provides service orchestration engines to construct both stateful (long-running) and stateless (short-running) processes from connected/plugged-in components.

- **Message Routing** - This service provides means for service components to exchange data based on standardized protocols and manages content-based routing and filtering of messages to/from connected/plugged-in components. It implements a transactional, secured and monitored MOM system.

2.3. Enterprise Service Bus

- **Transformation** - This service transparently mediates between differences in technologies, protocols and formats of messages between connected/plugged-in components. Examples are different XML Schemas for XML-based messages.

- **Management Tools** - This service provides real-time monitoring and management capabilities for system health and availability and includes functionalities to ensure configurable security control and management. It works in conjunction with a Dashboard that aggregated services from multiple sources connected/plugged-in to the ESB and allows developers to create SOA applications rapidly, often supported through a graphical service composition/orchestration user-interface. Using the dashboard, message formats, specific routing policies and necessary message transformation rules can be specified, configured and/or implemented.

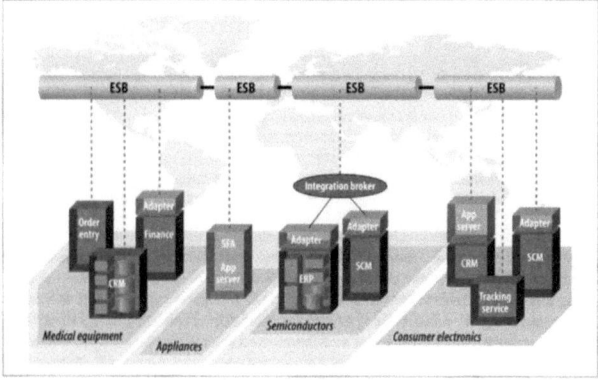

Figure 2.7: Enterprise Application Integration (EAI) across Partner Companies through Enterprise Service Buses (ESBs) [43]

Several software vendors offer commercial ESB platforms and advanced ones offer a number of additional value-added services. Typical ones are services for provisioning, discovering and dynamically integrating services, for dynamically adjusting SLAs based on performance and error events, for controlling service components interactions/invocations and for detecting, distributing and triggering a complex series of interrelated service events though Complex Event Processing [131, 137] (CEP) in an Event Driven Architecture (EDA) [37, 141].

When moving the focus from a single company with one location deploying an ESB to a multi-location company or a network of companies, further advantages of the ESB concept become clear. As illustrated in figure 2.7 departments or companies distributed all over the world are able to connect their independently deployed ESBs in the same transparent, loosely coupled, reusable, reliable, secure, managed, highly distributed and highly interoperable way as a single ESB connects services.

In this example a network of companies from different industry areas are collaborating and built a common ESB that allows them to specify business processes and create SOA-based applications that span across all companies and departments. As further illustrated at the Semiconductors company, also legacy systems can be included using adapters and Integration Brokers.

2.4 SOA Reference Architecture

The, in figure 2.8 illustrated, two dimensional Service Oriented Architecture Reference Architecture [251] (SOARA) for enterprise SOA platform implementation defines five horizontal and four vertical layers. The horizontal layers represent functional requirements and are further divided into the two tiers Service Provider and Service Consumer. The Service Provider encapsulates the back-end of an application while the Service Consumer tier includes everything related to the font-end serving the application users. The vertical layers define system-support facilities and enablement.

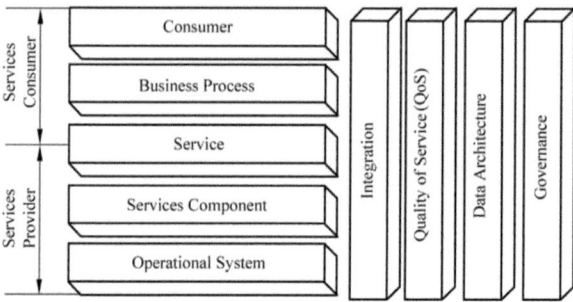

Figure 2.8: SOA Reference Architecture [251]

Horizontal Layers:

- **Operational System** - This layer contains all pre-packaged applications that are provided by Individual Service Vendors (ISVs), customer applications that are developed in-house and legacy system that were developed in a traditional way before a SOA deployment. All these applications and systems have in common that they can only be used for one purpose and serve one specific user. Through the integration into a SOA they can be exposed as services with standard interfaces and so, reused by upper level services.

- **Service Components** - This layer provides code containers that implement service interfaces for services that are defined on the Service layer above. A Service Component may aggregate some packaged components from the Operational System layer, some services from the Service layer as well as some business processes from the Business Process layer. A Service Component can be implemented in any implementation technology, may export selected methods from its interface on the Service layer and is responsible for an automated transformation of input as well as adaptation of output from/for an invocation.

- **Service** - This layer extends the known SOA Triangle Model with the features Service Registration, Decomposition, Discovery, Binding, Interface Aggregation as well as Service Lifecycle Management. It provides the capability to aggregate multiple service interfaces into a new service. It defines the concept of a Service Cluster, which describes a collection of Web Services that are serving a common business function. These services may be provided by different service providers and can be differentiated by their specific features. At business process decomposition, the Service layer is responsible for every service cluster to locate the appropriate service provider and to bind to the target Web Service interface.

- **Business Process** - This layer handles all business logic for services composition and decomposition. For service composition, it leverages the Service layer to compose services and choreograph business processes according to customer requirements. For service decomposition, it provides functionalities to decompose requirements into tasks encapsulating Service Clusters were each can be realized through existing business processes, services and service components. In contrast to workflow description languages such as BPEL, this layer does not focus on business process representation but on building SOA solutions based on business process through coordination and management of a collection of processes.

- **Consumer** - This layer is responsible for the presentation of a Graphical User Interface (GUI) for a SOA solution. It enables the simultaneous support of various types of users and clients (PC, Smart Phone, PDA). It leveraged the lower layers to build a user-interface for services based on customer requirements.

Vertical Layers:

- **Integration** - This layer mediates, routes and transforms service requests and responses between service consumer and service provider. An ESB is a typical conceptual and technical realization of the functionalities of this layer.

- **Quality of Service** - This layer provides SOA platform wide QoS management for aspects such as availability, reliability, security and safety and provides functionalities to support, track, monitor and manage SOA platform wide QoS control.

- **Data Architecture** - This layer provides a unified representation and enablement framework for an integration of domain specific data architectures of services developed by different parties.

- **Governance** - This layer provides analysis, design and implementation guidelines and rules to ensure a proper development of SOA application architectures. Typically, it summarized best practices, rules for application design and architecture, SOA-based development processes, principles of monitoring, rules for exception handling and more.

2.5 Service Delivery Platform

The term SDP has its origin in the Telecommunication industry and defines the combination of Telecommunication systems and Web/Internet technologies to provide CSPs with a middleware system that supports service creation, service exposure/third party access, service orchestration and support for an evolution, mediation or replacement of legacy service layer platforms.

SDPs have grown steadily in importance over the last five years [148] and their technological roots can be traced back to mobile content management/delivery systems, early approaches of replacing proprietary Intelligent Network (IN) platforms with standards-based Java environments and the more recent efforts of opening up services using technologies such as Web Services. In response to the ongoing innovation from the Web/Internet ecosystem CSPs are looking to tap into the innovation that smaller more agile companies can bring. Current SDPs provide an environment in which software developers can efficiently develop new applications by combining the capabilities of existing Telecommunication services (e.g. Voice/Video) and/or service enablers (e.g. Messaging or Presence Enablers) and enable efficient collaboration with content providers and third-party service providers.

In accordance to that, the minimum of functionalities an SDP needs to provide is summarized in the following overview [148]:

- **Service Exposure and Third-Party Access** - The SDP provides the infrastructure to support an ecosystem of developers using CSP service enablers to offer innovative new services and applications. Their aim is to enable developers to create Web 2.0 type services that incorporate the unique service enablers that a CSP can provide. Many large CSPs have projects underway to address this opportunity.

- **Service Creation** - CSPs need efficient platforms to develop innovative new services and applications of their own. Where fine control over the Telecommunication service logic and high performance are required, CSPs can use the sophisticated service creation environments that Telecommunication application servers provide. These servers need a high level of Telecommunication development expertise. Where fine grain control is not required, CSPs can use service orchestration on a service orchestration platform to build and execute the required work flows.

- **Content Management and Delivery** - CSPs have deployed a number of SDPs dedicated to specific types of content. CSP application stores are the area of highest interest at the moment and are strategically important. It is further important to rationalize existing mobile content management and delivery systems to support a broader range of content types and reduce operational costs.

- **Evolution, Mediation or Replacement of Legacy Service Layer Platforms** - The CSP's Telecommunication products are reaching the end of life or have limited support for new services and applications. CSPs want to replace or evolve existing legacy infrastructure to support new services/application and IN platforms are a major target for this. CSPs are investing in Telecommunication application servers as replacements or adjuncts to support TCP/IP-based control layers and to have access to more efficient service and application creation environments.

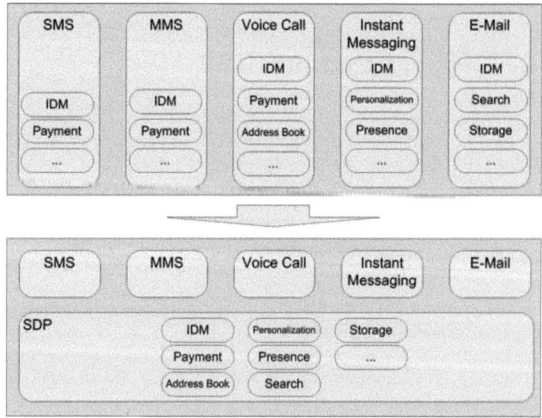

Figure 2.9: Transformation from Telecommunication Service Silos to SDP Services

2.6. Device Centric vs. Service Delivery Platform Centric

As depicted in figure 2.9, an SDP enables CSPs to transform their collections of separated services (Service Silos) into a pool of services that can be reused and combined to innovative end-user applications. SDPs enable CSPs to change their business model by opening up the service infrastructure to third parties and support rapid creation of new types of services and applications. SDPs are an enabler for innovation inside and outside the CSPs service and network infrastructure. [148]

As summarized above, there is a rough common understanding what an SDP represents, but there is no standard definition for the term or the components that constitute an SDP. Nokia and the Moriana Group give a good overview about this common understanding in [156, 113]. The TM Forum, Alcatel-Lucent and OMA published the technical specifications Service Delivery Framework [222] (SDF), the Service Delivery Environment [7] (SDE) and the OSPE, which are central references in the area of SDPs in the Telecommunication industry. Currently, the OSPE is the most widely used specification in SDP, middleware and service broker research and development projects in the Telecommunications domain.

2.6 Device Centric vs. Service Delivery Platform Centric

In the context of software architectures for Web-Telecom Converged applications, this research work defines a device centric architecture as depicted on the bottom of figure 2.10.

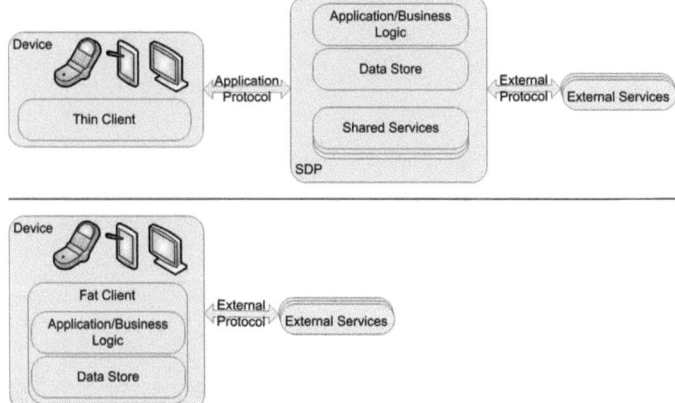

Figure 2.10: Device Centric vs. SDP Centric

An application is implemented as a Fat Client that is specifically tailored to the devices technology and platform and so, not compatible and difficult to port to other devices or platforms. All application-specific business logic, all data storage as well as access to external services such as Web/Internet services or Telecommunication services is implemented within the application on the device. Hence, every single application needs to implement and deal with the specifics of the protocols of the external services.

An SDP centric architecture is defined as depicted on top of figure 2.10. An application is distributed between the device and the SDP. A as device technology and platform independent as possible Thin Client implements the user-interface and is deployed on the device. All application-specific business logic and data storage is implemented on the SDP. Application functionalities that can be generalized and shared with other applications are provided as Shared Services on the SDP and Shared Services from other application can be reused during application development. Access to external services from the Web/Internet or Telecommunication networks is implemented and maintained as Shared Services on the SDP only once for every service.

2.7 Application Lifecycle

It is common to equate Application Lifecycle Management (ALM) with the Software Development Lifecycle (SDLC), but this view is too limiting. ALM includes every action that is performed on a software application during the entire time an organization spends money on it, from the initial idea until it is completely abandoned. Figure 2.11 illustrates this research work's view on ALM [112].

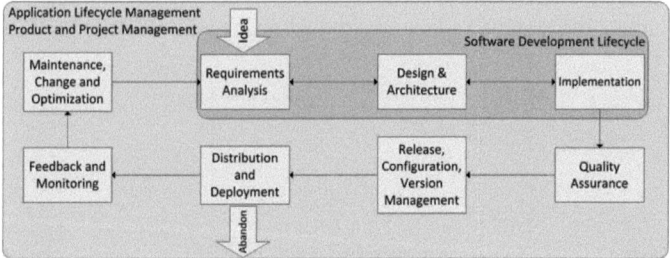

Figure 2.11: Application Lifecycle

As initial step, the idea needs to be developed into a business case by "Product Management". Once this case is approved, "Project Management" defines a project plan and supervises the development of the application, especially the SDLC. The SDLC can use any common, well proven and accepted software development methodology and typically includes "Requirements Analysis", "Design & Architecture" and "Implementation" in various forms. Once the application is developed, it needs to go through predefined "Quality Assurance" approvals and certifications. As next step, "Release, Configuration, Version Management" needs to manage the evolution of the application over time over different releases and versions as well as the combination of optional components and modules that can be used to assemble different configurations. Once application releases and configurations are available, these need to be distributed through online and offline sales channels as well as deployed over the Web/Internet or through on-site consulting and installation at the customers. While the application is utilized at customers, through "Feedback and Monitoring", their valuable end-user feedback needs to be gathered, the application needs to be monitored and its performance needs to be evaluated. Feedback and Monitoring data is used by "Maintenance, Change and Optimization" to define what errors need to be fixed, what new features need to be added and where the application could be optimized. From this, the SDLC is initiated again. In case an organization plans to remove an application from its portfolio, it is typically distributed and deployed one last time and then abandoned [44].

2.8 Convergence

The word convergence is derived from the Latin word "convergere", which means "to incline together". In the Telecommunication industry convergence defines the growing together of Telecommunication, Internet and Media technologies, services and applications. It can be seen as to enable the possibility to seamlessly provide all services on all networks and platforms to the end-users without any restrictions.

This research work distinguishes three types of convergence, (i) convergence of fixed (wireline) and mobile (wireless) networks, (ii) convergence of Telecommunication, media and broadcasting services and (iii) convergence of Web/Internet and Telecommunication services.

2.8.1 Fixed-Mobile Convergence

Since the introduction of digital mobile Telecommunication networks based on the GSM standard in Germany in the 1990s, fixed and mobile Telecommunication networks evolved independently in parallel. Fixed and mobile services were offered by different providers or by strictly separated subsidiaries of one CSP such as Deutsche Telekom. Through convergent devices, applications and technologies, Fixed Mobile Convergence (FMC) enables a ubiquitous and seamless delivery of the same end-user centric Telecommunication services over the fixed as well as the mobile Telecommunication networks. This opens new possibilities for flexible, intuitive and innovative private and enterprise communication services [193].

The evolution of FMC can roughly be structured in the following three stages [153]:

Virtual Convergence In this stage, fixed and mobile networks are virtually connected through simple service forwarding mechanisms such as call forwarding. One example (O2 Genion Product) would be that end-users receive a fixed as well as a mobile phone number for their mobile devices. Based on certain predefined rules such as being in a geographical region, calls to the fixed phone number are forwarded to the mobile device or, if this is disconnected, to the voice mailbox [59].

Functional Convergence In this stage several functionalities of the fixed and the mobile Telecommunication networks are centralized. Call signaling functionalities are combined, so a single phone number for end-users is able to ring at all of their mobile as well as fixed phones. Billing systems are connected, so end-users are able to receive a single bill for both networks. The voice mailbox is centralized, so all messages for fixed and mobile phone numbers are stored at one place and accessible from both networks. Basic information management systems are introduced centrally, so end-users can manage the same address books and even calendars from their fixed and mobile devices [10].

Full Convergence In this stage, fixed and increasingly mobile broadband Web/Internet connections are widespread, Telecommunication service and application alternatives are offered by ASPs through Web/Internet technologies and Telecommunication service revenues are declining. Core network technologies and system of fixed as well as mobile Telecommunication systems are fully converged by migrating them to novel Web/Internet technologies (TCP/IP)-based Telecommunication specifications and standards. This promises a more efficient development and delivery of personalized ubiquitous Telecommunication services. At the same time, through a simplified network structure and reduced bandwidth requirements, it reduces Capital Expenditure (CAPEX) and Operational Expenditure (OPEX) costs. By leveraging Web/Internet technologies, not only fixed and mobile Telecommunication networks are converged, but also non-

Telecommunication TCP/IP-based wireline and wireless access network technologies such as DSL or WLAN can connect to, and access services from the Telecommunication networks.

The driving force to realize Web/Internet technologies-based FMC resides within the Third Generation Partnership Project [217] (3GPP) and IMS (see section F.5.2). IMS was originally designed for mobile networks only, but when the standardization body "Telecoms and Internet converged Services and Protocols for Advanced Networks (TISPAN)" of the European Telecommunications Standards Institute (ETSI) was working on Next Generation Network (NGN) (All-IP Networks) specifications and standards it included IMS in its fixed network architecture. Thereby, IMS provides Web/Internet technologies-based Telecommunication services for both, fixed and mobile Telecommunication networks [110].

Even though fixed and mobile Telecommunication core networks are converged on Web/Internet technologies, as illustrated in figure 2.12, the access network technologies and so, also the end-user devices remain separated from this convergence. For fixed access networks these include Plain Old Telephone System (POTS) and Integrated Services Digital Network (ISDN) and for mobile access networks GSM, GPRS, EDGE and UMTS. As a result, at this point, Telecommunication networks are compatible with Web/Internet technologies at the core networks, but remain Telecommunication specific when delivering services to end-user devices through their access networks.

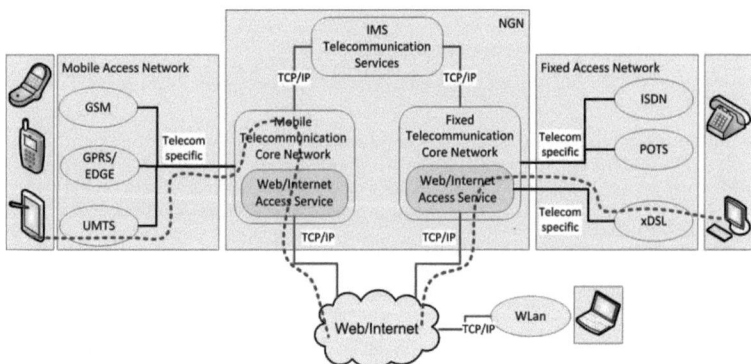

Figure 2.12: NGN Convergence

To still enable Web/Internet access on end-user devices, in mobile networks, "Web/Internet Access Services" are specified and included into the GPRS, EDGE and UMTS standards and deployed in core networks. Those services are strictly separated from and deployed in parallel to the "IMS Telecommunication Services". In figure 2.12, the dotted line on the left illustrates the data path of a mobile device that accesses the Web/Internet via a UMTS access network. The device is connected to the "Mobile Telecommunication Core Network" via Telecommunication specific protocols, in this example via ones from the UMTS standard. The "Mobile Telecommunication Core Network" separates access to Telecommunication services from access to the Web/Internet and so, forwards the Web/Internet data to the "Web/Internet Access Service". This translates from Telecommunication specific to Web/Internet technologies and from there the data is sent out to the Web/Internet.

2.8. Convergence

To enable Web/Internet access in fixed networks, additional Web/Internet access technologies that are able to work in parallel to POTS and ISDN, such as DSL are developed and deployed at end-users. In figure 2.12, the dotted line on the right illustrates the data path of a fixed device that accesses the Web/Internet via a DSL access network. Since DSL does not support Telecommunication services, the device is directly connected to the "Web/Internet Access Service" of the "Fixed Telecommunication Core Network" via a Telecommunication specific protocol from the DSL standard. Via DSL the device is not able to request any "IMS Telecommunication Services". The "Web/Internet Access Service" translates all data from Telecommunication specific to Web/Internet technologies and sends them out to the Web/Internet.

Technologies for convergence are constantly evolving and the latest specifications and standards for fixed and mobile Telecommunication core networks are IMS with SAE and EPC (see section F.5.1). For mobile end-user access technology, LTE (see section F.4.4) and for fixed Telecommunication service delivery, DSL with Voice-over-IP (VoIP) (see section F.3). Together, those realize a completely Web/Internet technologies-based Telecommunication service delivery infrastructure and enable convergence of all Telecommunication services via all networks all the way to the end-user devices. The resulting converged infrastructure and an exemplary application invocation is illustrated simplified in figure 2.13.

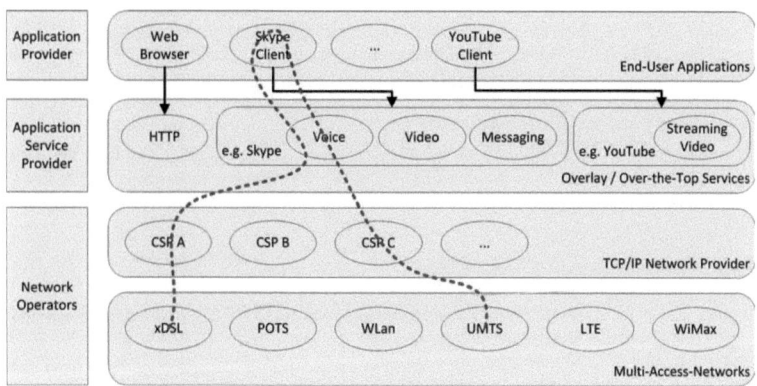

Figure 2.13: Convergence on All-IP (adapted from [226])

On the lowest layer, various access networks provide end-user devices with access to the infrastructure. On top of that, based on a TCP/IP network, CSPs as well as other network providers are connected worldwide. Those provide TCP/IP functionality as well as Telecommunication - Web/Internet technology translation and adaptation to access networks. In the figure, these two layers are strictly separated. In reality, the layers are entangled and many CSPs operate several access networks as well as provide the TCP/IP network at the same time. Above the "Network Operators", ASPs such as Skype or YouTube provide Over-the-Top (OTT) services. To enable the end-users to utilize their services, they provide end-user applications such as clients for various devices or platforms on top of them.

As exemplified by the dotted line, the converged infrastructure allows access network as well as provider independent access to applications. In this example, an end-user device is connected via a DSL connection provided by CSP A. The communication partner's device is connected via UMTS provided by CSP C. Since the example application, Skype, is solely based on TCP/IP, the end-user can use a Skype PC client to access the Skype voice service to call the intended communication partner on a Skype mobile client.

2.8.2 Media-Telecom Convergence

Over the last decade, media distribution specific technologies for terrestrial broadcast, cable and satellite evolved from analog to digital broadcast technologies. In recent years, broadcasters have increasingly adopted Web/Internet technologies to distribute their media. Radio via the Web/Internet has been around for some years now and since bandwidths of Web/Internet connections are growing steadily, existing TV broadcasters as well as CSPs are increasingly offering IPTV solutions to their end-users. For those, IPTV provides innovative features such as video controls (e.g. Pause, Rewind, Forward), Video-on-Demand (VOD) and interactive TV that traditional digital broadcast technologies are not capable of.

In 2008 the standardization body TISPAN of the ETSI published the second release of its NGN specification. It defines the convergence of fixed and mobile Telecommunication networks with IMS [5, 98, 4] and non-IMS [210]-based IPTV networks and technologies into a common service delivery network infrastructure based on Web/Internet technologies.

To enhance the capabilities of the TISPAN IPTV specifications, the Telecommunication industry standardization bodies OMA and Tele Management Forum (TMForum) specified additions such as the OMA Mobile Broadcast Service [171, 221]. Also, Vendors and broadcasters formed alliances and interest groups such as the Open IPTV Forum (OIPF) [159] to foster worldwide IPTV standardization and product commercialization [194].

Due to this intensive and still growing involvement of the various stakeholders from the media broadcasting and Telecommunication industries, in the next few years a growing propagation of the convergence of media services and Telecommunication services will be observable.

2.8.3 Web-Telecom Convergence

For many decades Telecommunication service development was based on proprietary Telecommunication technologies and only specially trained specialists were able to develop new services. The development process was a tedious work and deploying a new service on a Telecommunication network and publishing it to customers was extremely complex and difficult.

With the evolution of FMC (see 2.8.1) Telecommunication networks and services became increasingly Web/Internet technologies compatible. For Telecommunication service development, Web/Internet application development concepts were adopted, development became easier and less complex and large developer communities became available as sources for innovative ideas and developers.

To increase service and application innovation and reduce time-to-market for new services and application, CSPs are adopting Open Innovation [150] [128] [191] and Service Brokering [207] [29] [28] concepts. They are working on opening parts of their core Telecommunication networks to the Web/Internet on developer platforms. These are supposed to allow third party developers (Third Party Enabling [158]) to develop innovative services and applications by composing/reusing Telecommunication services with Web/Internet services. All resulting services and application are supposed to be deployed in the Telecommunication networks and distributed to end-users.

In this research work, this development is defined as "Web-Telecom Service and Application Convergence" and is, for the first time, enabling developers to combine features and capabilities from

2.8. Convergence

Web/Internet [176]-based services and applications, provided by ASPs, with Telecommunication services and applications, provided by CSPs. Thereby, the separated domains of Telecommunication services and Web/Internet services are converging to deliver future ubiquitous multimedia, communication and information services and applications seamlessly across all types of networks and technologies [111, 130, 128].

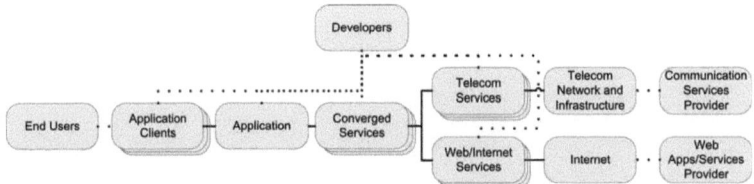

Figure 2.14: Distributed Web-Telecom Converged Services and Application

Figure 2.14 illustrates this general concept of a future Web-Telecom Converged Application that is accessible through different end-user clients. On the far right, CSPs and ASPs are offering their Telecommunication and Web/Internet services through the Telecommunication networks respectively the Internet. Developers are able to compose these services to innovative Web-Telecom Converged services that they can reuse in their applications. Finally, end-users utilize different client software products or client devices to access the applications provided by the developers.

Chapter 3

Web-Telecom Convergence Stakeholder Goals

In the research area of Web-Telecom Convergence, for this research project two layers of stakeholders were identified and are illustrated in figure 3.1. The inner layer defines a pentagon of the most relevant stakeholders Developers, Communication Service Providers, Application Service Providers, Device/Platform Manufacturers and End-Users. The outer layer defines peripheral stakeholders that influence Web-Telecom Convergence but do not have a major impact on the concept of a Web-Telecom Convergence Platform. Advertisers, Content Providers and Technology Providers mostly administrate their influence through one or several of the stakeholder in the inner layer as for example Communication Service Providers buy their hardware and software equipment from Technology Providers.

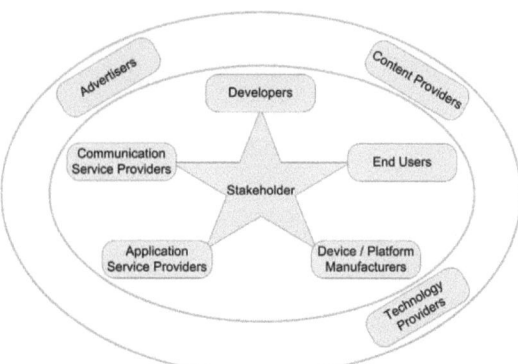

Figure 3.1: Web-Telecom Convergence Stakeholder

Based on an analysis of [148, 59, 128, 152, 63, 62, 83, 35, 153, 156, 125, 116, 81, 60, 231, 48, 84, 192, 82, 229, 47, 126, 144, 90, 58], this section presents some of the main characteristics of these stakeholder and illustrates their most important business and technical goals related to Web-Telecom Converged application development and delivery.

3.1 Communication Service Providers

A CSP provides Telecommunication services over fixed or mobile Telecommunication networks to end-users. Traditionally, these services were provided over a dedicated Telecommunication infrastructure in a circuit-switched manner. Over the last few years the Telecommunication industry has been transformed to increasingly use shared infrastructure and networks such as the Web/Internet using packet-switched technologies.

CSPs can be further structured by their different business models and levels of infrastructure deployment. Traditional fixed and mobile CSPs like Deutsche Telekom, Vodafone, O2, E-Plus own licensed frequency allocations of radio spectrum and deploy their own infrastructure such as copper or fiber cables and mobile base stations. Later, additional CSPs, often providing low cost services, entered the market as Mobile Virtual Network Operators (MVNOs) and have been building their own customer relationships, marketing strategies and product sales, do not own any spectrum license or infrastructure but rent that from established CSPs. Figure 3.2 provides an overview about the shares of mobile CSPs in the German market in 2011.

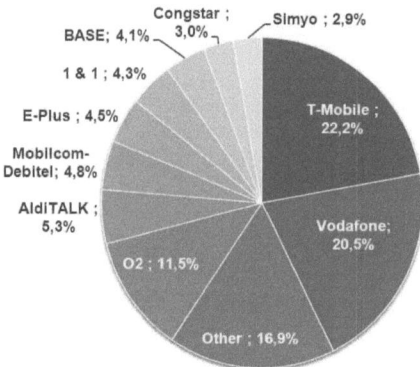

Figure 3.2: Distribution of mobile CSPs in Germany in August 2011 [116]

Goals

Several problems of CSPs were already illustrated in section 1.1. The following overview summarizes their most important goals

- **Increasing the Number of Customers and End-Users**

    In competition with ASPs, CSPs want to increase and transform their visibility at their customers towards being seen as a provider of innovative service and applications instead of plain Telecommunication services and data connections to the Internet. Through that, CSPs want to increase their overall number of paying customers for their traditional Telecommunication services and applications, while at the same time grow the number of end-users for each innovative service and applications they are going to offer in the future. If customers are satisfied with the portfolio and quality of services and applications they are getting provided by their CSP, then they are, on the one hand, less likely to use a similar service from an ASP and, on the other hand, less likely to move to a competitor CSP.

- **Strengthen Position in End-User Services and Applications Industry**

    As illustrated in detail in section 1.1.1, in this industry, CSPs compete with over-the-top ASPs such as Google, Apple and Microsoft. This leads to the trend that an increasing number of end-user applications are provided by those and CSPs are increasingly pushed into a position where they become a "bit pipe" and so, only provide the technical infrastructure and networks for data transmission.

    In order to be successful in this competition, CSPs plan to increase their visibility in the application developer space and present themselves as high-quality service providers to developers. They are exporting/offering Telecommunication services such as AAA, Identity Management (IDM), Location, Presence, QoS, rich Messaging, high-quality Audio/Video Communication, network management services and further to developers. They are extending their business intelligence capabilities to learn more about needs, habits, interests, etc. of their customers and to provide excellent recommendation services in all sorts of areas such as mobile applications, shopping, multimedia etc.

    On developer platforms, CSPs are publishing/marketing exported services and are offering support, tools and business/marketing models to attract developers (e.g. Developer Garden [56], BetaVine [234], Orange [72], etc.). CSPs plan to combine Open Innovation through third party developers on developer platforms with an increase in own and internal service and application development.

- **Migrating from Circuit-Switched Networks to Packet-Switched Next Generation Networks**

    To enable an efficient and flexible delivery of new services and application, CSPs are investing into new hardware and software infrastructure components. Those migrate their core Telecommunication networks from former Telecommunication specific circuit-switched technologies, standards and specifications to Web/Internet standards, protocols and specifications-based packet-switched technologies. Since those technologies build the foundations of the Internet, the CSPs Telecommunication networks and systems become compatible with Web/Internet services and applications.

- **Deploying Service Delivery Platforms (SDPs)**

    For many decades Telecommunication service development was based on proprietary technologies and only specially trained Telecommunication specialists were able to develop new services. The development process was a tedious work and deploying a new service on the network and publishing it to customers was extremely complex and difficult. CSPs are planning to buy and deploy NGNs-based SDPs from Telecommunication technology vendors to acquire the ability to create and implement services more easily and quickly, to offer a comprehensive service portfolio on the market and to introduce/adapt new services in line with changing market requirements. Since different vendors have different understandings of what and SDP is and what components it is constituted of, CSPs have to make sure to choose the right one for their organization and plans. CSPs are combining their SDP plans with their services and applications development Open Innovation concepts mentioned above.

- **Fostering High-Quality of Service and User Experience for Converged Applications**

    CSPs plan to develop and deploy means to combine existing Web/Internet-based services with internal Telecommunication services in order to offer value-added services to external developers and so, innovative applications to their customers. Since Web/Internet services do often not comply with the high-quality standards of Telecommunication services, CSP standardization bodies are working on several proposals for convergence without drawbacks in the high-quality user experience customers are expecting and CSPs have to deliver.

- **Global Marketplace for Mobile Applications**

    In February 2010, 24 major CSPs (e.g. AT&T, Deutsche Telekom, Vodafone, China Telecom) together with the three handset manufacturers LG, Samsung and Sony Ericsson founded the, since then steadily growing, WAC initiative. The general goals are to build a counterweight to device-centric application stores, to reduce the fragmentation of CSPs application stores and to simplify application development and distribution for themselves as well as for third party developers. Besides building an active developer community, WAC will provide a centralized white label application store solution that all partners can launch under their own brands in their Telecommunication networks/markets. For application developers WAC will provide means to develop and deploy their Web-, BONDI- and JIL-based [185, 224] applications once on a central wholesale marketplace and to monetize them by selling them through all associated partner application stores.

- **Supporting Long-Tail Business Models**

    The growing mobile services industry has a large number of successful high-revenue general-purpose services for large markets on the one side and a growing number of long-tail services for niche markets on the other side. CSPs want to extend their portfolios of services and applications they can offer to their customers and are looking for solutions to support and include more long-tale services. As in the transition from left to right in figure 3.3 illustrated, they need to find means to decrease their costs per services (OPEX) while keeping or even increasing the quality of service and end-user experience.

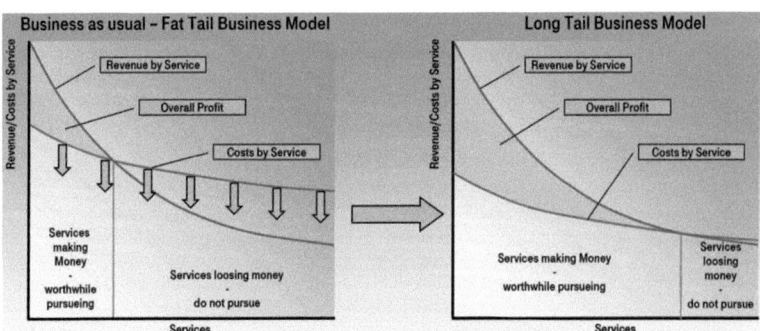

Figure 3.3: Longtail Business Model [16]

This way they loosen themselves from the burden of only being able to pursue services and applications with large numbers of paying customers, but can also support and gain revenue from niche services.

- **Supporting and Providing Enterprise Services and Applications**

    Future enterprise applications need to be flexible, modular, extensible and quickly adaptable in order to stay competitive in a changing enterprise environment. In the future, innovation in the enterprise applications market will not only come from the current big players for enterprise applications, but equally from new players from adjacent industries, small companies or independent developers. Most legacy and current Information Technology (IT) concepts and infrastructures are not able to cope with these new requirements. Enterprises are reorganizing their IT departments in order to evaluate or launch cloud computing strategies to outsource IT infrastructures, services and applications immediately or in the future. In this transforming enterprise environment CSPs plan to take a significant role in the value chain and to generate additional revenue through two strategies, (i) collaborating with ASPs and enterprises and supporting their services and applications through cloud computing offerings or (ii) competing with ASPs and providing services and applications to enterprise customers themselves.

CSPs drive standardization in cloud computing Infrastructure-as-a-Service (IaaS) and Platform-as-a-Service (PaaS) areas focusing at enterprise application provisioning, management, hosting, maintenance, delivery, etc. Thus, they achieve credibility and a competitive advantage over other players (e.g. Microsoft with Azure, Google with AppEngine, Amazon with Web Services) when offering enterprise products in the cloud computing industry. They can combine their existing technologies, platforms and third party development concepts with flexible, scaleable, professional and SLA-backed cloud computing infrastructure/platform offerings. Thereby, on the one hand, enabling a cooperation with ASPs and enterprises by creating a platform for managing their existing services and applications. While, on the other hand, allowing professional and independent developers to develop and deploy innovative enterprise services and applications on top of their platforms.

CSPs extend their internal services and applications development departments and combine these with their technologies, platforms, future cloud computing infrastructures and third party development concepts. Through that, they will be able to develop a selection of high-quality enterprise applications that they can offer and provide to enterprise customers directly. Hence, since enterprise customers are more willing to pay for services and applications than private customers, CSPs can apply a traditional business model to generate more revenue through new services and applications.

3.2 Application Service Providers

Traditionally, an ASP is defined as a company that offers computer-based services/applications to consumers via a data network. Today, through the spreading of cloud computing, an ASP can be defined as a Software-as-a-Service [202] (SaaS) provider offering services/applications that are accessible as on-demand software over the Internet. Through the reduced effort and lower costs of the distribution of the software over the Internet, ASPs can base their software development on a larger number of customers and so, provide higher quality software for a lower price than traditional software companies. Consumers use thin software clients on their client devices such as PCs or smart phones to work with the software. Nowadays, web browsers are the most popular universal thin software clients than can be used to access Web/Internet-based SaaS products. Popular ASP companies in the B2B and B2C industries are Salesforce, SAP, Oracle, Zoho, Google, Microsoft, Facebook, Xing, LinkedIn, Skype, Twitter, etc.

In the B2B industry, ASPs satisfy the growing need of enterprises to reduce their large investments in IT hardware and software upgrades (nowadays often surpassing budgets of mid-sized companies), to transform those into running costs on a per-use, monthly or yearly basis and to reduce in-house IT hardware and software management complexity, effort and expenditures. The responsibility for IT hardware and software availability, management, maintenance, technical support, security, safety, stability, etc. is shifted from the enterprise to the SaaS providing ASP. They typically offer specialized enterprise applications for Enterprise Resource Planning (ERP), Customer Relationship Management (CRM), project management, process management, etc.

or enterprise grade productivity applications such as office suits, collaboration tools, knowledge management, unified communications etc.

In the B2C industry, ASPs are typically relatively young companies that work in a rapidly changing market and that need to be able to adapt their business models fast and often. They satisfy the growing need of private users to be entertained or to work with personal data using any device and from anywhere in the world through free or relatively cheap Web/Internet technologies and mostly web browser-based applications. They typically offer innovative productivity, communication, media and entertainment applications such as web mail, office suits, social networking, VoIP, instant messaging, music/video downloads/streaming, IPTV etc.

Goals

The following overview summarizes the ASPs most important goals.

- **Competition for Subscribers/Users in B2C Market**

    On the Internet, private customers expect free or "freemium" applications for their personal use. Hence, nowadays, most ASPs base their B2C business models on non-customer focused revenues such as advertisement, access to customers or selling customers' information. Ultimately, success of an application is often measured by number or user registered, or number of users that use the application regularly. Due to that, ASPs ultimate goal is to maximize the number of users that use their applications, to draw them to their advertisements supported application user-interface and to lock them to their applications as tight as possible.

- **Building Monopoly Applications in B2C Market**

    ASPs are trying to build monopolies in the areas in which their applications fulfill the users' needs and to lock the users to their applications. An open platform/technology or any standardization together with competitors or partners from other fields is contradicting with the ASPs business models and success factors for their applications. Hence, most communication services provided by ASPs such as Skype, MSN and GoogleTalk are incompatible and isolated. Most ASPs did not yet figure out how to combine openness with their business models and so, are not even trying to use their successful applications to define open "defacto" technology standards on the Internet. Some ASPs, especially in the social networks area, started providing Application Programming Interfaces (APIs) to connect other applications or websites to their applications to provide them with features such as authentication using an existing profile. These connections are basically unidirectional towards the ASPs applications and aim at drawing more users, user generated content and user context information (e.g. browsing history, interests, location information, social attributes) to the ASPs applications. Hence, cooperation between ASPs applications and competitors or partner companies is difficult, very limited and if there is one, mostly unidirectional or based on financial compensation of some sort.

- **Convergence of Communication and Information**

    Traditionally, for users, the Web/Internet has been a medium and source for all kinds of information. Through the spreading of Web 2.0 concepts, users are shifting into an active role where they are publishing general or even personal information on Web/Internet-based applications provided by ASPs. Today, with the ubiquitous availability of broadband fixed and mobile data networks, ASPs are providing sophisticated and innovative Web/Internet-based communication applications and combine them with their already existing Web 2.0 information applications.

- **Fostering Third Party Development and Integration**

  ASPs have recognized the value of third party developers and integration much earlier than CSPs. Over the last decade, they have built many mature developer platforms (e.g. Google Code, Facebook, MSDN, DeveloperForce) that allow rapid service and application creation based on common Web/Internet technologies. These platforms have specifically low entry barriers for third party developers to allow them to drive innovation by extending/enhancing the applications and technologies the ASPs already offer. Based on the successful App Store examples from Device/Platform Manufacturers, ASPs are starting to build marketplaces on top of their developer platforms (e.g. Google Apps Marketplace, Windows Azure AppFabric, Salesforce AppExchange and DeveloperForce) in order to provide third party developers with a distribution channel to customers. Since enterprise customers are typically more willing to pay for a high-quality service or application than private users, most of the ASPs platforms have been focusing on providing high-quality enterprise services and applications. Several have created a two-sided market with third party developers on developer platforms on one side and small/medium size enterprises on application marketplaces on the other side. The values of the ASPs developer communities are growing steadily. Hence, they are going to nurture this excellent source of innovation even more in the future.

- **Expansion to Mobile Web/Internet**

  Established ASPs are adjusting and extending their applications and platforms to provide their users access through mobile devices such as smart phones or tablets. Some ASPs tailor their applications to provide a good user experience when accessed by mobile device browsers. Most develop specialized apps for mobile platforms such as Android, iOS, Windows Phone to provide their users with access to their application. Popular services such as Facebook announced more than 100 million users accessing their applications over the mobile Web/Internet regularly. This number is expected to be growing rapidly and ASPs are going to focus even more on application delivery using the mobile Internet.

- **Fostering Use of Context Information in B2C Industry**

  Context aware computing has evolved from traditional applications such as portal personalization and has become a disruptive technology that has the potential to improve user experience drastically, to build up loyalty and to provide a competitive advantage. ASPs are aiming to include context data elements such as location, presence, social attributes and other environmental information from various sources into their applications. They will be able to anticipate their end-users momentary needs and based on those provide sophisticated and situation-aware applications.

3.3 Device and Platform Manufacturers

Device Manufacturers (OEMs) design and produce the high-end consumer devices (e.g. mobile phones, smart phones, tablets, IPTVs, etc.) that are used to access current Telecommunication as well as Web/Internet services and applications. They build their sophisticated technology solutions according to worldwide fixed and mobile Telecommunication standards and specifications that are defined by industry associations/unions/partnerships/alliances/communities (e.g. ITU, 3GPP, GSMA) they are mostly also part of. Device manufacturers have to cope with shortening product lifecycles that require them to launch new products with up-to-date designs and new/enhanced hardware features such as faster/multicore CPUs, enhanced screen sizes and resolutions, high-definition cameras or Near Field Communication (NFC) components several times a year. The overall market for innovative, sophisticated high-end devices has been growing rapidly over the last years but also competition has been increasing heavily. Revenue margins of device sales have been decreasing and new market players like HTC or ZTE have announced to conquer the market by pursuing a price aggressive strategy. Due to that, device manufacturers have to develop new selling propositions and business opportunities in the future. Figure 3.4 (left) provides an overview about the distribution of mobile phone device manufacturers in the German market in 2011.

Since the complexity of mobile phone hardware platforms has been rising rapidly over the last decade, device manufacturers have been struggling with keeping up with implementing their Operating Systems (OSs) that provide the software platforms for all new features, services and applications. Hence, costs for software development have been rising dramatically and so, similar to the PC industry, a separation of hardware and software/OS evolved. At first, several device manufacturers joint forces and built foundations/alliances such as the Nokia driven Symbian Foundation to develop a common platform for services and applications that all of the members could tailor to their needs and use to run their devices.

Together with these first device manufacturer driven approaches the use of the mobile Web/Internet started rising and companies started sharing the idea that the one who will provide the platform for future devices is about to control the mobile Internet. As a result, several ASPs and IT companies such as Microsoft, Google and Apple entered the market with own mobile phone platforms (e.g. Windows Mobile, Windows Phone), with own alliances like the Open Handset Alliance (Android) from Google or with tightly coupled and closed combinations of devices (iPod, iPhone, iPad) and platforms (iOS) like Apple. Due to the maturity and universality of these current smart phone platforms, this research work focuses mainly on them. Figure 3.4 (right) illustrates the distribution of smart phone platforms in the German market in 2011.

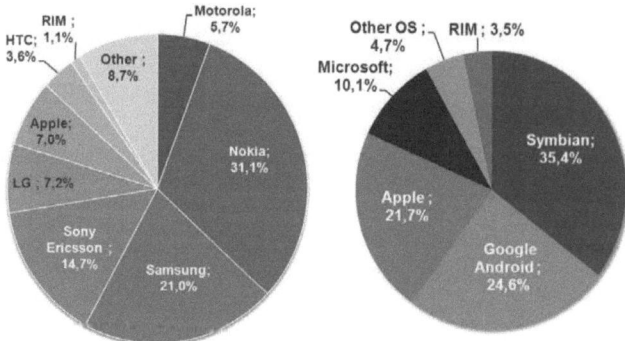

Figure 3.4: Distribution of mobile phone OEMs and smartphone OSs in Germany in August 2011 [116]

Goals

The following overview summarizes the manufacturers most important goals.

- **Drive Sales through Usage Scenarios and Services**

    Device manufacturers are following two parallel approaches to increase the value of their devices for the customers in order to increase sales. On the one hand, they have shifted their advertisements and selling propositions from hardware features centric campaigns to use-case and added value centric campaigns. They are using the new hardware and software features, including their common platforms, to develop and advertise the most appealing and innovative every-day or business usage scenarios in which the device supports the customers. Through that they are trying to increase the demand and adoption of high-end devices in the society in order to archive a wider market penetration.

On the other hand, many device manufacturers such as Nokia, shift their focus from the in-house development of semiconductors to new sources of revenue in the domain of (mobile) services they can offer in combination with their devices. They outsource their device manufacturing and enlarge their software services and applications divisions. ASPs, such as Google or Apple, that entered the platform manufacturers market in the last couple of years, have been building popular proprietary information, data and multimedia services and applications such as Search, E-Mail, Contacts, Maps, Messaging, VoIP on top of the Web/Internet over the last decade. They are using these now to revolutionize the Telecommunications and (mobile) Web/Internet industry though high-tech service platforms with diverse innovative and advanced mobile services and applications. Through providing such value-added services, applications and platforms with the devices, manufacturers are planning to intensify their relations to customers, increase the overall value of their devices and ultimately increase device sales, their customer base and service/application users.

- **Provide Excellent User Experience**

    Device and platform manufacturers are constantly striving to provide their customer with the best user experience possible on their devices, meaning the best combination of user-interface design and usability. With the increase in diverse high-tech hardware features, services and applications on the devices, the complexity for creating an excellent user experience has been rising constantly. With the maturation of touch screen technology in the last years, a major shift from small screen keyboard/keypad devices to large screen touch devices has taken place. In contrast to the static layout of keyboards/keypads, the dynamic nature of touch interfaces allows manufacturers to create an excellent and intuitive user experience for modern devices and platforms even when they are filled with large collections of diverse high-tech features, services and applications.

- **Provide Open vs. Closed Platforms**

    In the platform manufacturer market approaches for how much access or influence on a platform customers, partners or third party developers get diverge drastically. On the one hand manufacturers like Apple or RIM follow a "Closed Platform" approach that ensures them to have full control of all hardware and software features of their platforms. They are designing their own hardware devices and are implementing their software platforms in-house without company external influences. They are certain that only through such tightly coupled hardware and software development their excellent features, services and applications provided together with an excellent user experience are possible. A few years ago, these manufacturers adopted third party service and application development including platform-specific application stores for their platforms. Even though this was a small break in their closed ideology, they still aim to control as much about the third party services and applications as possible. They limit the developers' access to platform and hardware features wherever they identify a possible loss of control over their platforms and restrict any adaptation of pre-installed platform features. They enforce testing and certification of all applications before they are allowed to be distributed through their applications stores and limit or define the types of content the services and applications are allowed to provide to the end-users.

On the other hand, platform manufacturers like Google and Microsoft follow different levels of an "Open Platform" approach that enables them to work closely with partners and developers to enable high-end devices with excellent features, services and applications. Some of their platforms are open source projects, maintained and developed by an alliance of device manufacturers, platform manufacturers and developers. They aim at reducing the complexity of the mobile world by setting standards for a platform that consolidates the heavily fragmented mobile devices and platforms market. Other platforms are closed source projects that are maintained and developed in-house by a platform manufacturer. The platform manufacturers aim at establishing cooperations with many device manufacturers who use their platforms to run their devices. Through that they can broaden the user base for their legacy Internet-based services and applications (e.g. Search, Maps, E-Mail, Calendar, Office, VoIP), acquire mobile customers for those and target business models like advertisement towards them. Similar to above, also these platform manufacturers adopted third party service and application development including platform-specific application stores. In contrast, here developers gain almost full access to platform and hardware features and are even encouraged to extend or substitute pre-installed features, services or applications of the platform. The platform manufacturers' influence on applications on their application stores is very limited and the stores are generally open to all sorts of applications with all types of content. Quality assurance is driven by the market participants through rating, ranking and feedback mechanisms.

- **Foster Third Party Development**

    Platform manufacturers have gained positive experience with their shift of service and application innovation and development towards external third party developers. They are going to foster their existing developer communities by continuously enhancing their hardware and software platform technologies, promoting new features to the worldwide developer communities and providing easy-to-use, top-quality developer tools for their platforms. Some manufacturers are planning to implement innovation processes such as "Open Innovation" that allows them to bring company-internal innovation, services, applications and features together with external developers in a more efficient way.

    All platform manufacturers are trying to attract many skilled and innovative developers to grow the developer communities around their platforms and to assure a continuous process of innovation. Developers have become a major success factor for a manufacturers' platform and so, for platform manufacturers, they are seen as a specific group of customers that has to be won and convinced of their product. Competition for developers in this market will grow.

- **Foster Platform-Specific Application Stores**

    Through the combination of application store concepts and third party development, platform manufacturers have created a very successful distribution channel for applications directly accessible from the devices that run their platforms. By utilizing a revenue share model with developers, they have created a win-win situation for both sides and so, attract many professional and leisure developers. The worldwide generated revenue through the stores of, for example, 4.2 billion USD in 2009 is typically only a fraction of the platform manufacturers' total revenue. Nevertheless, the conveniently accessible large selection of third party applications for their platforms attracts customers to buy devices that are based on their platforms, builds a direct access to these customers and increases brand awareness and loyalty. Hence, platform manufacturers are going to foster their platform-specific application stores and are unlikely to build any cooperations between platforms and stores.

- **Dominate Mobile Advertisement Market**
  As illustrated in the previous section, on the Internet, many ASPs apply an advertisement-based business model for their B2C services and applications. The ASPs that became platform manufacturers are now pushing to bring this business model to their platforms, which will lead to a rapid growth of advertisement over the next years. The platform manufacturers control their platforms and so, in some ways, the access to their customers. To also control advertisement, they are integrating easy-to-use advertisement feature APIs into their platforms Software Development Kits (SDKs), which allow targeting customers more precisely and efficiently with advertisement. This enables developers to integrate advertisement into their applications. Thereby, platform manufacturers provide the developers with means to finance their applications while at the same time, they further control and dominate the advertisement market on their platforms.

- **Foster Cooperations with Content Providers**
  Content providers are continuously looking for new profitable distribution channels for their multimedia content. Especially now, when print media revenues decline they are looking for ways to distribute more of their content digitally. Several platform manufacturers realized this need and positioned their platforms as future media content platforms that can be used to distribute high-quality multimedia content through multimedia applications on their application stores. Platform manufacturers are partnering with content providers to distribute multimedia content to customers and to generate revenue for both sides. However, some platform manufacturers are following a very stringed concept defining very strictly what types of content can be distributed in what ways and for what price. Others are following a very open concept allowing content providers to distribute their content according to their individual innovative ideas, marketing and business plans. Nevertheless, media content providers will use these platforms, partnerships and their own applications extensively to distribute multimedia content in the future.

- **Foster Device Distribution Partnerships with CSPs**
  Traditionally, close cooperations with CSPs have been very important distribution channels for device manufacturers. CSP have been subsidizing devices so customers could buy them in combination with a Telecommunication services contract at a low price. Device manufacturers rarely sold devices independent of CSPs and they put limited effort into own marketing of devices. The CSPs were the ones with direct access to customers and device manufacturers were eager to cooperate with them in order to sell devices. Hence, CSPs were in control of the terms and conditions of these cooperations.

  With the introduction of the iPhone by Apple in 2007, this CSPs centric model shifted to a more balanced. Device manufacturers have started to market their devices independently and CSPs have been eager to collaborate in order to offer these popular devices, sometimes even exclusively, to their existing and potentially new customers. This fact that some device manufacturers established own marketing and distribution efforts leads to rising CSP-independent sales of devices. Nevertheless, a collaboration between them and CSPs will continue to be an important worldwide distribution channel for their devices and a success factor of their business.

3.4 Developers

Developers are conceptualizing, designing and implementing services and applications based on platforms, technologies, services and devices provided by CSPs, ASPs or device/platform manufacturers. Often developers are roughly divided into two groups, Commercial/Professional and

Non-Commercial/Independent Developers, which clearly sometimes blend into each other. Developers that are not employed at the CSP, ASP or device/platform manufacturer they are contributing innovative services and applications to but are independent and external, are typically referred to as "Third Party Developers".

Non-Commercial Developers typically conceptualize their own innovative ideas and implement an application or service that provides a solution to this idea to end-users. Their motivation originates from intrinsic and extrinsic sources. They enjoy the activity of creating something innovative and useful, learning new technologies, following their ideology and feeling self-fulfillment by being altruistic. They like to fulfill the need for solving specific problems through software, enjoy their growing reputations in developer communities and at end-users and sometimes hope to build a career from that.

Commercial Developers design and implement services and applications as a profession. Several companies from other software industries like game development and enterprise application development shifted their focus to mobile and Web/Internet services and applications. Several specialized companies were founded over the last years and have been growing successfully since then. Many Commercial Developers design and implement their software to customers' orders based on the ideas, use-cases and requirements the customers provide them with. In contrast to Non-Commercial, they typically also have the resources and expertise to design, implement and roll out complex large scale enterprise applications. Besides customer focused development, several also dedicate some of their resources into creating innovative ideas in the Web/Internet and mobile industry and, based on those, design and implement innovative products for end-users.

Goals

The following overview summarizes the developers' most important goals.

- **Economic Criteria-Based Mobile Platform Adoption**

  Developers have a growing selection of mobile platforms they can develop their services and applications for. These platforms can be differentiated by a large number of technical as well as economical parameters. Figure 3.5 illustrates the importance ranking of the criteria that developers use to select the platform they focus development resources and expertise on. It can be observed that the top three and the fifth are economic criteria and only the fourth constitutes a technical.

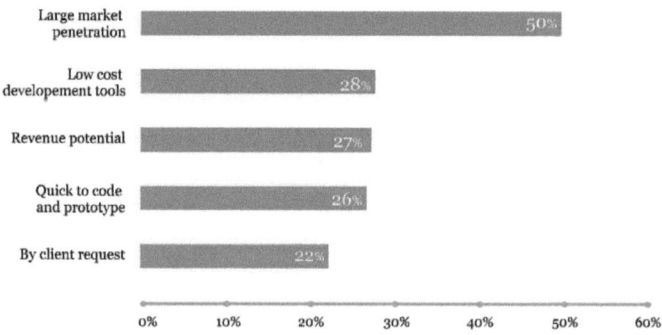

Figure 3.5: Platform Adoption Criteria [231]

3.4. Developers

A large market penetration, meaning to reach many end-users, is the most important criteria for developers to decide what platform they develop their services and applications on. Important factors are the size of the market, growth perspectives as well as support, possibilities and restrictions in terms of publishing and distribution of services and applications in that market. Distribution channels have evolved over the last years and developers shifted their focus to application stores. In the past, CSPs portals on the Web/Internet and on the mobile device in combination with the Wireless Access Protocol (WAP) were important distribution channels. Further, distribution through an own website, through aggregator websites or shops as well as through preloading on the end device by device manufacturer or CSPs were important. Today, the importance of all these channels declines and application stores are for 45% of developers across the eight major platforms the primary distribution channel. Developers want platforms that provide mature distribution channels that allow them and assist them at promoting, selling and distributing their applications to end-user devices worldwide. When all this is provided, developers are still looking for attractive pricing conditions and options, but are also happy to accept the typical current revenue share models of 70% for the developer and 30% for the application store owner.

The availability and access to development tools at low costs that allow developers to quickly code and prototype is ranked second among the criteria. This is one factor that supports a low entry barrier for developers, which constitutes a goal that is discussed further below.

The potential to generate revenue with services and applications developed for a specific platform ranks third. Developers typically generate revenue through commission/salary for contract work, direct sales of applications on platform stores, purchases made by the end-user within an application and advertisements placed in the applications. Apple's iOS platform is still ahead by generating 3.3-times more revenue than Symbian, followed by Java ME with 2.7-times, BlackBerry with 2.4-times, Android with 1.7-times and Mobile Web with 1.6-times. Nevertheless, there are also many developers that are losing money with their applications. Around a third is generating less than $1000USD per application in total, which does not cover the costs of resources and implementation time invested in developing the application.

Alongside revenue potential, for some developers career opportunities are an important factor for platform selection. If they can contribute to a young and growing open source platform they can be recognized as important contributor and ultimately even be hired by one of the companies supporting the platform.

- **Mature and Active Developer Community**

    Developers, especially independent ones, want to work in and contribute to an active developer community that provides mature, powerful and high-quality community tools such as technical documentation, technical support, How-Tos, example case studies, blogs, wikis, discussion forums, chats, webinars, personal trainings etc. The community needs to have an efficient registration process, efficient financial tools to pay fees and to receive payments from sales as well as an excellent overall usability. It needs to support the developers precisely and quickly and allow an efficient interaction between developers as well as developers and device/platform manufacturers. A great advantage and opportunity that developers highly appreciate is to promote and bring together the whole community through the organization and/or the support of regular offline events all over the world.

- **Low Entry Barrier**

    For developers, the entry barrier of a platform is typically composed of the factors costs and technology. Developers want to get access to a developer platform, community and their resources with low initial and minimal or no running costs. So, for developers, a platform needs to provide tools and resources together with pricing models that attract large professional development companies while at the same time ensure a low barrier for independent developers.

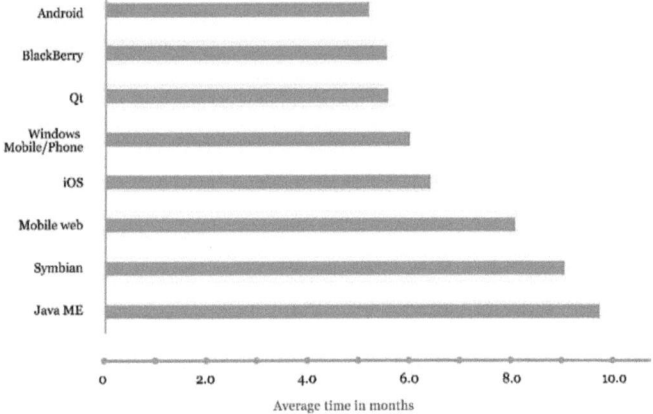

Figure 3.6: Learning Period [231]

On the technology side, developers want platforms that require small investments in necessary hardware and software and that are easy to learn and use. There are quite significant differences in how much time and effort it requires to learn and apply a platform for own service and application development. Figure 3.6 illustrates the ranking of the most popular platforms in terms of average required learning period.

It shows clearly that native platforms such as Android, iOS, BlackBerry and Windows are easier to learn than the upcoming cross-platform compatible Mobile Web platform and so, have a lower entry barrier for developers. This is due to the fact that native platforms typically use one specific implementation technology whereas for Mobile Web, developers need to learn a complex stack of languages, technologies and frameworks across client and server environments. Further, today, they also have to cope with cross browser/platform compatibility challenges that will be removed in the future.

Recently, the entry barrier at the distribution channels of the platforms has been rising for independent developers. Professional development companies increasingly use their visibility among end-users to promote new applications though cross application promotions and distribution. This makes it harder for independent developers developing for niche markets to promote and distribute their applications.

- **Creative Freedom**

    Developers want the possibility to distribute whatever innovative idea they implement through as many distribution channels and as fast as possible. They want platform manufacturers to provide open platforms with access to distribution channels for every developer and to put as little rules, restrictions, policies, licenses, terms and conditions on their services and applications distribution processes as possible. They want the whole application

3.4. Developers

distribution process on every platform to be fast, uncomplicated and completely transparent.

Currently, platform manufacturers' strategies in this area vary heavily. All of them somehow rely on customer community parameters such as ratings, comments and numbers of downloads to rank, promote and recommend applications on their stores. In contrast to these open and community driven mechanisms, some manufacturers implemented restrictive platform features that evaluate and allow or reject every application based on intransparent criteria and that censor applications by strictly restricting the types of content an application is allowed to present/publish and rejecting or removing applications that do not comply.

- **Access to High-Tech Platforms and Features**

  Developers want the latest and most innovative devices and platforms that contain the newest technical components and leverage the newest design concepts. They want full and early access to the newest features of these platforms through SDKs and APIs, so they can be used to generate and implement innovative ideas that had not been possible before.

- **Access to Simple yet Powerful Development Tools**

  Developers aim to have access to developer platforms with well documented APIs and professional SDKs providing extensive frameworks, rich libraries and powerful development tools. The platforms need to be mature, high-quality and based on common standards and well-known programming languages and technologies. Developers want an Integrated Development Environment (IDE) that simplifies the development process that includes state of the art source code editors, debuggers, testing tools, device/platform simulators, user-interface design tools and that ideally supports the management of the whole application lifecycle. Platforms need to evolve regularly, but backward compatibility needs to be ensured so that applications run stable on all devices of a platform. If this is not provided, for independent developers it is especially difficult to maintain their growing number of applications to adapt them to changing platform features and APIs.

  To support distributed applications by leveraging cloud computing concepts, developers want PaaS or IaaS-based sandboxes for testing, management tools and professional service and application deployment and execution environments.

- **Cross-Platform Multi-Screen Development and Distribution**

  Developers are increasingly expanding their development focus and expertise to additional devices and platforms. On average, developers currently develop their applications for 3.2 platforms concurrently. Since the architectures, development environments, frameworks and programming technologies of all major platforms are very different, in order to make their applications work there, developers have to partly or sometimes completely redevelop them. For the developers, this is very time consuming, inefficient, and expensive and so, they are constantly looking for technologies and solutions that allow them to develop an application only once and still distribute it across all major platforms to a larger potential customer base. Over the last years, several proprietary solutions such as the PhoneGap, Titanium and Rhodes frameworks evolved. At the same time, advancements and standardization of mobile web technologies including Hypertext Markup Language Version 5 [247] (HTML5) and related continued and developers increasingly plan to adopt these standards to meet their cross-platform development requirements in the future. From a usage perspective, 67% of developers are using Android, 59% iOS and mobile web is currently already on third position.

Even after developing applications that are cross-platform compatible, the fragmentation of the distribution channels for applications poses a great challenge for developers. Currently there are around 50 different application stores available and each of them has its own registration process, submission process, artwork and paperwork requirements, application evaluation, certification and approval process, revenue sharing model options and payment, taxation and settlement terms. The effort of distributing an application through one more distribution channel is significant and developers want some common standards, compatibility or cooperation.

Aside from cross-platforms and distribution, with the increased spreading of smartphones, tablets, programmable IPTVs, set-top boxes and car entertainment systems developers are increasingly expending their development focus on applications that are compatible with all screens end-users utilize. Almost 50% of developers work with smartphones and tablets and nearly 25% are planning to adopt IPTV and set-top box development in the near future. Currently, mobile web is the best suitable and most versatile platform for multi-screen development and developers using this platform target an average of 2.5 screens.

- **Access to ASP Services and Applications**

    Since the introduction of Web 2.0 and, through exported APIs, programmable web services and applications of ASPs, Web/Internet developers have been building numerous innovative services and applications as mashups enriched with own ideas and features. Programmable Web lists 4,658 APIs including geo information (Maps, Qype), music (Last.fm), telephony (Ribbit, Twilio), messaging (Jabber, Google Talk), advertising (AdSense), shopping (eBay), multimedia (Flickr, YouTube) and enterprise (Salesforce.com, Amazon S3, Microsoft Azure). Recently, more social networking APIs were published. As content can be more easily shared within an established social network with millions of users, developers adopt them to reach potential new users.

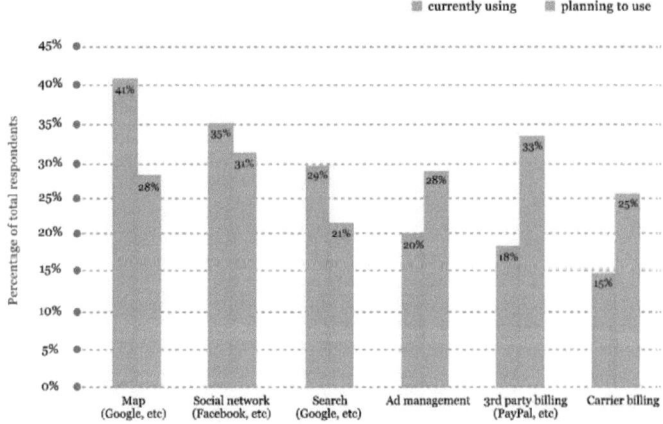

Figure 3.7: Adoption of ASP Services [231]

With the introduction of powerful mobile devices, platforms and the ubiquitous availability of mobile Web/Internet, also mobile service and application developers are increasingly adopting Web/Internet service and application APIs from ASPs to build their mobile services and applications. Especially developers for the new smartphone platforms iOS and Android are active users of these APIs, while Blackberry, Java(ME) and Symbian developers were late adopters. Figure 3.7 illustrates the ranking of the most popular ASP service and application APIs.

Over 40% of mobile developers are already using map APIs from popular ASPs such as Google and Microsoft and 28% more are planning to adopt them in the near future. This makes maps the most common ASP APIs used. Maps can be used for various use-cases from visualization of locations on a map graphic, over routing to retrieving local points of interest. They are closely followed by social networks with 35% and search with 29%. Since a large number of their potential users are already registered at one of the social networks, developers are increasingly collaborating with social networks and use their APIs to outsource authentication and authorization features. Besides that, one of the fastest growing segments is third party billing. 33% are planning to use ASP and 25% CSP offers for their billing functionalities in their applications in the future.

Even though many ASPs services and applications provide back-end functionalities such as authentication, messaging, contacts and document/data storage that mobile applications could share, most are still largely standalone and do not provide a cross-application experience for end-users. Developers require more generic Shared Services (e.g. user profile management) that they could use to realize common features of their applications and that are shared across many applications and preferably across many platforms and screens.

- **Access to White Label Telecommunication Functionalities**

  Traditionally cooperation between developers and CSPs has been very limited. Web/Internet as well as increasingly mobile developers have been building services and applications on top of CSPs data transmission networks and have not been using any further features, functionalities or services from CSPs or their networks in new services and applications. For developers it has been unclear what other role, than delivering data access, CSPs could play in the services and applications (development) industry.

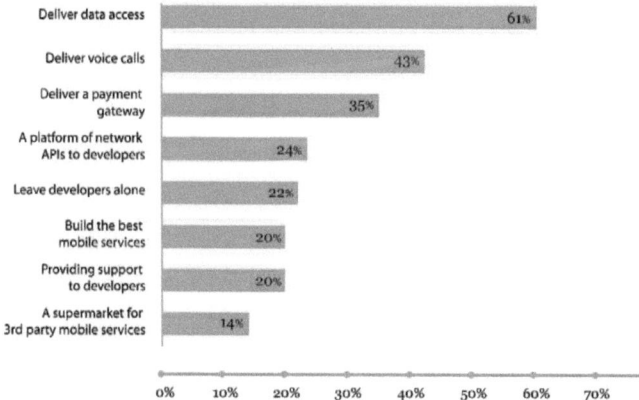

Figure 3.8: CSPs roles in service and application development [231]

Recently, this situation has changed and the effort of CSPs to make some of their network services accessible through APIs and to publish/market them has elevated their recognition at developers. Figure 3.8 provides an overview about in what areas developers would like to cooperate with CSPs in their service and application development in the future.

It can be seen that, although declining, 22% of developers still hold the opinion that CSPs should not interfere with service and application development and that these two industries should stay strictly separated. With 61%, developers clearly see CSPs responsible for providing efficient and high-quality data transmission and access for their services and applications. A growing number of developers, 43% respectively 35%, see the CSPs most professional and high-quality assets, voice communication and payment systems, as viable services they could leverage in their future services and applications.

In terms of service and application development, developers are indecisive whether CSPs should provide a platform with APIs to network services, build services and applications themselves or provide tools and platforms that support developers at their work. Additionally, there are growing regional differences in how developers perceive CSPs as possible cooperation partners. In Asia, 14% more than the global average of developers are planning to use CSPs payment systems and see CSPs as API platform providers. In Europe and North America developers prefer to be CSP independent and so, 20% more than the global average of developers have the opinion that CSPs should deliver data and voice but not offer own services and applications or build application stores.

Over the next years, CSPs will extend their portfolios of services and APIs and developers will increasingly adopt these high-quality and highly reliable services from CSPs instead of re-implementing them for their new services and applications.

- **Revenue Share Business Cooperation with CSPs**

  In contrast to ASPs and device or platform manufacturers, CSPs have not yet managed to implement a viable revenue-share business model with developers on their developer platforms. CSPs are treating developers as a secondary group of customer and are charging them for the use of their services and platforms.

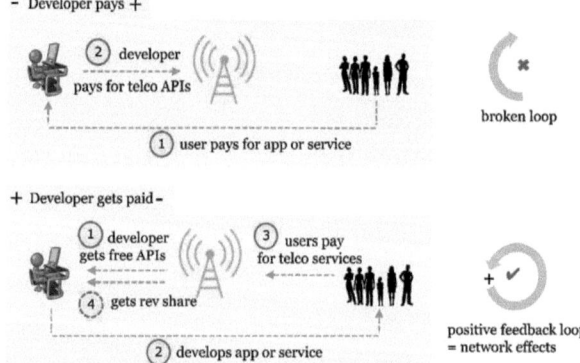

Figure 3.9: CSP - Developer Business Cooperation Models [231]

Developers are requesting a drastic shift in this model and want to be seen as resellers of CSPs network services/APIs that elevate service usage and/or network traffic for CSPs. Thereby, driving more end-users to CSPs core business and increasing revenue. CSPs need to establish partner programs with developers and share the additional revenue that their services and applications generate with them. Developers want to focus on inventing innovative services and applications that leverage CSP services and APIs instead of worrying about their associated costs. Figure 3.9 illustrates the two different models.

In the currently applied model, illustrated on top, developers are responsible for paying the CSPs for service APIs usage, hence they need to charge their users to cover these costs. This model does not encourage developers to include any CSP services into their services or applications. It entails costs from the start and increases charging/billing complexity for the developers but generates additional revenue mainly for the CSPs.

In the, for developers, optimal model, illustrated on the bottom, developers are enabled to use CSPs service APIs at no costs. Developers implement and distribute services and applications leveraging CSP services to end-users. Those pay CSPs directly for the usage and developers receive a revenue share from that. This model builds a positive feedback loop that generates network effects, meaning it encourages all parties to foster their partnerships as well as to constantly expand service and application development.

- **Deliver Enterprise Grade Business Applications**
  As already discussed in section 3.1, innovation in the enterprise applications market will not only come from the current big players for enterprise applications, but equally from new players from adjacent industries, small companies or independent developers. As noted in section 3.2, through third-party developer platforms, many professional developers and increasingly independent developers are already contributing new features or services to enterprise applications provided by ASPs. They are interested in continuing these contributions while at the same time, in developing completely new innovative enterprise services and applications independent of existing ASP applications. In order to provide high-quality enterprise services and applications that are customizable to the specific requirements of the enterprise customers, developers want flexible, scaleable, professional and SLA-backed cloud computing infrastructures/platforms as foundation for their services and applications. To keep maximum flexibility at selecting and switching between cooperation partners, developers require an increase in standardization in cloud computing IaaS and PaaS areas. It is necessary especially in those focusing at enterprise service and application provisioning, deployment, hosting, execution, management, maintenance and delivery.

3.5 End-Users

End-users are individuals that use the innovative applications created and distributed by developers on their devices such as laptops, netbooks, smart phones or tablets. Roughly, end-users can be divided into the two categories, (i) Private End-Users who use their applications for personal tasks and use-cases such as communication and entertainment, and (ii) Enterprise End-Users who use their applications for business tasks and use-cases at work. In recent years these boundaries have become increasingly blurred since many end-users have started to request from their employers to being able to use for work the same devices, tools and applications to which they have become accustomed to in their private lives. In the literature, there is typically a distinction between the customer who acquires and pays for a product and the end-user who utilizes it. In the following of this research work this distinction is disregarded.

Goals

The following overview summarizes the end-users most important goals.

- **Sophisticated and Innovative Services and Applications for Private End-Users**

    End-users want providers to offer innovative and mature productivity, communication, media and entertainment applications that support them in their daily life tasks and use-cases. They want applications that fully leverage all new opportunities that the latest high-end hardware and software features embedded in their latest home and mobile devices have to offer.

    For their personal productivity tasks and use-cases, end-users want powerful applications such as office suits, task management and collaboration tools that they can use at home and mobile.

    End-users want multimedia entertainment applications that allow them to consume multimedia streaming content from anyone and anywhere, to create and publish their own multimedia content worldwide, to watch high-quality IPTV at home and mobile and to access and manage one's personal multimedia seamlessly anytime and anywhere.

    End-users want innovative quick, open and easy communication solutions. With 85%, e-mail is still the most utilized communication system on the Internet. Increasingly, end-users are preferring VoIP solutions such as Skype over traditional Telecommunication services. They want ubiquitous communication features such as video call, conference call and instant messaging on the Web/Internet as well as on all of their personal home and mobile devices.

    Social networking has become increasingly successful over the last years with current growth rates of 200% and above. Social networks fulfill the end-users needs to extend their offline social environment and to increase their interaction with other users on the Web/Internet. End-users want social networking features and applications to organize their personal contacts, to communicate and stay in touch with friends and colleagues, to share information and multimedia content and to find users with similar interests. End-users want to use their social communities as information and recommendation sources in various areas such as product and service recommendations and discussions, updates about upcoming parties and events and more.

    End-users increasingly want to learn from other users on the Web/Internet as well as share their own knowledge with others on sites like Wikipedia. They are publishing Web 2.0-based User Generated Content on the Web/Internet in blogs, wikis, photos sharing sites, online/streaming music/video portals, journalism/news sites, forums, social networks and similar. They are tagging, sharing and commenting content they regard as interesting or important for others. End-users want similar possibilities and features in future applications for their home and mobile devices.

    End-users increasingly utilize mobile Web/Internet applications for their high-end mobile devices. Especially location-based, video/audio communication, multimedia, instant messaging and social networking applications are rising quickly. Upcoming technologies and features such as mobile payment, IPTV and augmented reality applications will follow soon.

- **Low Costs for Services and Applications for Private End-Users**

    On the Web/Internet advertisement revenue-based business models are widespread and accepted by providers as well as end-users. They are accustomed to receiving the applications for their personal use free of charge and that in return those are augmented with advertisements in diverse ways. Payment plans on a per-use or monthly basis, are typically only necessary if end-users want to remove the advertisements or access some premium features the applications offer in addition.

3.5. End-Users

It can be observed that this trend spreads to mobile applications and the mobile Web/Internet. Two thirds of Web/Internet end-users in the US and Germany and three quarters of 13 to 24 year olds in the US would like to keep their digital content and applications freely accessible and would choose advertisement-based models over end-user-paid ones.

Nevertheless, the acceptance of advertisement on mobile devices highly depends on the way it is conveyed and presented. End-user do not want any TextMessaging-based advertisements sent to their mobile devices since they feel this to be too intrusive and privacy invasive. Fortunately, the latest mobile devices with large touch screens provide enough screen space to present advertisements in a similar way as on the Web/Internet browser on a traditional computer. This form of advertisements in applications is increasingly accepted by end-users and therefore increasingly used by developers.

- **Sophisticated and Innovative Services and Applications for Enterprise End-Users**

  The percentage of enterprises with broadband Web/Internet access has remained nearly constant for a few years now whereas the one for mobile Web/Internet access has been rising constantly to over 60% today.

  For enterprise end-users the overall "cost to benefit ratio" influences buying decisions for applications most. Enterprise end-users require all applications to meet high standards regarding data security and privacy and especially for critical processes all applications need to be highly reliable. An easy integration of new applications into the existing IT infrastructure of the enterprise needs to be guaranteed and B2B interoperability needs to be ensured through standardization.

  Enterprise end-users want innovative business applications that enable an effective and integrated data management across the whole enterprise. Applications need to lead to efficiency improvements in the enterprises primary activities and tasks such as unified communications, logistics, CRM, ERP, knowledge management, supply chain management (including B2B E-Commerce and E-Procurement Marketplaces), sales and marketing. Enterprise end-users are increasingly requesting mobility solutions for their business applications to support their mobile and distributed workforce.

  Over recent years, social networking has become increasingly important for enterprise end-users in a B2B and also B2C environment. Collaboration with other enterprises is crucial and professional social networking tools such as Xing or LinkedIn enable enterprise end-users. Increasingly, enterprises need to use social networks to communicate with their customers in order to market their products, publish information or provide support. Enterprise end-users require applications that support them in both, the B2B and B2C sector social networking.

- **Excellent Usability and Quality of Experience**

  Usability and QoE have become increasingly important for the acceptance and success of new applications. Advancements in multimodal user-interface technologies such as touch, voice and haptic together with technological advancements at device displays and computing hardware capabilities have transformed traditional small screen keyboard-based user-interfaces to large screen touch-based user-interfaces. This has enabled application developer to provide such excellent user experiences that would not have been possible a few years back. Hence today, for every new application they utilize, end-users expect certain high levels of usability and QoE that are similar to the ones they experience at the latest applications on state-of-the-art platforms such as iOS, Android and Windows Phone 7.

- **Cross-Platform and Cross-Screen Applications**

  End-users utilize an increasing number of devices with an increasing number of available screen sizes such as PCs, laptops, netbooks, smart phones, tablets, IPTVs and car entertainment dashboards to work with their personal and business applications. From various manufacturers, there is a growing number of competing and mostly incompatible platforms available for all these devices.

  End-users do not want to be put in the middle of the competition between device and platform manufacturers and do not want to make their decisions about devices based on the platform compatibility of applications they intent to make use of. End-users want every available application to be fully accessible from all of their devices simultaneously with all of their application data and settings fully synchronized.

  End-users do not want to be bound to a specific device or platform manufacturer, but want to freely move any applications including all related data and settings to any additional or new device they might purchase and utilize in the future.

- **Cross-Application Features**

  Most current Web/Internet and mobile applications are explicitly separated from each other and are managing their application data and settings independently. Some of the latest applications leveraging cloud computing concepts provided by ASPs, share data such as sign-on credentials, profile information, contacts, events/tasks, documents, multimedia, etc. End-users experience the benefits of application features and data to be shared across several applications and across the Web/Internet and their mobile devices. For future applications, end-users want more innovative cross-application features that relieve them from managing their personal data for each application independently.

- **Access Network Independent Applications**

  Typically, applications provided by CSPs are limited to their, mostly regional, networks and so, only accessible through end-user devices that are connected to these networks. Applications provided by ASPs are typically accessible by all end-user devices connected to the Web/Internet worldwide.

  To ensure the end-users worldwide mobility, they need to be able to switch between networks, even across providers, arbitrarily without any interruption in their applications. Hence, they want access-network and provider independent applications.

- **Growing Influence on Application Development**

  In a few years, the majority of end-users will be from the generation of digital natives and will have grown up with technology, computers, the Web/Internet and smart phones. A growing number will become consumers and producers at the same time (Prosumers) and will develop or want to customize their, sometimes long-tale and niche, applications themselves. Future applications need to provide these possibilities and enable personalization, customization and even extension through visual tools (e.g. Yahoo Pipes [209], Microsoft PopFly [249], IBM Mashup Center [95]) as well as end-user software development.

- **Discovering Suitable Applications from a Large Selection**

  For end-users, the primary decision characteristic for a mobile device is the selection of applications that is available for the platform the device is based on. For the most popular platforms iOS, Android and Windows Phone 7 selections exceed 500.000, 400.000 and 50.000 respectively.

  This growing selection of applications is offered on proprietary application stores that are just as strictly separated and incompatible as the platforms themselves. With their goal to

3.5. End-Users

have "Cross-Platform and Cross-Screen Applications" (see above), end-users also want to have consolidated application stores that are easy to access and offer as well as distribute all available applications to all of their devices.

To cope with the large selection of applications in such a consolidated application store, end-users require means to find, retrieve, install and configure relevant and suitable applications for their personal and business tasks. In current stores, roughly 90% of end-users accept features such as community ratings, community reviews, discussion forums and social recommendations whereas only 54% trust application advertisements. In order to advance application discovery features, end-users must be willing to share certain information such as personal interests, buying habits, their social network, their location with ASPs and CSPs. Thereby, those can use their business intelligence systems to realize excellent discovery features.

Current application stores apply different levels of certification for applications in terms of stability, virus scans, malicious code identification, etc. End-users want a certain level of quality assurance and certification for all applications on a consolidated application store.

- **Trust and Security**

  Many future applications will reveal most of their potential and benefits only when working with or sharing personal end-user data such as their social network, interests, habits, profile information, etc. End-users require high privacy protection, trust and security standards/guarantees from the application developers and ultimately providers.

- **Home and Mobile Office**

  Mobile Web/Internet access among German companies has significantly increased over the last three years. Companies worldwide are increasingly equipping their employees with laptops and mobile phones instead of workstation computers and fixed office phones. The number of people working primarily mobile is predicted to grow to nearly 1.2 billion in 2013.

  Mobile working can be categorized in the four types, (i) "Full Mobility" that is characterized by a high degree of mobility and frequent changes of the workplace, (ii) "Site Mobility" that is characterized by mobility in geographically restricted areas (e.g. hospitals), (iii) "Multi Location Workplace" that is characterized by regular travels between fixed locations where work is carried out for a certain period of time, and (iv) "Networked Workplace" that is characterized by limited physical mobility while working collaboratively with many sites using online IT systems and applications. Enterprise end-users will need business applications that can cope with all these mobile working models. Future enterprise applications will need to cope with novel and often complex requirements due to increasing mobility.

  Concepts from (ii) are already evolving new forms of offices. In a large number of enterprises, workers are already sharing desks and choose a different workplace regularly in order to work close to the people they are collaborating with on projects and tasks. For special purposes, there are rooms specifically designed for concentrated working, meetings and conferences.

  Home office work, as an instance of (iii), is increasingly offered by companies today. Enterprise end-user need sophisticated applications that connect them from home to the corporate network and allow efficient multimedia communication, interaction and collaboration.

  End-users especially in category (i), but also in (iii), are traveling between workplaces regularly. They need enterprise applications that let them work on their business tasks efficiently and securely while using public mobile Web/Internet access in train stations, at airports, in hotels and other public places.

3.6 Technology Providers, Content Providers, Advertisers

Technology Providers are Telecommunication equipment, network equipment, server hardware and mobile device vendors as well as software companies. CSPs, ASPs and device/platform manufacturers are their customers and end-users. They are closely working together with them in terms of technology research, hardware/software system development and standardization. Thereby they use their insights into the industry in order to identify system requirements and to provide innovative technology products that fulfill those. Technology Providers are commercializing hardware and software products to equip their end-users with the IT infrastructure they need to provide services and applications to their private and enterprise end-users.

Content Providers create and distribute media content such as text, images, music and film/movie/video in different formats such as print media, music/video discs, digital media through different distribution channels such as online, store, mail order. Many are confronted with declining revenues and difficult business situations in their respective markets. Print media is increasingly substituted by online media and so, advertisement revenues of publishers are declining. The music and film industry needs to cope with the increase in illegal distribution of their content on peer-to-peer networks as well as with an increasing competition through user generated audio/video content sites. Content Providers are commonly looking for new profitable ways to offer their content. On the one hand, they are planning to publish their own innovative mobile applications to allow end-users to consume their content for a fee or financed through advertisement. On the other hand, they are offering their digital content as a service and are extending their cooperations with mobile application developers, CSPs and ASPs so they include the content into their end-user applications.

Advertisers are entities such as companies or individuals that market their products and services in CSPs', ASPs' and developers' services and applications through various types of paid advertisements. For providers and developers advertisers can constitute a profitable revenue source. Hence, they provide increasingly sophisticated tools and technologies for them, so they can run their campaigns highly efficient and precisely aimed at their target customer groups.

Chapter 4

Analysis

4.1 The Evolution of Telecommunication Service and Application Development

Over the past century, the Telecommunication industry has served the society's need to communicate over distances with an evolving portfolio of Telecommunication services and applications. Due to their high complexity and large development efforts, for several decades, Telecommunication systems had been specifically designed and standardized for only one specific service. This approach even continued when services were evolving or new services were designed.

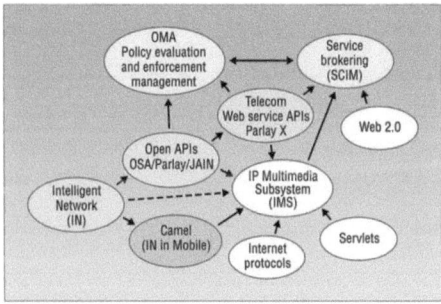

Figure 4.1: Evolution of Telecommunication Service and Application Development Concepts [132]

Nevertheless, over the years, Telecommunication systems were constantly supplemented with additional services, resulting in deployments of many independent and separated service specific hardware and software systems in CSPs networks. The central standardization body International Telecommunication Union (ITU) has even been fostering this approach through its three-stage process. For every new service, it starts with a detailed description of its capabilities and end-user applications from a high-level end-user focused perspective. The next step specifies a functional architecture and the last step defines service specific hardware and software elements together with service specific protocols between them. This development has been leading to so called "Telecommunication Service Silos" as already illustrated in section 2.1. [109, 132]

Over the past 30 years, the Telecommunication industry has transformed, invented supplementary or enhanced Telecommunication services and expanded into the Mobile and Web/Internet industry. In the 1980s, the goal of the development and standardization of new service architectures was to separate the physical network from the services. It was to create a programmable Telecommunication environment that allows introducing new services almost independently of the evolution of the underlying physical network. In early service architectures, such as ISDN, services are integrated in the protocols running at the end-users' access network devices. Thus, deployment of enhanced or additional services is inefficient as all devices and network components have to be updated.

Over the last 10 years, mobile Telecommunication systems were enhanced by mobile Web/Internet technologies in order to repeat the enormous success of fixed Web/Internet access again in mobile environments in the mobile Telecommunications industry. The emphasis of upcoming (mobile) Telecommunication networks is on enhancing network control and management capabilities while providing multimedia distributed services. CSP are exploring technologies and network architectures capable of offering value-added network-centric services. Thereby, Telecommunication service and application development has been evolving from IN over Parlay and IMS to Web Service, Web 2.0 and Web/Internet technologies-based concepts and, as illustrated in figure 4.1, ultimately resulted in Service Broker and Policy middleware specifications.

4.1.1 Intelligent Networks

In the 1980s, for IN, an overlay service architecture was defined on top of the physical (e.g. Public Switched Telephone Network (PSTN)) network. The service functionalities were extracted from the physical network and implemented in central Service Control Points (SCPs), as illustrated in figure 4.2. To connect all components within the overlay architecture as well as with the physical network in real-time, the IN Application Protocol (INAP) was standardized on top of the physical network protocol, Signaling System 7 (SS7). Even though it is simpler to deploy and remove services in such a centralized service platform architecture, the fact that a central network server is the main platform for hosting services often raises scalability problems.

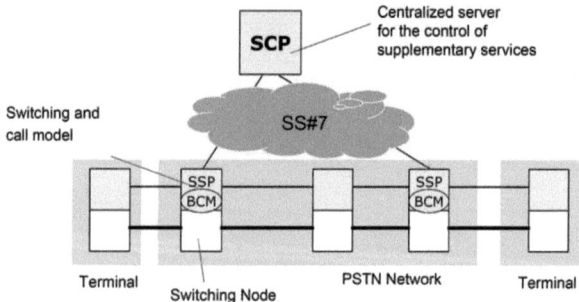

Figure 4.2: Intelligent Networks [110]

4.1. The Evolution of Telecommunication Service and Application Development

To realize service development in IN the ITU defined an IN Conceptual Model that adds one stage to the three-stage service development process. In this stage, based on a market-driven evaluation, common services were analyzed and decomposed into independent service features that could be reused by other services. All identified feature were transformed into IN Service Independent Building Blocks (SIBs) and the IN architecture provided means to define sequence graphs to chain these SIBs together to new services. Thereby, the IN architecture makes services independent of the network in principle, but limits the available features and functionalities through the selection of a limited number of common services.

For service developers, IN provides Service Creation Environments (SCEs) that enabled a comfortable, often even visual, development of new service logic. The execution of IN services cannot be initiated by an end-user directly. It is defined and configured by trigger points in the physical network "Switching Nodes" that react to different states of a Telecommunication service such as a phone call. [109, 132, 110]

4.1.2 Customized Applications for Mobile Enhanced Logic

The service platform of the European second generation mobile Telecommunication system, GSM, includes as core components the Mobile Services Switching Center (MSC) and Home Location Register (HLR), illustrated in figure 4.3. The MSC is responsible for all call control while the HLR includes all functionalities of a SCP in an IN, such as hosting end-user data like location for mobility as well as supplementary custom services. All services supported by the HLR are limited by a strict focus on the end-user (e.g. Call Forwarding on Busy) and are triggered from the MSC.

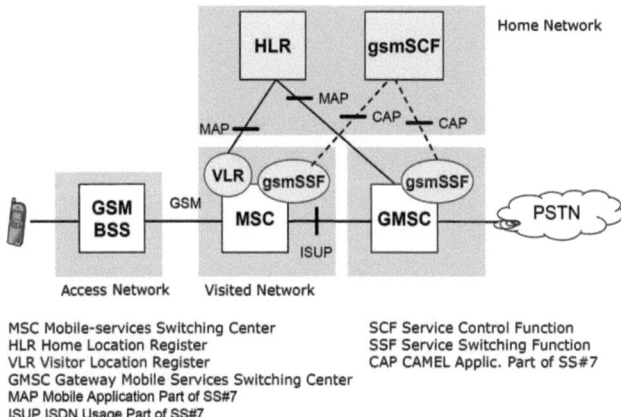

Figure 4.3: CAMEL (adopted from[110])

To support global services such as "Number Translation for Free Calls", "Virtual Private Networks" or "Short Messaging Service" independent of the end-user, Customized Applications for Mobile Enhanced Logic (CAMEL) was embedded into the GSM standard. In addition to the HLR service control point focusing on end-user services, CAMEL introduces "gsmSCF" service control points that cover global services independent from basic call control. In order to trigger such services, the "gsmSSF" service switching function was added to the MSC to detect service requests. [109, 132, 110]

4.1.3 Telecommunication Information Networking Architecture

In the mid-90s, the concept of a Distributed Processing Environment (DPE) was introduced in the software development industry. In a DPE, a middleware, such as CORBA by the OMG, supports the development of a distributed system. This middleware manages system components that are distributed over several heterogeneous platforms without requiring any adaption at the end-user applications. For such as distributed system, the DPE manages the collaboration of all components including the exchange of information in standardized messages using abstract communication concepts such as Remote Procedure Call (RPC). [109, 132, 110]

The goal behind the definition of Telecommunications Information Networking Architecture (TINA) was to standardize a global architecture for multimedia Telecommunication systems based on the latest software concepts and technologies. TINA applies a common software model to all components such as end-user device applications, service components and switching nodes, which enables CSPs to assemble new services from reusable, distributed and interacting components. The overall structure of TINA is composed from three architecture components, (i) the "Computing Architecture" that describes the distributed system based on the DPE concept as an application of distributed object-oriented software design through an extension of CORBA, (ii) the "Service Architecture" that describes the component-based platform responsible for service delivery and (iii) the "Network Resource Architecture" that manages and controls all physical network components and resources. [109, 132, 110]

With the quick evolution of Telecommunication systems to Web/Internet technologies and the initial incompatibility of TINA with those, TINA was never implemented and deployed outside of research labs. Nevertheless it provided many concepts and architecture ideas that were reused by later Telecommunication standards such as Parlay, IMS and SAE.

4.1.4 Open Application Programming Interface

In the software development industry, object-oriented programming became increasingly accepted. Newly available programming languages like C++ and Java enabled concepts of powerful distributed middleware platforms that could be used for scalable and distributed service delivery. Just as intended with TINA, a few years earlier, these make service development easier than with traditional IN and define a clear abstraction of the services from the underlying physical network, signaling protocols and transport protocols (e.g. ISDN, SIP, INAP). These technologies introduced the concept of creating own APIs for a software system to the Telecommunication industry. Thereby, for the first time, non-Telecommunication expert third party service providers could be provided with access to features of CSPs networks and service platforms. [109, 132, 110]

4.1.4.1 Parlay

Parlay [214] is a Telecommunication standard standardized in 1998 by the Parlay Consortium, which was composed from operators and manufacturers worldwide. Parlay standardizes an API that provides access to network-internal data as well as market-oriented Telecommunication related control and monitoring capabilities such as Call Control, User Interaction, Conferencing, Messaging, Location Information, Charging, Presence Information and Group List / Address

Book Management. Thereby, it defines a common interface on top of all types of independent and sometimes even incompatible Telecommunication networks.

The Parlay standard defines two different interfaces:

- **Parlay Framework Interface** - Provides functionalities to ensure a secured access to "Parlay Services" (e.g. AAA), for the management of "Parlay Services" as well as for the selection and access to the "Parlay Service Interface". It does not provide any functionalities for end-user profile information management.

- **Parlay Service Interfaces** - Provide interfaces to access "Parlay Services". "Parlay Services" are not intended to be invoked from outside by an end-user device, but are consolidated in an internal Parlay API to allow services and applications to access and control network functionalities and resources. Using a Parlay internal interface, "Parlay Services" are registered at the "Parlay Framework".

"Parlay Services" are categorized in the five groups Call Control Services, User Interaction Services, Mobility Services, Messaging Services and Connectivity Services. Each group includes interfaces of various sizes from which each represent one class of network services. Unfortunately several services, such as the INAP Call Control Service, are very specific to the underlying Telecommunication protocol from which they are actually supposed to abstract. This is probably due to the fact that "Resource Interfaces" to the actual physical network resources and protocols are not part of the Parlay specification and so, this important abstraction is often omitted.

All Parlay interfaces are specified completely technology and programming language independent in UML. The actual technology to access the interfaces from a client service or application is solely the Parlay platform vendors choice (e.g. C++ or Java using a CORBA middleware).[109, 132, 110]

For mobile communication systems the Parlay specification has been adopted by the 3GPP as Open Service Access (OSA) and is currently jointly developed further

4.1.4.2 Java API for Intelligent Networks

Sun Microsystems published the first version of Java API for Intelligent Networks (JAIN) in 1998 and from then, had been enhancing it in cooperation with the developer community up until about 2004. Basically, JAIN is a Java specification combined with a reference implementation of the Parlay standard in version 1.2. Thereby, it defines the implementation technology and programming language for Parlay including the network communication technology that Telecommunication applications use to access Parlay Services through Parlay Interfaces.

By using Java technology, JAIN brings a large number of advantages to Parlay Telecommunication application development. Through Java's standardized programming and runtime environment, all JAIN applications and services are fully portable between different JAIN systems. Through Java's standardized component technology, Java Beans, JAIN services and application can integrate interfaces and their implementations dynamically, even at runtime. In comparison to earlier concepts, such as IN, were developers had to deal with proprietary SCEs, Java is a well-known and understood programming language backed by a huge developer base. Thereby, JAIN service and application development is more tangible and a potentially large number of developers could join the Telecommunication service and application development community. [109, 132, 110]

In addition to the Parlay API, JAIN introduced a number of additional components and APIs illustrated in figure 4.4.

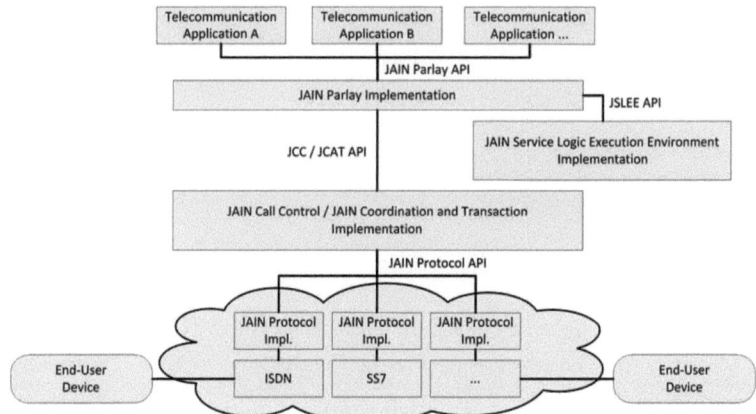

Figure 4.4: Java API for Intelligent Networks

- **JAIN Protocol APIs** - On the lowest abstraction layer, these APIs map the physical network and Telecommunication protocol details, events and messages to the Java environment. In the Parlay standards, they represent the Parlay Resource Interfaces.

- **JAIN Call Control (JCC) APIs / JAIN Coordination and Transaction (JCA) APIs** - Those provide physical network and Telecommunication protocol independent functionalities for Telecommunication service (e.g. Call) control and processing. Examples are monitoring, initiation, response, route manipulation and handling of multi-end-user calls across different physical Telecommunication networks. Only in combination with the functionalities provided by the JSLEE does this API comply with the Parlay standard.

- **JAIN Service Logic Execution Environment (JSLEE) APIs** - Provides Telecommunication network independent, non-Telecommunication service related functionalities for management and security of JAIN services and applications.

4.1.4.3 Conclusion

The idea to provide APIs that provide applications, hosted by CSP or third parties, access to exposed network capabilities could have created win-win business models for both sides.

Although this technology was promising and seamed to include everything that is required, such as secure access, API extensibility to cope with future market demands and innovation, service discovery and SLA features, the acceptance at CSP was too slow. Most were not ready to actually open up parts of their networks, the APIs were still too complex for non-Telecommunication developers and the object-oriented concepts to new for traditional Telecommunication engineers.

4.1.5 Adoption of Web/Internet Servlet Development Concepts

In 2000, the Web/Internet's success at providing increasingly powerful applications motivated Telecommunication standardization bodies to adopt web application development concepts. Since the Java platform has been the most successful professional web application development platform, the Java HTTP Servlet specification, since 2009 at version 3.0 in Java Specification Request (JSR) 315, was selected as a paradigm. The idea was to specify a similar concept for SIP-based Telecommunication networks and the result was the SIP Servlet specification, since 2008 at version 1.1 in JSR 289. Several vendors have been implementing the specification in their SIP application server products, which allow deploying and managing Telecommunication services and applications based on the Servlet concept.

In 2004, the 3GPP adopted the SIP application server concept for their standarization of IMS (see section F.5.2). Since SIP Servlet is, next to JSLEE, one of just very few technologies for SIP application servers, it will become a very important concept for Telecommunication service and application development and will probably be available in all major Telecommunication networks in the future. [109, 132, 110]

4.1.6 Web Service-Based Concepts

Web Services (see section 2.2.2) provide a programming language, technology and platform independence for distributed service and application development. The server application hosting a Web Service provides it through a platform independent interface and communication protocol to the client application. Both can be implemented in any common programming language such as C++, C# or Java.

The Parlay [214] APIs (see section 4.1.4.1) were standardized to enable non-Telecommunication development experts to develop Telecommunication functionalities enabled services and applications. Unfortunately, their abstraction from the physical Telecommunication network and its protocols was not pushed far enough. They are still quite low-level, requiring developers to still have an extensive know-how of Telecommunication service concepts and technologies. [127, 132]

Through the combination of that, in 2002, the Parlay consortium had started to standardize a Web Services-based abstraction from Parlay, called Parlay X. The first draft was published in 2003 and further enhancements on the path to a European standard were driven by ETSI and 3GPP.

Similar to the evolution steps illustrated above, also the Parlay X Web Services are intended to stimulate the development of next generation network applications by enabling developers who are not necessarily experts in Telecommunication technologies. The choice of what Web Services will be provided to developers is mostly driven commercial utility rather than technical integrity. [127, 132]

Figure 4.5 depicts the resulting standardized Parlay X architecture.

The main goals of Parlay X are that [127, 132]:

- each Web Service is abstracted from the set of Telecommunication capabilities exposed by the Parlay Gateway, or, if essential for services and applications in the future, may abstract Telecommunication capabilities currently not exposed by Parlay.

- the capabilities abstracted by a Parlay X Web Service may be homogeneous (e.g. Call Control only) or heterogeneous (e.g. mobility and presence)

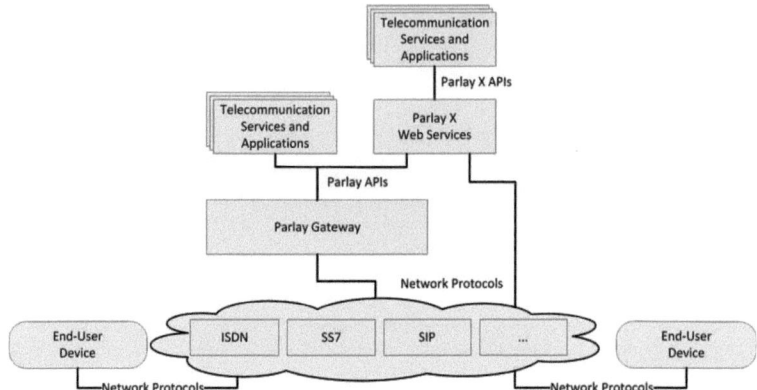

Figure 4.5: Parlay X Architecture

- it is preferred that Parlay X Web Services implement a synchronous message request/responses model that is initiated by the service or application.
- it is preferred that Parlay X Web Services are implemented stateless and that invocations are uncorrelated.
- a Parlay X Web Service is neither service or application nor network technology or protocol specific.
- Parlay X Web Services are not unnecessarily complicated or overloaded and so, should support 80% of services and applications through only 20% of their functionalities.
- the set of Parlay X Web Services has to be extensible by proven, reliable and standard compliant Web Services provided by third parties.

Through the use of Web Service technologies, further enhancements could easily be achieved by adopting concepts from Web Service-based BIS development. One such concept is the application of an ESB (see section 2.3) to abstract and manage the link between Parlay X Web Services, Web Service-based third party services and applications as well as CSP internal Web Service-based Operations Support System (OSS) and Business Support System (BSS). [179]

4.1.7 Telecommunication Service Orchestration

Service orchestration has been an important concept in BIS development long before the Telecommunications industry felt the need for it. In an early version, the IMS specification standardizes a Trigger Point-based mechanism, adopted from IN, that allows developers to define triggers based on Telecommunication signaling protocol (e.g. SIP) states and event. This allows services and applications to chain IMS application servers and so, in some sense, to orchestrate their functionalities. [155]

Since the initiation of this mechanisms the need for a more flexible and, from signaling protocols abstracted, way to orchestrate services has arisen. In the current version of the IMS standard the Service Broker concept from BIS development was introduced by the Service Capability Interaction Manager [225, 107, 146] (SCIM) component (see section F.5.3.2). Since, in this standard, the SCIM is not specified in detail, but only the basic functionalities are outlined, the actual realization, architectural decisions and choice of technologies is left to vendors providing an IMS implementation. This results in a broad range of heavily varying products using all sorts of Telecommunication technologies such as Parlay/OSA, Parlay X, JAIN as well as various BIS technologies such as BPEL or WSCI that all claim to implement a SCIM [230].

4.2 Evaluation of Web-Telecom Convergence Concepts and Platforms

This section introduces and discusses the most relevant state-of-the-art concepts for Web-Telecom Convergence that are currently available from Telecommunication standardization bodies as well as from research institutes.

4.2.1 Comparing Established Web-Telecom Convergence Platform Concepts

In this section, the evaluation and comparison of the established Web-Telecom Convergence Platform proposals "OMA Service Environment [163] (OSE) [164, 163]" [163], the "Fraunhofer FOKUS SOA Telco Playground [29, 135, 28]" and the " Service Platform for Innovative Communication Environment (SPICE) [93, 92, 211]", conducted in the CDTM research project [125], is presented.

4.2.1.1 Comparison Methodology

The topic of software architecture evaluation and comparison has been mainly driven by the IT industry and IT consulting in cooperation with academia. Thereby, most architecture evaluation methodology concepts have been derived from industry projects at IT companies on deployed and productive software systems.

The evaluation methodology of this section is based on the "Domain Specific Software Architecture Comparison Model (DoSAM)" [24] supplemented by the "Asset-Based Architecture Design Methodology for Rapid Telecom Service Delivery Platform Development (AADM)" [196, 9], for the elicitation of the functional requirements, and by the IEEE Standards for a "Software Quality Metrics Methodology (SQMM)" [203], to define quality attributes for the comparison. Figure 4.6 provides an overview of the designed architecture evaluation and comparison process.

The process can roughly be divided into two parts. In the first part, until the "Two Dimensional Evaluation Framework", a, as complete as possible, Telecommunication domain specific summary of business and functional requirements for a generic Web-Telecom Convergence Platform is compiled. In the second part, this summary is used to qualitatively evaluate the fulfillment of these requirements for every Web-Telecom Convergence Platform proposal and to generate a consolidated comparison.

Business Requirements To enable new business from new market opportunities, IT systems need to support business processes of a company in all forms. Therefore, the elicitation of the core Business Requirements is the first step of this evaluation process. They are seen as a high level, and in a company's core business applicable, abstraction of the underlying software features

Figure 4.6: Comparison Methodology (adapted from [125])

provided by the architecture. The Business Requirements represent the capability models within the AADM.

Functional Requirements The Functional Requirements consist of two integral parts, (i) the creation of a DoSAM Architectural Blueprint and (ii) breaking the blueprint down into Architectural Services.

The blueprint represents a basic understanding of the main system components and their relationships to each other. It defines the scope of the system and defines its borders.

The services break the main components down into clearly defined functionalities, which the system is required to fulfill. It is essential to specify these functionalities correctly and completely, as they map the business goals and requirements to the system that will be developed.

Quality Requirements A Quality Requirement is defined as a description of a property or characteristic that a software system must exhibit or a constraint that it must respect. The architecture provides the foundation for quality characteristics, hence it is essential to take quality attributes into account in the architecture design process.

The IEEE SQMM provides a standardized framework to describe as well as to evaluate quality characteristics of a software system. In a first step, based on business goals and requirements, Quality Factors need to be compiled and structured. In the second step, the Quality Factors

4.2. Evaluation of Web-Telecom Convergence Concepts and Platforms

need to be broken down into Quality Subfactors or groups of Subfactors. In order to compare architectures, these are then qualitatively evaluated.

Two-Dimensional Evaluation Framework   This framework combines the structured collections of requirements from Architectural Services and Quality Subfactors into a unified and well-structured collection of requirements. In order to being able to evaluate the architectures in a qualitative process, the framework aligns the requirements on similar levels of abstraction. The framework is not specifically tailored to the three platform proposals being evaluated, but is also adaptable to others in the future.

Evaluation of Platform Proposals   The platform proposals are structured similar to the requirements structure of the "Two-Dimensional Evaluation Framework". At first, the proposals are evaluated based on the Blueprint and its derived Architectural Services. Then, they are evaluated based on the Quality Subfactors. Finally, a qualitative comparison and analysis is compiled from the results of the first two steps.

4.2.1.2   Defining Comparison Methodology Parameters

In the following, the necessary domain specific comparison methodology parameters for a generic Web-Telecom Convergence platform are defined. The parameters for the initial step of the evaluation and comparison process, the collection of Business Requirements, can be found in appendix A.1 [125].

Architectural Blueprint   The Architectural Blueprint, illustrated in figure 4.7, represents a high-level view on the architecture of the Web-Telecom Convergence Platform concepts. It was designed through the combination of project partner expert interviews with an architecture analysis of the major components from several platform research results, concepts and vendor products. A further decomposition of the high-level components follows at the specification of the Architectural Services.

- **Service Creation Environment** - Needs to provide tools and high-level features to assist internal and third party developers at the rapid creation of new services and applications. It needs to manage the usage of reusable services and enablers, and support developers at creating and deploying new ones through service creation/development concepts such as service orchestration. For this, graphical tools for chaining and composing services to value-added services or business processes, without the need of extensive source code programming, are desired.

  Service creation does not only include the development, but also the thorough testing. Certain quality assurances and testing methodologies/concepts need to be supported to ensure a high-quality for all services before they are deployed to the Service Execution Environment.

- **Service Control Environment** - Is a gateway that allows partners secured and controlled access to Telecommunication network resources and services. With the increase in network capabilities and services to be exposed to third parties, security mechanisms such as AAA with user and role management as well as Access Policy Management and Enforcement become increasingly important, but also complex, and must be simple to handle. With the introduction of SLAs between service consumer and the platform as service provider, some

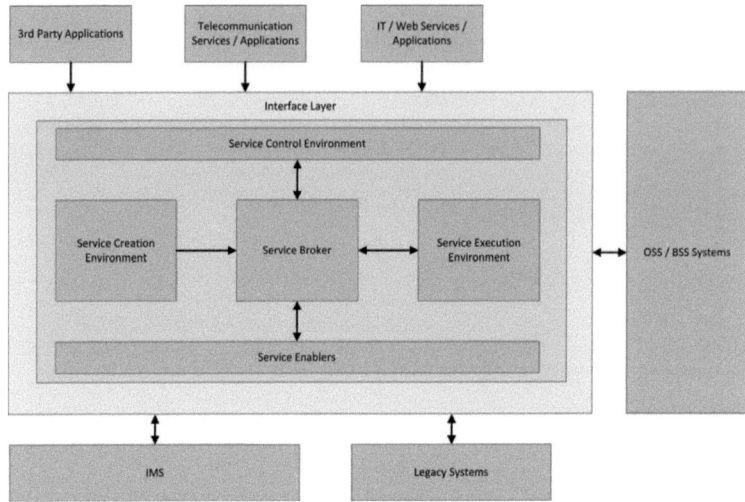

Figure 4.7: Web-Telecom Convergence Platform Concepts Blueprint (adapted from [125])

control mechanisms such as monitoring and enforcement of predefined parameters need to be provided.

- **Service Execution Environment** - Provides a homogeneous service lifecycle management (see section 2.2.4) for all services deployed on the platform. This includes functionalities such as service discovery, service execution as well as the execution of service orchestrations designed in the Service Creation Environment.

- **Service Broker** - Manages the exchange of messages/data between the Execution Environment, the Control Environment and the Creation Environment. Typically it provides some sort of generic message bus or middleware that is able to handle the interaction between a large number of heterogeneous services efficiently. To do so, it maps and adapts service interfaces entirely transparent for the services. To administrate and to analyze the performance and state of this component, it needs to provide management and monitoring functionalities.

- **Interfaces** - Enable CSP internal as well as third party services and applications to access the services on the platform. They need to be provided using state-of-the-art and, for developers, common development technologies and programming languages bundled in APIs or even complete SDKs.

  In addition to the external services and applications interface, the Interfaces component also provides access for OSS/BSS to include the platform into the CSPs operational processes.

- **Service Enablers** - Are the buildings blocks that expose and abstract the underlying physical Telecommunication network protocols, technologies and capabilities through common software development technologies for non-Telecommunication experts. Enablers represent

4.2. Evaluation of Web-Telecom Convergence Concepts and Platforms

reusable Telecommunication specific service components, which can be used to build higher-level services through composition or to build complete Telecommunication applications.

The parameters for the next step of the process, the Architectural Services, are derived from the blueprint. An overview about these can be found in appendix A.2.

Quality Factors   In parallel to the functional aspects of a Web-Telecom Convergence platform, also the quality aspects are taken into account. As parameters for this step, the following Quality Factors were identified as the most important ones [125]:

- **Interoperability** - The platform has to include the ability to adjust to different end-user applications, devices, partner platforms, underlying networks as well as legacy systems and networks. It has to provide open standardized interfaces to be combined with platforms of CSP and ASP partners in the future. It has to provide standardized interfaces to attract third party developers, leading to more innovative services and applications.

- **Reliability** - The platform has to have the ability to operate correctly without failure over a defined period of time. It needs to ensure a consistent and stable environment for the deployment, execution and the delivery of its services. It has to ensure a reliable delivery of messages between services on the platform as well as between the platform and third party services and applications.

- **Availability** - The platform needs to provide a high degree, to which it is operational and accessible for use. In the Telecommunication industry this is means it needs to achieve near carrier grade (99,999%) availability. It needs to be tolerant to system failures and overload situations, and be capable of solving and isolating problems to ensure the availability of the platform. Since contractual measurements of availability are usually included in SLAs, the platform needs to include the functionalities to provide monitoring information in order to analyze the availability status of the platform constantly.

- **Usability** - The platform needs to provide a high measurable quality of end-users experience in interaction with devices, platform functionalities, services and data. It needs to be easy for developers to create and deploy services on the platform. The platform needs to abstract from Telecommunication technology specifics in a meaningful way, so developers can quickly adopt service and application development in this, for them, new environment. It needs to provide mature and powerful services and enablers that are simple to adopt and integrate into other services and applications to ensure a fast time to market.

- **Security** - The platform needs to provide the ability to resist unauthorized attempts of usage or behavior modification, while still providing services to legitimate end-users. Data integrity and confidentiality play major roles on every professional software platform. State-of-the-art mechanisms for configuring and enforcing permissions for users, groups and roles need to be provided.

- **Performance** - To comply with Telecommunication standards, the platform should perform in near real time, which is measured by the maximum response time of deployed services. Especially platform internal functionalities such as access and authorization functions should not impact the performance of services. This is especially crucial, because the platform has to manage high volumes of data in a high number of transactions.

- **Scalability** - The platform needs to exhibit the ability to function without degradation of quality attributes when the platform is changed in size due to an increase in volume.

Due to the massive amount of end-users, especially within the Telecommunication industry, scalability of systems is extremely important.

As parameters for the next step of the process, the Quality Subfactors are defined by decomposing the Quality Factors. An overview about these can be found in appendix A.3.

4.2.1.3 Comparison of Web-Telecom Convergence Platform Proposals

In the following, the methodology and parameters are applied to compare the OSE, "FOKUS Open SOA Playground" and SPICE platform proposals. The complete qualitative evaluation of every platform, based on every domain specific business, functional and quality parameter of the evaluation process, can be found in [125]. The summary of the results is illustrated in figure 4.8. A green indication represents a major fulfillment of the evaluation parameters, a yellow indication points-out some major parameters to be not fulfilled in this area, while a red indication highlights requirements to be not specified at all, or to be failing fulfillment completely.

	OSE	Fokus	SPICE
Architectural Components			
Service Creation Environment	-	~	+
Service Execution Environment	~	~	+
Service Control Environment	~	+	+
Service Broker	~	+	+
Interfaces	-	+	+
Enabler	+	+	~
Quality Requirements			
Interoperability	~	+	+
Usability	-	~	+
Security	~	~	+

+ ... fulfilled
~ ... partially/limited fulfilled
- ... not fulfilled

Figure 4.8: Web-Telecom Convergence Platform Proposals Comparison [125]

OSE focuses strongly on its enablers, thus lacking enhancing functionalities necessary for a future proof Web-Telecom Convergence platform. It offers a very abstract solution and is limited in scope, but it can be used as a foundation for more advanced Web-Telecom Convergence platform specifications or products in the future.

Fraunhofer FOKUS offers an abstract overall design of a rich Web-Telecom Convergence platform, proposing the use of either published standards or own enhanced specification upon standardized specifications. It fulfills the requirements of the Service Control Environment, the Service Broker, the Interfaces and Enablers from the functional point of view in a satisfying manner. At the Service Creation Environment and Service Execution Environment it needs more detailed specifications and tools for service creation and development.

SPICE offers the most matured and complete architecture specification within this comparison.

Besides the Enabler requirements, in which it lacks more detailed specifications, SPICE fulfills the requirements in every other category on functional as well as quality side.

4.2.2 Discussing Web-Telecom Convergence Research Results

V. Danciu, et. al. discuss in [52] the abstraction and composition of existing cloud services in a new Cloud Broker middleware. This Cloud Broker manages Authentication, Authorization, Accounting, Auditing and Charging (A4C), and dynamically discovers/selects, aggregates, binds and manages cloud services. It provides compositions of these cloud services to mobile applications transparently. For a dynamic composition of services according to a changing environment and requirements, the Cloud Broker provides workflow-based orchestration components and tools. The Cloud Broker focuses on shared Web/Internet services and leaves shared Telecommunication services, application-specific services and cross-platform client development aspects out of scope.

N. Blum, et. al. propose in [30] and [27] a SDF based on SOA concepts and present a prototype implementation and test-bed deployment. Their platform allows for an autonomous composition of Telecommunication services within the Telecommunication domain using SOA service description and orchestration concepts. Web-Telecom Convergence of services and applications is out of scope of their platform. They define it as to take place on layers above their Service Delivery Framework, which developers should design themselves.

N. Blum, et. al. present in [28] a concept for a policy-based service broker that allows for an integration of Telecommunication services based on IMS enablers into Web/Internet mashups and other third party applications. The broker mediates between the real-time Telecommunication services and third party applications. The broker's policies serve as service access definitions as well as an expression for user/service specific capabilities and rules.

F. Deinert, et. al. propose in [54] an approach to combine Web 2.0 enabled widgets with Telecommunication services exposed by an IMS. They introduce a new abstraction layer with interfaces and a widget engine that provides access to the Telecommunication services. It allows rapid development of Web 2.0 widget applications but is restricted to use-cases where widgets are suitable as end-user clients.

J. Yang and H. Park propose in [248] an Open Service Access Gateway (OSAG) that allows Telecommunication operators to leverage W3C Web Services to provide integrated services. It further describes how Telecommunication and W3C Web Services can be combined on the OSAG to build Web-Telecom Converged services and how applications can use these services through defined interfaces. An application architecture or end-user client support is out of scope of this research work.

C. Gbaguidi, et. al. propose in [76] the concept of Hybrid Services as services that span across multiple, especially IP-based, networks such as telephone, Web/Internet and cellular. They describe an architecture for the provisioning of such services. Their architecture allows the programming of new elements of the platform in order to develop new services that can used in new applications. Further, they introduce a concept of orchestration on Telecommunication features such as call control, security, address translation etc. and expose them as higher-level services for reuse. Finally, they implement a Java-based prototype of the platform and a prototype service/application on top.

X. Shao, et. al. describe in [195] an integrated Telecommunication and IT SDP for converging IMS Services, W3C Web Service and underlying services. They propose a combination of their SIP-based Micro Service Orchestration with a Service Bus to achieve the orchestration. At the end, they present a prototype multimedia service implementation and discuss the support of their SDP for rapid development and deployment of new Web-Telecom Converged multimedia services.

H. Ohnishi, et. al. present in [158] a SDP concept that goes beyond the ones discussed in section 2.5. Their goal was to develop an SDP architecture that co-exists with Enterprise and Web/Internet architectures and so, they use Enterprise/Internet compatible Web/Internet and W3C Web Service technologies such as ParlayX, BPEL [157], ESB [43] and WSDL to realize their SDP. They extend the technologies used in order to fulfill Telecommunication service specific requirements identified from a CSP's viewpoint.

4.2.3 Evaluation Conclusions

In this section the current state-of-the-art of Web-Telecom Convergence was presented and evaluated by comparing the three most popular Web-Telecom Convergence Platform concepts as well as discussing the most widespread and recognized research results. By additionally taking into account less recognized but relevant supplementary research results from [163, 168, 170, 120, 3, 94, 39, 105, 122, 227, 132, 19, 129, 31, 32, 253, 69, 182, 20], the following summary discusses the most important conclusions that can be drawn.

- **No End-to-End Platform Concepts** - The concepts evaluated in this section do not specify any solutions or architectures that would allow to design and build an application from the low-level "end" of the physical Telecommunication all the way to the highest-level "end", the end-user application on the end-user devices. They do not provide concepts and solutions for reusing Web/Internet as well as Telecommunication services, for security, for scalability, for data/message transmission in a distributed application, for the integrated software development process on the platform and more.

- **No Distinction Between Services and Applications** - The concepts evaluated in this section do not separate between functionality that can be reused by other services or applications and functionality that is applications specific and useless for other services or applications. The first is typically encapsulated in services whereas the later is typically encapsulated in the client and server parts of a distributed application.

- **No Clear Separation of Network and Application** - The concepts evaluated in this section do not separate services that abstract from physical core Telecommunication network capabilities, technologies and protocols, from those that provide higher-level functionalities for applications. Further, most don't even include into their concepts, the applications that ultimately deliver the implemented functionality to the end-users on their devices.

- **No Cross-Platform Support** - The concepts evaluated in this section do not provide any concept or solutions for end-user client development and distribution. Hence, they do not provide any concept or solution for platform features, components or services that would support developers at providing end-user clients that are able to run seamlessly, in parallel and fully synchronized across all the various types of client devices and platforms. Further, they do not provide any platform features that would support the transformation and adaptation of the service/application content or data to different types of end-user clients.

- **No Application Lifecycle Support** - The concepts evaluated in this section do not support the lifecycle of the end-user applications. They only cover the initial steps by abstracting from the Telecommunication capabilities and providing reusable services for them. They do not provide developers with any concepts or support for end-user application development, hosting, distribution, etc.

4.3. Evaluation of Mobile Application Development Technologies   79

- **Limited Cross-Access Networks Support** - Most concepts evaluated in this section do not include any concepts or solutions for how to allow seamless service and application access from across heterogeneous operators domains as well as from the Telecommunication networks independent Web/Internet. They do not include solutions for how to migrate components like security, charging and accounting from an access network provider level to a higher and provider abstracted level so they can be used seamlessly across providers' domains worldwide.

- **Limited SOA Concepts Adoption** - Most concepts evaluated in this section adopt, mostly technical, SOA concepts only for Telecommunication network abstraction service exposure as proposed in Parlay X (see section 4.1.6). They do not adopt supplementary concepts such as the SOA Triangular Model, SOA Service Layers or a SOA Reference Architecture (see section 2.2) to structure their platforms better in order to build Telecommunication applications that are provided to the end-users completely based on SOA concepts.

- **Limited Web/Internet Services Support** - Most concepts evaluated in this section do not include concepts or solution to dynamically import services from other domains that are outside of the platform or the network of the CSP. They do not support an import of external Web/Internet services into the platform in order to manage them with the tools the platform provides. They do not support to compose them with Telecommunication services to value-added reusable services or full end-user applications right on the platform. Most propose the Web-Telecom Convergence to take place above the platform they are specifying. For the evaluated concepts the scope for Web-Telecom Convergence is mostly very limited, often it is completely out of scope.

- **Limited Service and Application Developer Support** - Most concepts evaluated in this section do not provide any tools or solutions to support end-user application development. They do not provide any concepts for the service and application deployment process such as SDKs, service and application hosting, beta testing and live roll-out. Most don't provide means for service publishing, discovery and access/invocation for application developers and their applications. For all concepts evaluated, binding SLA negotiation, supervision and enforcement are out of scope.

This Web-Telecom Convergence Concepts and Platform evaluation, the comparison results, the discussions above and this summary of conclusions build the foundation for this research work's requirements definitions and platform design presented in the following chapters.

4.3 Evaluation of Mobile Application Development Technologies

For every Web-Telecom Converged application, the client applications deployed on the end-users' devices are an essential part of the distributed application. In order to identify, support and provide developers with the most suitable technologies and tools to create application clients with great user experiences, the currently available technologies and tools need to be structured, compared and evaluated.

This section summarizes the two-part evaluation of development platforms and frameworks conducted in the CDTM project [121]. In the first part, the evaluation introduces the currently most successful mobile device platforms and structures the comparison of their technological details into 4 categories, 18 criteria and 44 sub-criteria. Following that, for each platform, it rates the criteria's and sub-criteria's individual availability, fulfillment or maturity by distributing points in the range from 0 to 3.

In the second part, the evaluation introduces the currently most popular mobile development frameworks. Similar to the first part, it structures their technological details by deriving 4 categories, 19 criteria and 25 sub-criteria. Following that, similar to the first part, it rates the criteria and sub-criteria for each framework.

From the resulting structured rating tables, criteria or sub-criteria that may be important for a certain mobile development use-case, such as Web-Telecom Converged application clients, can be selected or weighted. Thereby, both mobile platforms as well as mobile development frameworks can be compared and evaluated explicitly for this use-case. See section C for the complete comparison tables.

4.3.1 Mobile Platforms

The evaluation focused on the three popular and fast spreading mobile platforms iOS from Apple, Android from Google and Windows Phone 7 from Microsoft.

- **Apple iOS**

    iOS is a proprietary mobile platform developed, maintained and fully controlled by Apple that can only run on devices designed and sold by Apple. Originally, it was designed and created for the introduction of the iPhone in 2007. Three years later, it had been extended to other Apple devices like the newly introduced iPad, iPod Touch and Apple TV.

    By the end of Q3 2011 Apple had shipped 146 million devices and published about 500,000 applications on the Apple App Store. Apple controls applications and digital content for the iOS through the App Store and iTunes, which are the only places where end-users can purchase, download and install applications or content [231, 233, 232].

    The iOS is based on a scaled-down version of Apple's Mac OS X desktop/laptop platform that was optimized for touch-screen user-interfaces and adapted to cope with the limitations of mobile device hardware resources. Technologies shared between iOS and Mac OS X include the OS X kernel, BSD sockets for networking, Objective-C and C/C++ compilers for native performance. Apple distributes open source portions of the kernel and Mac OS X through its sponsoring of the Darwin project.

    The iOS belongs to the newest generation of operating systems that contain five layers: the kernel, the middleware layer, the Application Execution Environment (AEE), the application/user-interface framework and the application suite layer. For developing native iPhone/iPad iOS applications, Apple provides an SDK for Mac OS. This contains all tools a developer needs to create an iOS application, such as the IDE Xcode, a simulator, a user-interface builder and analysis tools to both optimize and monitor iOS applications for memory leaks in real time. In addition, recently, Dashcode, an IDE that simplifies the development of future web-based iPhone and iPad applications, was added.

- **Google Android**

    The Android OS was originally developed by Android Inc., which was acquired by Google in 2005. Following the acquisition, the Open Handset Alliance was created by Google to foster and distribute Android to manufacturers, CSPs, developers and end-users. Android is fully open-source and every device manufacturer can adapt it to fulfill his user experience and business requirements. Therefore, Android applications can be downloaded from the central Android Market or installed from an Android Application Package (APK) and run on various different mobile and tablet devices from various different manufacturers.

4.3. Evaluation of Mobile Application Development Technologies

Android was launched in November 2007 and since then, 225 million devices have been sold and 300,000 applications have been published on the Android Market. Roughly 10 billion Android applications have been downloaded, and in Q4 2010, with 32.9 million shipments, the Android platform outran Nokia's Symbian platform with 31 million shipments and became the leader of the smartphone platforms market.

Similar to iOS, Android is a new generation mobile operating system with five layers. Android relies on Linux version 2.6 for the core system and all libraries on the middleware layer are written in C/C++ and used by components of the AEE on top. The middleware provides support for audio and video multimedia, 2D and 3D graphics, wireless, networking, location services, sensors, Bluetooth, etc.

The application framework and pre-installed applications are written in Java and typically, third-party developers create their Android applications in Java as well. Every Java application on the Android platform runs as an independent process with an independent instance of the Dalvik virtual machine executing the application. For special purposes, through the Android Native Development Kit (NDK) or the Java Native Interface (JNI), the platform can also run performance-critical C/C++ components or applications.

For developers, Google provides a mature SDK that is built around an Eclipse IDE Android plugin and includes a wide range of powerful tools for developing, testing, debugging and deploying Android applications.

The Android platform is distributed with pre-installed applications that integrate the platform with many Google cloud services such as Google Search, Google Voice/Talk, Google Maps, Google Mail, Google Calendar/Contacts, Android Market etc.

- **Microsoft Windows Phone 7**

  Windows Phone 7 is a mobile device platform that is designed, developed and controlled by Microsoft and was launched at the end of 2008. Based on the experience from previous Windows Mobile versions, Microsoft created a Windows Phone 7 certification standard that enables all device manufacturers to deploy Windows Phone 7 on their certified devices. Since 2011, Nokia is the largest device manufacturing partner of Microsoft. Since the platforms launch, 10 million devices have been sold and about 30,000 mobile applications have been published in the Windows Phone 7 Marketplace.

  The Windows Phone 7 platform architecture is built upon the four components Runtimes, Tools, Portal and Cloud Services. Runtimes support developers in writing secure and graphically rich applications. As Tools the platform provides two well-known Microsoft IDEs: Visual Studio and Expression Blend. Portal Services help developers to manage application lifecycles in the Marketplace and Cloud services connect the platform to Microsoft Azure.

  Microsoft offers two frameworks for developing Windows Phone 7 applications, Silverlight and XNA (XNA is Not an Acronym). Web developers know Silverlight as a powerful framework for creating rich web-based user-interfaces. Silverlight was extended for Windows Phone 7 to enable developers to create innovative applications with a great user experience. XNA is Microsoft's game platform that was originally developed for the Xbox. It supports both 2D sprite-based and 3D graphics with a traditional game-loop software architecture. XNA was extended from the Xbox game console to enable developers develop applications for Window Phone 7 and Zune HD environments.

Figure 4.9 provides a consolidated overview of the results of the evaluation of these three platforms. A detailed overview can be found in section C. An extended discussion of the results and a detailed explanation of the categories, criteria and sub-criteria is illustrated in [121].

Categories	Criteria	iOS	Android	Windows Phone 7
Application Development				
	Development Workflow Support	2	1	1
	Developer Community and Support	1	1	1
	Development Environment	4	7	4
	Learning Curve	0	2	1
	Hardware Capabilities	12	14	14
	Programming Language	0	2	1
Software Stack and Architecture				
	Cloud Computing	1	1	1
	API Capabilities	25	24	21
	Memory and Process Management	1	1	1
	Multiple Screen	1	1	1
	Open Source	0	1	0
	User Interface	2	1	1
	Web Browser	1	1	0
Capabilities and Constraints				
	Devices	1	1	0
	Ecosystem	2	2	2
	Runtime Speed	2	1	1
Market Success and Issues				
	Fragmentation	2	1	1
	Mobile Platform Race	2	1	0

Figure 4.9: Consolidated Mobile Platforms Comparison

For Web-Telecom Converged applications it can be concluded that currently, iOS and Android are the primary mobile platform choices for mobile application client development. The distinction between those heavily depends on the use-case and the experience and know-how of the developers that implement the mobile application. iOS provides a more coherent support for user-interface design with a common usability across all devices, and does not allow any fragmentation of the platform by device manufacturers or developers. Android, provides an open development environment, uses a common, wide-spread and easy-to-learn programming language and, through its device manufacturer cooperation model, has the potential to spread quickly to a large user-base in a multi-device and multi-screen market.

4.3.2 Mobile Development Frameworks

The evaluation focused on the four most popular, most mature and fastest spreading mobile development frameworks PhoneGap, Titanium, RhoMobile and WAC.

- **PhoneGap**

    PhoneGap intends to bridge the gap between Web/Internet technologies and native mobile application development while providing access to more platform and device capabilities than current HTML5 applications have. It is a mobile application development framework that enables developer to implement mobile web applications that are able to run across several native platforms that have access to platform APIs, services and hardware capabilities, and that can be published in the platforms' respective App Stores. PhoneGap leverages the Web/Internet technologies HTML and JavaScript that many developers either already know or easily learn.

    PhoneGap was created by Nitobi, which was acquired by Adobe in October 2011. It was initially developed for the iPhone and was soon extended to support many other mobile platforms like Android, Windows Phone 7, Blackberry, WebOS, etc. PhoneGap is an open source project and was contributed to the Apache Software Foundation (ASF) under the name Apache Callback in October 2011.

    PhoneGap supports the native mobile development IDEs XCode, Eclipse, Visual Studio, etc. Alternatively, developers can write HTML and JavaScript files in any editor of their choice and upload them to the Web/Internet-based PhoneGap Build Service. The Service compiles the application files and returns a distributable application package.

    Since PhoneGap applications are basically Web/Internet technologies-based applications, developers can use many other powerful JavaScript-based libraries such as jQuery, MooTools, XUI, jQTouch, etc. to enrich their applications. In addition, PhoneGap enables developers to extend the PhoneGap framework to provide additionally desired functionalities by writing and sharing plug-ins.

- **Titanium**

    Titanium is a, partly commercialized, open-source and Web/Internet technologies-based (HTML, JavaScript, CSS, etc.) mobile development framework for building native desktop and mobile applications. It offers a free Community Edition ready for building and distributing applications as well as commercial Professional and Enterprise Editions that provide additional support and services.

    A Titanium-based application can be deployed and run on the three desktop/laptop platforms Windows, Mac OS X and Linux as well as on the two mobile platforms iOS and Android. A package that supports the Blackberry platform will be released in the near future. For developers, Titanium offers a package of the Titanium Studio IDE together with an SDK that provides an application development API.

    The Titanium Studio is a powerful Eclipse-based IDE that is built upon the patent-pending development technology acquired from Aptana. It provides development support features like a simulator, compiler, debug/test, deploy, repository support, etc.

    The Titanium SDK provides a platform-independent API that abstracts access to native user-interface components as well as to platform and hardware capabilities such as sound, file system, network, local database, 2D and 3D animations, camera etc.

    In addition to Studio and SDK, Titanium offers the commercial Appcelerator Network, which is a cloud service for testing, packing, distribution and analytics for desktop and mobile applications.

- **RhoMobile Rhodes**

    Rhodes is a mobile application development framework created by RhoMobile. Rhodes aims to offer a complete suite of products for building and managing enterprise mobile applications. It was initially released in December 2008, is available for the major mobile platforms iOS, Android, Windows Phone 7 and Blackberry and is a commercially-supported open-source product licensed under the MIT License.

    Rhodes is a framework that fosters a Model-View-Controller pattern to clearly separate business logic from presentation and that supports the programming languages HTML, CSS, JavaScript and Ruby.

    It offers its own Object-Relation Mapping (ORM) solution Rhom to simplify database access as well as its own GUI logic concept Embedded Ruby (ERB) to support developers at implementing logic on the application front-end. Rhodes provides RhoSync, a cloud service to synchronize data of mobile platforms and allows extending the application development framework through native extension.

    Applications built by Rhodes are platform-specific native applications that have access to platform and hardware capabilities such as GPS, maps, camera, calendar, etc. They are compiled into Ruby byte code, which can be executed by the Ruby runtime that is included in the Rhodes versions for the different mobile platform.

    For developers, RhoMobile provides the state-of-the-art Rhodes Studio IDE for Windows and Mac OS X.

- **Wholesale Application Community (WAC)**

    As briefly illustrated in section 3.1, WAC is an open global alliance that was created by the world's largest CSPs and device manufacturers such as AT&T, Vodafone, DoCoMo, Deutsche Telekom, Nokia, Samsung to support developers at creating and distributing compelling future mobile applications and digital content.

    WAC's four major goals are to enlarge the worldwide market for mobile applications, to standardize mobile technologies, to give developers more opportunities to distribute their applications and to encourage the use of CSPs' network APIs.

    The WAC application development framework is based on the five specifications (i) the standardized Web/Internet technologies HTML5 and JavaScript that many developers already know and that are easy to learn, (ii) the device APIs Bondi and JIL that provide access to platform and hardware capabilities through JavaScript, (iii) the OneAPI that provides access to CSPs' network capabilities, (iv) the Compliance certification that ensures that Web/Internet technology runtimes are consistent across platforms and devices, and (v) the security policies.

    For developers, WAC provides an SDK that is compatible with most common desktop/laptop platforms and a development plugin for the popular IDE Eclipse. A final WAC application is packaged according to the World Wide Web Consortium (W3C) Widget standard in a WGT file format. WAC provides a WGT runtime for most current mobile platforms and a web-based WGT emulator for testing and debugging. Before an application can be distributed through the WAC App Store it needs to pass the WAC testing and certification process.

Figure 4.10 provides a consolidated overview of the results of the evaluation of these four frameworks. A detailed overview can be found in section C. An extended discussion of the results and an explanation of the categories, criteria and sub-criteria is illustrated in [121].

For Web-Telecom Converged applications it can be concluded that current mobile development frameworks are mature enough to support probably most of the possible future applications

4.3. Evaluation of Mobile Application Development Technologies

Categories	Criteria	PhoneGap	Titanium	RhoMobile	WAC
Context					
	Open Source	1	2	2	2
	Cross Platform	2	1	2	2
	Application Type	1	1	2	1
	Services	0	0	2	0
Application Development					
	Debugger	1	1	1	1
	Build Process	2	1	2	1
	Test Process	1	1	1	2
	IDE	2	3	3	4
	Programming Language	1	3	2	1
	Community	2	1	2	0
	Learning Curve	1	1	0	1
	Tutorials, Documentation	1	1	1	0
Device API					
	Access to Mobile Platform	1	1	1	0
	Hardware Capabilities	11	13	18	8
	Network API	0	0	0	1
	Extensibility	1	1	1	0
	Multiple Screen	1	1	0	0

Figure 4.10: Consolidated Mobile Development Frameworks Comparison

developers will implement. From the four frameworks evaluated, RhoMobile and PhoneGap are the most suitable for cross-platform compatible Web-Telecom Converged application clients. RhoMobile provides access to a wide range of mobile platform services and their underlying hardware capabilities. It allows developers to choose from a large selection of Web/Internet development technologies and provides a great development environment including an IDE, a debugger and test/build tools. PhoneGap provides the widest range of cross-platform and cross-screen support, fosters a growing and active developer community, provides great tutorials and documents, is based on common Web/Internet technologies and so, is easy to learn for developers. It provides access to platform services and underlying hardware capabilities that are sufficient for a wide range of mobile Web-Telecom Converged applications.

Chapter 5

Design of Web-Telecom Converged Applications

This section develops the very general concept of Web-Telecom Convergence from section 2.8.3 further and applies it to the development of an application. It provides an overview about a few exemplary Web-Telecom Convergence application scenarios that will be used as case studies throughout the rest of this research work. Further, it presents a generic logical architecture of a distributed application that builds its application logic upon the convergence of services and functionalities from the Web/Internet with some from Telecommunications. Finally, this architecture is mapped to a technical architecture of one of the applications scenarios.

5.1 Web-Telecom Convergence Application Scenarios

This section presents some exemplary scenarios that illustrate how Web-Telecom Convergence could be used in future innovative application development.

5.1.1 Unified Address Book

By using many Web/Internet service and hardware devices, a typical end-user has a number of different address books stored under different Web/Internet accounts, in CSP managed Telecommunication address books as well as on different devices such as smart phones, tablets, laptops, etc. The concept of the Unified Address Book is to tap into all these source of contact data and provide them as one well sorted and structured address book in an end-user application on all devices and screens. In figure 5.1 the concept is illustrated as a one- and a two-level approach incorporating exemplary contact data sources.

The Address Book services aggregate the contacts data from the sources below, synchronize data changes in both ways and (semi-)automatically map data sources with each other in order to combine data for the same contact into only one contact data element. In the one-level approach (top), there is only one service interface, so all applications have access to the whole collection of contacts data from all types of sources. In the two-level approach (bottom), there is not just a Unified Address Book service that provides the whole data collection, but there are also Web/Internet, Device and Telecommunication Address Book services that provide only subsets. Thereby, applications can choose to only retrieve the collection of contact data they can or would

88   Chapter 5. Design of Web-Telecom Converged Applications

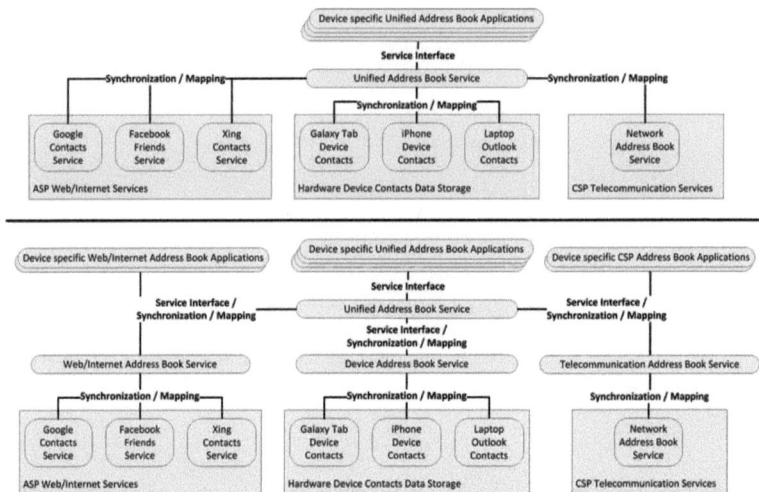

Figure 5.1: Unified Address Book as One- and Two-Level Approach

like to process. The data subsets are smaller and from more homogeneous sources, so aggregation and mapping of contacts is more efficient.

5.1.2 Social Notification Application

End-users are increasingly active on ASPs Web/Internet social network applications. Those can easily be accessed using web browsers on fixed (e.g. PC, Laptop) as well as increasingly using mobile web browsers or dedicated mobile applications on mobile devices. To receive updates from their networks, end-users need to, in a so called Poll-Model, actively log-on to the social network applications and check for them.

The concept of the Social Notification Application is to transform this update mechanism into a so called Push-Model, in which end-users are automatically notified about social network updates on all of their devices using various types of Web/Internet and Telecommunication data/communication channels. Figure 5.2 illustrates such a Social Notification Application using some exemplary Telecommunication and Web/Internet data/communication services.

The Social Notification Application is able to receive status updates from all of an end-user's social networks. Once a status update event is received, based on the end-user's preferences, this status update information is transmitted via (i) an automatically initiated audio/video call to the end-user's Telecommunication device, (ii) a text/multimedia message sent to the end-user's Telecommunication device, (iii) an e-mail sent to the end-user's e-mail system, or (iv) some status update data sent directly to the Social Network Application clients on one or many of the end-user's devices.

To enable an end-users to also respond to such status update events even when they are not logged-in to them on their (mobile) web browsers or dedicated mobile applications, the Social

5.1. Web-Telecom Convergence Application Scenarios

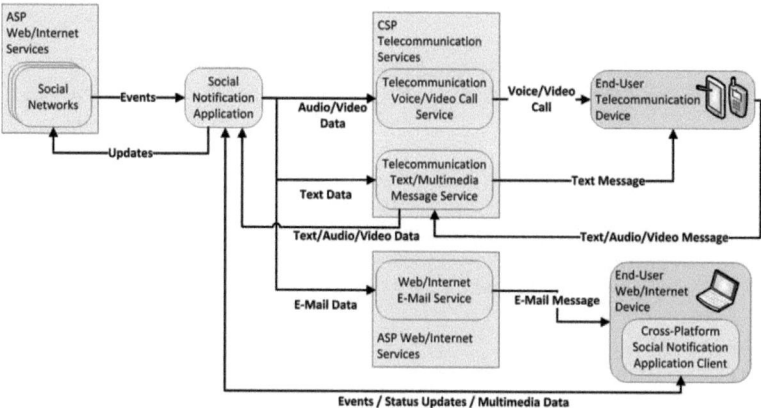

Figure 5.2: Social Notification Application

Notification Application provides a reply channel. An end-user can use a Telecommunication network Multimedia Message containing text, graphics, audio and video to respond right from a Telecommunication device. Further, an end-user can also use the Social Notification Application client to respond with Web/Internet-based social network status updates and multimedia messages.

5.1.3 Postal Service Notification

A popular illustration for Web-Telecom Converge is instant end-user notification about the current status of a service process that is in progress. One example is worldwide letter or package delivery by the traditional postal service. The internal shipment tracking and management systems are mostly updated to Web/Internet technologies-based systems and so, could easily be converged with Telecommunication services. The postal service system could automatically initiate Multimedia Messages or text-to-speech enabled voice/video calls to the shipment receiving customers' Telecommunication devices in order to inform them about exact delivery or pick-up details regularly. Further, the systems could even automatically initiate instant voice/video communication between the receiving customers and the postal service delivery staff, so they can provide up-to-the-minute information. This could increase the rate of successful delivery and satisfied customers drastically.

5.1.4 Dynamic Voice Mail Message

In current Telecommunication systems, voice mail messages are typically static and so, do not provide much information about the actual whereabouts or current appointments of the callee. The idea of this scenario is, to tab into the end-users data in popular Web/Internet-based tools such as online calendars, Facebook or Twitter to customize the voice mail message automatically. Based on the end-users preferences, the system could take a specifically formatted Twitter tweet, the headline of the current calendar appointment, or the current Facebook status message and transform them into audio data using text-to-speech technologies. This audio data can be transmitted to the Telecommunication voice mail service in order to set it as current voice mail message. Through such an automated mechanism, an update of the voice mail message can be done as often as necessary, for example when end-users progress from one appointment to the next, or when they actively post new tweets or social network status updates.

5.1.5 Automated Telephone Conference

The concept of this scenario is to automate the initiation of a scheduled telephone conference using Web/Internet-based calendar systems. The organizer of the conference schedules it in a personal calendar and invites all participates to this event. Responders are able to accept or decline this invitation. An automation system monitors the calendar and triggers once the time for the conference has come. The system reads the list of responders that accepted the conference, gathers all phone numbers the responders defined for this call and uses a Telecommunication conference call service to initiate a conference call between all of their Telecommunication devices.

5.1.6 Click-to-Call Supplement to Business Software

A very popular, and in some cases already implemented, scenario is Click-to-Call. The concept is to add Telecommunication functionality to desktop or Web/Internet-based business applications such as Address Book or CRM software products. The software is personalized for all employees including the definition of their work and mobile phone numbers. Once employees want to call their customers or contacts, they can click on them and the software uses a Telecommunication phone call service to initiate a call between their and the customers Telecommunication devices automatically.

5.2 Logical Reference Architecture of a Web-Telecom Converged Application

The logical Web-Telecom Converged application reference architecture maps the concept of an Model View Controller [201] (MVC) architecture to a distributed end-user application that uses Web/Internet services as well as Telecommunication services to realize its functionalities. Figure 5.3 illustrates this generic reference architecture.

- **Web/Internet Layer** - This layer represents all services and applications on the Web/Internet that can be consumed through openly accessible interfaces using common Web/Internet technologies. Typical examples are popular ASP services such as Google Mail, Google Contacts, Facebook, Salesforce, etc.

- **Web Protocol** - Generally, this could be any TCP/IP-based protocol. For most non-browser-based applications such as instant messaging, e-mail or VoIP these are open and standardized or closed and proprietary protocols based on TCP/IP. For most popular and common browser-based services and applications on the Web/Internet this is HTTP, sometimes in combination with concepts such as REST or SOAP.

- **Telecommunication Layer** - This layer provides implementations of Telecommunication functionalities. It provides TCP/IP-based multimedia Telecommunication services such as voice call/streaming, video call/streaming, text/multimedia messaging as well as extended IMS service enablers such as network address book or presence.

5.2. Logical Reference Architecture of a Web-Telecom Converged Application

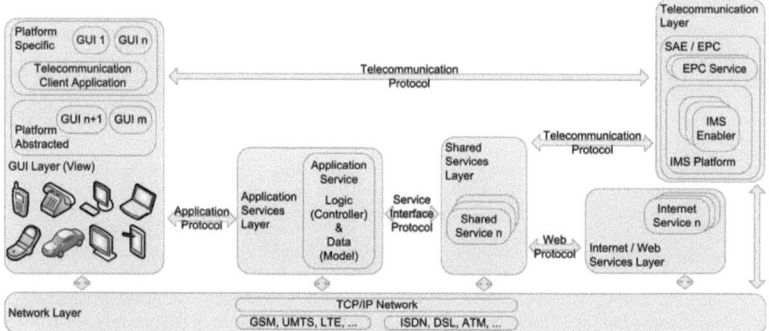

Figure 5.3: Generic Web-Telecom Converged Application Reference Architecture

- **Telecommunication Protocol** - There are several different protocols used to build the connections between the Telecommunication Layer and the Shared Services Layer as well as between the Telecommunication Layer and the legacy Telecommunication Client Applications. Such client applications are typically device or platform manufacturer specific and Telecommunication standards-based Phone, SMS and MMS applications deeply embedded into the end-user device platform (GUI Layer). Telecommunication protocols in NGNs and IMS are for example SIP and Diameter. Protocols and specifications used in legacy Telecommunication systems are defined in GSM, UMTS, SS7, etc.

- **Shared Service Layer** - This layer provides reusable services that can be accessed through clearly specified service interfaces. These services provide access to Telecommunication functionalities from the Telecommunication Layer as well as Web/Internet service functionalities from the Web/Internet Services Layer. The Shared Services' lifecycles are typically managed and monitored by some service container or a Web-Telecom Convergence platform infrastructure.

- **Application Services Layer** - This layer hosts the application logic (Controller) and data (Model) as a bundled or packaged software components, typically leveraging some database functionalities of the container or platform that manages them. In combination with the Shared services, this component is the center of the application, responsible for all major processing and coordination. Thereby, freeing the end-user clients from these tasks and enabling them to be very lightweight. A container or platform for these application components could be provided and managed by a professional hosting company or a CSP, which then, in turn, would be able to ensure that the deployed applications meet predefined CSP quality standards for end-user applications.

- **Service Interface Protocol** - These protocols connect the application logic (Controller) with the shared and reusable services it uses from the Shared Services Layer. Typical examples for a Web-Telecom Converged application would be SOAP, REST, HTTP and TCP/IP etc.

- **GUI Layer** - This layer represents the different GUIs (Views) for the different types of platforms for the different types of end-user devices the application supports. These GUIs are thin clients for the application logic on the Application Services Layer and can be implemented as (i) native/platform-specific (e.g. Java, C++, Objective C ...) or, (ii) platform-abstracted/independent (e.g. J2ME, HTML5, BONDI [34], ...) GUI clients.

- Native/Platform-Specific GUI clients have full access to all client platform APIs and so, to all cutting edge features a device supports. Unfortunately, in order to be ported to other platforms, expensive and time-consuming reprogramming of major parts of the clients is necessary.
- Independent/Platform-Abstracted GUI clients have reduced access to client platform APIs and so, to a reduced device feature set, but are automatically portable to all platforms that support the same platform abstraction technology.

Independent of the type, in order to conserve the limited resources of the end-user device and to be able to easily port them to new platforms in the future, all clients have to be implemented as thin as possible. Meaning, as much functionality as possible needs to be implemented on the Application Services Layer and the clients are only responsible for a high-quality data presentation and the end-user input. Overall, the clients are the end-users' only contact points of the application, so those need to exhibit and ensure an exceptional usability and an excellent user experience of the whole Web-Telecom Converged application.

Over the last few years, an increasing number of platform abstraction technologies and standards (often even solely Web/Internet browser-based technologies) such as HTML5 and BONDI has emerged and gained more importance. They have been steadily expanding their client platform APIs and functionalities access possibilities. This leads to the conclusion that the installation of native/platform-specific applications will be obsolete in the near future, and that applications will be delivered in a Web/Internet technologies-based SaaS model leveraging thin independent/platform-abstracted end-user clients.

- **Application Protocol** - These protocols connect the application logic on the Application Services Layer with the GUI Layer clients on the end-user devices. They are responsible for data and signaling information transport/transmission, are application-specific and can be any TCP/IP-based protocol. A container or Web-Telecom Convergence platform supports the application developer at choosing a suitable protocol for his application and provides APIs and interfaces in order to simplify the usage of common protocols and standards such as REST, SOAP, JavaScript Object Notation (JSON) etc.

5.3 Technical Architecture of a Web-Telecom Converged Application

This section exemplifies the architecture of the distributed Web-Telecom Converged Unified Address Book application (see section 5.1.1), for which technical implementation decisions were made, so it can be deployed onto a technical infrastructure.

- **Telecommunication Network and TCP/IP Network** - These two networks are clearly separated from a technologically point of view. They are built upon different stacks of protocols, specifications and standards, defined by different standardization organizations. Over the last years, concepts to bridge the gap have been defined and built from two sides. On the one hand, modern Telecommunication standards like UMTS specify gateways to the TCP/IP network. On the other hand, end-user devices (e.g. smart phones, netbooks) leverage these standardized gateways to access the TCP/IP network through the Telecommunication network they are connected to, or leverage built-in WLAN technologies to connect to the TCP/IP network independently of the Telecommunication network.

5.3. Technical Architecture of a Web-Telecom Converged Application

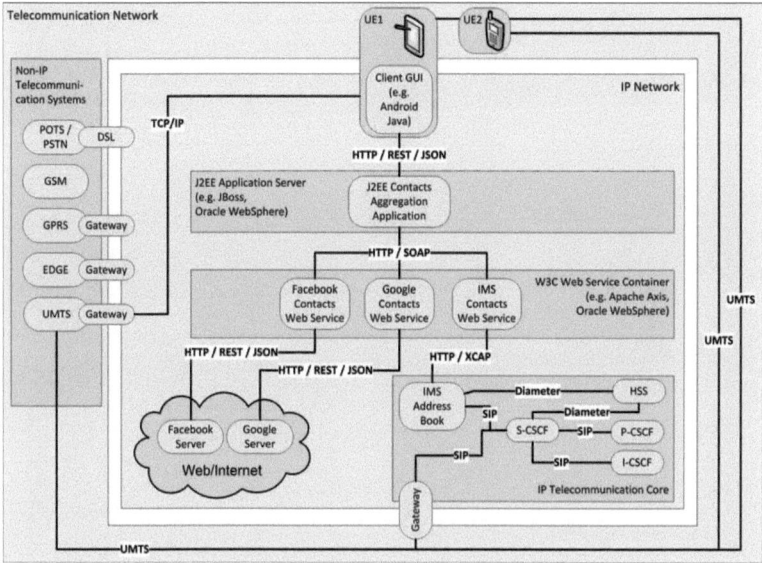

Figure 5.4: Exemplified Technical Web-Telecom Converged Unified Address Book Application Architecture

- **Web/Internet** - Represents the protocols and standards built on top of the TCP/IP network and includes the services and applications provided by ASPs on top of these Web/Internet protocols and standards.

  For the Unified Address Book, the Facebook friends/contacts service on the Facebook server as well as the Google Contacts service on the Google server are consumed through their clearly defined and openly accessible HTTP, REST and JSON-based service interfaces.

- **IP Telecommunication Core** - Represents the multimedia service components of the fully TCP/IP-based Telecommunication NGN. The central part is the IMS (see section F.5.2) with its three types of CSCFs, the HSS and the VoIP and authentication protocols SIP and Diameter. To bridge the gap to the Telecommunication network's standards and protocols, the IP Telecommunication Core specifies a bidirectional Telecommunication media and signaling gateway.

  For the Unified Address Book, one of the earliest Enablers for the IMS, the Converged Address Book [169] (CAB), is leveraged using its HTTP and XML Configuration Access Protocol [189] (XCAP)-based interface.

- **Non-IP Telecommunication Systems** - Represents the traditional Telecommunication system standards that were defined before the core architecture shift towards TCP/IP. This includes traditional fixed Telecommunication POTS/PSTN that added the DSL technology to provide TCP/IP network and so Web/Internet access for end-users. It also includes all current mobile Telecommunication standards from GSM over GPRS and EDGE to UMTS, from which the later all included some sort of gateway definition to provide some level of TCP/IP network access for end-user's mobile devices.

- **W3C Web Service Container** - This container implements the W3C Web Service specification illustrated in section 2.2.2. The container provides an environment to deploy the services and to manage their lifecycles as illustrated in section 2.2.4. Most current containers such as Oracle WebSphere or Apache Axis provide further supplementary functionalities such as database management, transaction coordination etc. that deployed services can leverage. All services deployed in this container clearly define an open HTTP and SOAP-based interface that can be used by any TCP/IP-based services and applications located inside or outside of the container to access and consume the service.

  For the Unified Address Book, the container hosts three Web Services that gather the data from the Web/Internet as well as the Telecommunication services of Google, Facebook and the CSP. These Web Services are implemented generic and completely Unified Address Book application-abstracted. Thereby, they can be reused by any other service or application that needs access to the contacts data from any of these Web/Internet services. Quality metrics such as availability and performance can be monitored at one single spot. If interfaces of the Web/Internet services change, fixes can be applied transparently and quickly at one single spot, meaning, without the need of updating all components all the way to the client applications on the end-user devices.

- **J2EE Application Server** - The application server implements a software development technology specific enterprise application development standard. In this example, the JBoss or Oracle WebSphere application servers implement the latest J2EE specification developed by the Java Community Process (JCP). Just like the W3C Web Service Container, the application server acts as a container for the application components, manages their lifecycle and provides supplementary functionalities that the deployed applications can leverage.

  For the Unified Address Book, the application server hosts an application component that implements the business logic (Controller) and data (Model). To communicate with the different Client GUIs on the different end-user devices, it provides an application-specific and proprietary HTTP, REST and JSON-based interface. Every application component on the J2EE Application Server has to be clearly completely application, in this example Unified Address Book, specific, and must not include any functionalities that could be reused by any other service or application. Such functionalities would have to be extracted and deployed as Web Services on the W3C Web Service Container.

- **Client GUIs** - Are thin native/platform-specific or platform-abstracted/independent client applications for all types of platforms for all types of devices the end-users might utilize. The clients are responsible for data presentation and end-user input and need to ensure an excellent usability and a great user experience of the application.

  For the Unified Address Book, a Java-based client application for the Android platform is illustrated. The advantage of Android for such an application is that it can substitute the address book application that comes with the platform and so, can become the main address book of the end-users on all their Android devices.

  Since JBoss and Oracle WebSphere are able to serve HTML5 to end-user devices, an additional, not illustrated, client applications could be an HTML5-based platform independent Web/Internet application.

Chapter 6

Requirements for a Web-Telecom Convergence Platform

In this chapter, the results from the "Stakeholder Goals" as well as from the "Analysis" and the "Design of Web-Telecom Convergence Applications" are transformed into two structured sets of requirements for an optimal Web-Telecom Convergence platform.

6.1 Deriving Requirements from Stakeholder Goals

This section illustrates the process that derives a first set of requirements for the Web-Telecom Convergence platform from the major goals of the identified stakeholders, illustrated in chapter 3. It applies results and learnings from definitions and concepts in chapter 2, evaluations in chapter 4 and Web-Telecom Converged applications design in chapter 5 to define the following set of requirements.

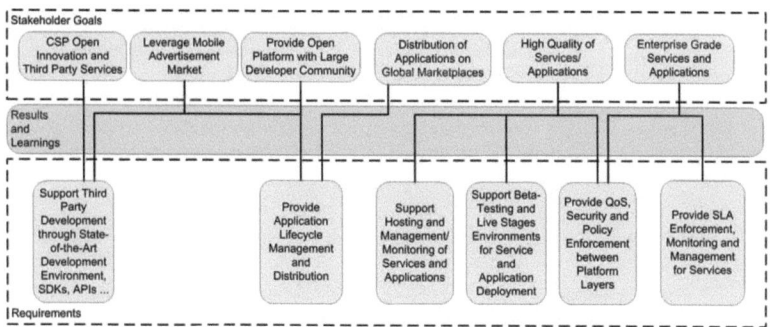

Figure 6.1: Requirements derived from major Stakeholder Goals

For clarity reasons, the process is divided into three independent parts that are discussed consecutively based on figures 6.1, 6.2 and 6.3. The figures illustrate the stakeholder goals, the resulting requirements and the primary mapping paths, for which the previous results and learnings were applied. Since any additional applicable mapping paths would render the figures confusing, they are not illustrated.

In figure 6.1 the first part of the mapping process is depicted for the first set of major stakeholder goals.

R1.1 Support Third Party Development through State-of-the-Art Development Environment, SDKs, APIs

The platform needs to provide a software development environment that is based on common software development technologies and programming languages. It needs to provide a mature IDE or some IDE-integration that is available for several common computing platforms such as Windows, Apple and Linux. Based on that, it needs to provide rich and mature SDKs and APIs that enable developers to easily utilize services provided by the Web-Telecom Convergence platform that hosts their Web-Telecom Converged application, as well as services provided by the device platforms that execute their Web-Telecom Converged applications clients.

R1.2 Provide Application Lifecycle Management and Distribution

The platform needs to manage the lifecycle (see section 2.7) of all applications deployed in it. It needs to support them from the initial provisioning of resources, over the development and testing, the final productive (live) deployment to future improvement or maintenance updates.

The platform needs to support developers at distributing their deployed applications to the target end-users' devices. It needs to provide means to distribute them directly via a link or download as well as to support registering/submitting, managing and advertising them on a broad range of global marketplaces.

R1.3 Support Hosting and Management/Monitoring of Services and Applications

The platform needs to provide a PaaS inspired hosting and runtime environment were developers can deploy their services and applications. It needs to provide storage space for service and application packages/archives that can include executables, clients for all supported device platforms, libraries and multimedia resources. To support developers at application internal data handling, the platform needs to provide database storage functionality that can be used by any service and application deployed on the platform.

This hosting environment needs to provide means to manage and monitor all hosted services and applications. Thereby, the provider of the platform will be able to control and ensure service and application quality on all platform levels and developers will be able to easily identify implementation and performance problems of their deployed services and applications.

R1.4 Support Beta-Testing and Live Stages Environment for Service and Application Development

The platform needs to provide a two stage service and application deployment approach, which needs to clearly illustrate the differentiation between services and applications that have no quality guarantees and those that guarantee a high-quality.

- Beta-Testing Stage services and applications are deployed by developers to be shared with other developers at an early stage, to be tested and enhanced by the whole developer community and to be transferred to the Live Stage at some point in the future.

- Live Stage services and applications are deployed by the platform provider after they have completed a platform provider specific certification process. Services and applications on this stage are considered high-quality and fully stable. If services, they are ready to be shared and reused in other services or applications. If applications, they are a high-quality product and ready to be delivered to end-users.

R1.5 Provide QoS, Security and Policy Enforcements between Platform Layers

The platforms needs to provide a certain basis of QoS, A4C, and policy management and control. This basis needs to be distributed throughout the platform, so that for different sections or layers of the platform, such as Beta-Testing Services or Live Services, appropriate security strengths and parameters can be configured. The platform needs to provide means to allow developers to enhance and adapt the basic functionalities to the specific needs of their deployed services and applications.

R1.6 Provide SLA Enforcement, Monitoring and Management for Services

In tight cooperation with the previous functionalities, the platform needs to provide a basic SLA monitoring and management functionality. It needs to allow developers and partners to define basic QoS SLA parameters for certain services. Since the platform typically acts as a middleware and so, is service consumer and service provider at the same time, such SLAs need to be definable in both directions and with both roles. Once defined, the platform needs to monitor these specified parameters in real-time and report any SLA violations to the relevant stakeholders.

In figure 6.2 the second part of the mapping process is depicted for the second set of major stakeholder goals.

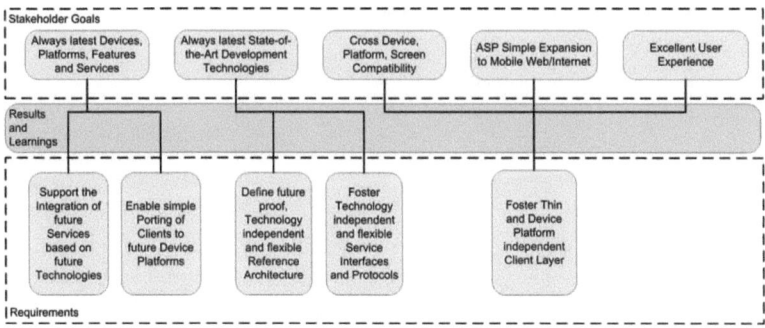

Figure 6.2: Requirements derived from major Stakeholder Goals

R1.7 Support the Integration of future Services based on future Technologies

The platform needs to provide developers with means to use any of their choices of development technologies for their service and application development. By relying on software development technology and device platforms independent standards, the platform needs to enable the import and management of services based on future technologies.

R1.8 Enable simple Porting of Clients to future Device Platforms

For the implementation of native/platform-specific clients (see also section 5.2), the platform needs to encourage developers to implement thin application clients with low complexity. Such implement just data presentation and user input functionalities, and outsource all application logic, data processing and data management to services on the platform. The platform needs to foster the use of Cross-Platform Mobile Development Frameworks (see section 4.3.2) such as PhoneGap or Titanium to enable a, by default, porting of all application clients to a wide range device platforms.

R1.9 Define future proof, Technology independent and flexible Reference Architecture

The logical reference architecture of the platform, including all features and components, needs to be specified in a fully technology independent way. The choice of implementation and deployment technologies must be made by the platform vendor that implements the platform in a software product. This vendor needs to ensure that the technology specific parts of the platform can be updated to, or easily integrate additional and future technologies that developers might want to use for their service and application development.

R1.10 Foster Technology independent and flexible Service Interfaces and Protocols

Service development, service deployment, service interfaces and protocols used between services and application clients need to remain as software development technology independent/abstracted as possible. The platform needs to foster generic and universal (defacto-) standards that are applicable across many service development technologies and device platforms.

R1.11 Foster Thin and Device Platform independent Client Layer

The platform needs to foster, in the future maybe dictate, a device platform independent implementation of the thin application clients, introduced in the requirement "Enable simple Porting of Clients to future Device Platforms", by endorsing technologies such as current Web/Internet technologies like HTML5.

The platform needs to define an architectural layer that supports, manages and delivers these clients. This layer needs to provide functionalities that support developers by simplifying the implementation of the connections between their clients and their application logic. It further needs to support the developers at implementing application clients that dynamically adapt their GUI and content rendering to varying target-device platform-specifics such as screen size, resolution and user input options.

In figure 6.3 the third part of the mapping process is depicted for the third set of major stakeholder goals.

R1.12 Provide SOA Platform with Services Repository, Composition, Lifecycle Mgmt. and Execution

The platform needs to be thoroughly based on a SOA (see section 2.2) implementation that provides the SOA concepts of a Service Repository, Service Composition, Service Lifecycle Management (see section 2.2.4) and a Service Execution Environment. All services on the platform need to be specified, implemented and deployed as SOA compliant services such as Web Services (see section 2.2.2).

The Service Repository needs to store all services on the platform, and upon request, needs to provide/deliver those to the Service Execution Environment. This needs to provide functionalities to load, start, stop and pause all services on the platform and is responsible

6.1. Deriving Requirements from Stakeholder Goals

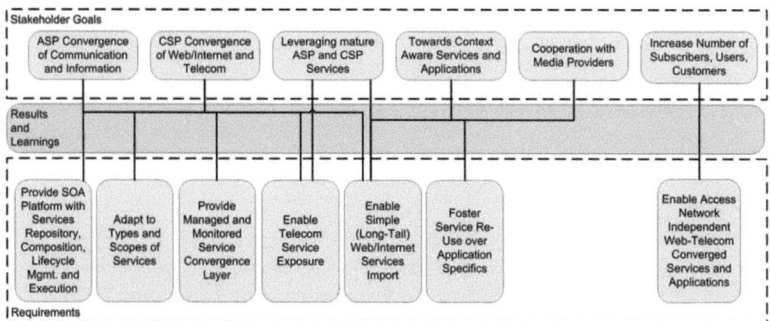

Figure 6.3: Requirements derived from major Stakeholder Goals

for resolving possible dependencies between services by, for example, defining a suitable loading/startup sequence.

R1.13 Adapt to Types and Scopes of Services

The platform needs to manage services that can be categorized in the types, (i) Telecommunication services that access and import functionalities from the CSPs' Telecommunication systems, (ii) Web/Internet services that access the APIs of the ASPs' programmable services and applications on the Web/Internet to import their functionalities, (iii) Web-Telecom Converged services that access the Telecommunication and Web/Internet services on the platform to combine their functionalities to a higher-level value-added service, and (iv) Application services that access Web/Internet, Telecommunication and Web-Telecom Converged services on the platform to combine and use them in order to realize all business logic of a Web-Telecom Converged application.

The platform needs to manage the scope of services that can be divided into Shared services, including (i), (ii) and (iii) that are shared among all services and all applications on the platform, and Application services, including (iv) that are application-specific, not relevant for any other service or application and so, not shared outside the actual Web-Telecom Converged application.

The platform needs to provide means to adapt to the different characteristics that come with the different types and scopes, and enable the service and application developers on the platform to leverage those means.

R1.14 Provide Managed and Monitored Service Convergence Layer

The platform needs to provide a service convergence layer that builds the foundation of all Web-Telecom Converged applications. This layer needs to manage all Web/Internet and Telecommunication services, needs to leverage SOA Service Composition to provide means to orchestrate them to Web-Telecom Converged services, and needs to provide all of these Shared services to the Application services of the Web-Telecom Converged applications.

Since the services on this layer are the foundation and core of all Web-Telecom Converged applications on the platform, this layer needs to leverage functionalities from the requirements "Provide QoS, Security and Policy Enforcements between Platform Layers" and "Provide SLA Enforcement, Monitoring and Management for Web/Internet and Telecom Services" to precisely monitor all available service parameters in real-time and to inform all relevant stakeholders about their status and possible problems.

R1.15 Enable Telecom Service Exposure

The platform needs to be fully compatible with current TCP/IP-based Telecommunication protocols and systems. It needs to be able to access Telecommunication functionalities within the Telecommunication systems' Cores and Enablers, and import them into the platform. It needs to expose these functionalities as shared Telecommunication services to all other shared as well as all application-specific services on the platform.

R1.16 Enable Simple (Long-Tail) Web/Internet Services Import

For mature, successful and widespread Web/Internet services and applications, the platform needs to provide means to manually and programmatically access and import their full functionalities into the platform. The platform needs to provide these imported functionalities as shared Web/Internet services to all other shared as well as application-specific services on the platform.

For long-tail niche-market Web/Internet services and applications, a manual import is too costly, so the platform needs to provide a (semi-) automatic way to import their main functionalities. Similar to above, it also needs to provide them as shared Web/Internet services to all other shared as well as application-specific services on the platform.

R1.17 Foster Service Reuse over Application Specifics

In accordance to the concepts illustrated in the SOA Manifesto in section 2.2.1, the platform needs to foster a large collection of shared Web/Internet, Telecommunication and Web-Telecom Converged services to be deployed and managed on the convergence layer. By aggregating and sharing all services on a common layer, the platform needs to foster the innovative combination of their multimedia and communication functionalities as well as their available data, such as context information, in future Web-Telecom Converged applications.

The platform needs to support and encourage the developers to divide their Web-Telecom Converged applications into reusable and application-specific functionalities. These need to be implemented and deployed as separated shared and application-specific services on the platform. To foster such a separation, the platform needs to support the developers by simplifying the implementation of the connection between the platform's Shared Services and the developers own application-specific services.

R1.18 Enable Access Network Independent Web-Telecom Converged Services and Applications

The platform needs to support the successful "App Development" concepts that were introduced by modern smartphone platforms such as iOS, Android and Windows Phone 7. By abstracting from the underlying wireless data networks and technologies, these concepts support developers on mainly focus on creating and implementing innovative end-user application ideas on these modern platforms.

As discussed in sections 1.1 and 2.1, in contrast to how traditional Telecommunication services and applications were specified, and to enable rapid Web-Telecom Converged application innovation, the platform needs to support that applications can be implemented completely decoupled from the details of the shared underlying data or Telecommunication networks and systems. The underlying networks and systems need to be abstracted by the platform and the Web-Telecom Converged applications can choose to leverage and access networks functionalities and network parameters such as latency or available bandwidth if necessary for the implementation of certain functionalities.

The platform needs to provide and deliver all deployed Web-Telecom Converged applications to any supported end-user device connected via any TCP/IP-compatible access network worldwide.

6.2 Deriving Requirements from Analysis and Applications Design

In this section, from the analysis in chapter 4 and the applications design in chapter 5, a second set of requirements is derived. Results and learnings from definitions and concepts in chapter 2 combined with results from the CDTM research project in [152] are applied to define the following set of requirements. This set is limited to supplementary requirements that have not yet been derived in the previous section.

R2.1 Provide Layered Architecture

The platform needs to be designed in a strictly layered architecture inspired by SOA Service Layers concepts presented in sections 2.2.5. The platform needs to, at least, clearly distinguish between the domains Data and Telecommunication networks, Web/Internet services and applications, Telecommunication systems and services, Shared and Application services, Web-Telecom Converged applications and end-user clients.

R2.2 Dictate a Separation of Networks and Services/Applications

The platform needs to ensure that all services and applications delivered to the end-users' devices abide by the platform's layered architecture concepts. It needs to ensure that the underlying networks and systems are abstracted by the bottom layers of the platform and that no application bypasses any of the platform's layers. It needs to ensure that none implements or uses any Web/Internet or Telecommunication services, standards or protocols directly within an application or application client implementation, but instead utilizes the platforms functionalities and services to access network features.

R2.3 Foster Equal Treatment of Applications on Device Platforms

The platform needs to foster that all services and applications are delivered to the end-users equally. On the devices' software platforms, services and applications provided by a CSP, such as Voice/Video Call and TextMessaging, should not receive any advantages or preferred treatment over any Web-Telecom Converged applications.

For end-users, all services and applications installed on a device platform should be presented and accessible in similar ways, on modern smart phones typically as "App" shortcuts or "Web App" links.

For developers, all services and applications installed on a device platform should be able to access the same platform and API functionalities and features with the same options and rights.

R2.4 Provide High Performance and Reliability

The platform needs to ensure that performance and reliability of all Web-Telecom Converged applications are similar compared to what end-users experience from traditional Telecommunication services and applications on fixed and mobile Telecommunication networks. The platform needs to support developers at achieving and monitoring the high-quality standards defined and required from traditional Telecommunication services and applications.

R2.5 Foster Personalized Services and Applications

The platform needs to provide functionalities and services that allow developers to personalize Web-Telecom Converged services and applications deployed on the platform. It needs to support combining end-user related internal context data with context data from external services or applications provided by ASPs or CSPs.

R2.6 Foster Applications with an Exceptional User Experience

The platform needs to foster Web-Telecom Converged application client technologies that enable developer to provide an exceptional user experience within their applications. The platform needs to support, on the one hand, native smart phone technologies that currently still have some advantages over Web/Internet-based ones, but also Web/Internet-based technologies such as HTML5 that are rising rapidly through ongoing standardization and their utilization in Cross-Platform Mobile Development Frameworks (see section 4.3.2) such as PhoneGap or Titanium.

R2.7 Publish, Advertise, Discover, Access and Compose Services Across Domains

The platform needs to provide means to enable different individual deployments of the platform from different vendors to collaborate across their individual domains. It needs to support the distributed publishing, advertising, discovering, accessing and composing of all heterogeneous Shared Services on all platform deployments by leveraging SOA ESB concepts illustrated in section 2.3.

Chapter 7

Design of the Application Delivery Platform

This chapter illustrates the design of the Web-Telecom Converged ADP that extends existing Telecommunication SDP proposals and Web-Telecom Convergence concepts to deliver Web-Telecom Converged applications end-to-end. It provides an overview about the core concepts of the ADP, illustrates the logical reference architecture and presents an exemplary technical architecture.

7.1 Core Concepts of the Application Delivery Platform

This section summarizes the major core concepts that were derived from the learnings and results of the analysis, design and requirements in chapters 4, 5 and 6. They build the foundation for the design of the logical and technical ADP architectures.

7.1.1 C1 - Extending the Concepts of Service Delivery Platform to an Application Delivery Platform

As discussed in sections 2.5 and 4.2, current SDPs focus on delivering services to any application that end-users use to utilize the service. For the SDP, everything beyond the service itself, such as applications that reuse it or application clients that allow end-users to utilize it, are typically completely out of scope.

SDPs are typically designed for one specific domain such as Telecommunications or Web/Internet. The majority of current SDP concepts and solutions exist for the Telecommunications industry, and none of those are designed to bridge the technological and conceptual gaps between the Telecommunications domain and other domains such as the Web/Internet.

The ADP extends these existing SDP concepts by

- focusing on the delivery of entire Web-Telecom Converged applications to end-users' devices.
- bridging the technological gap between Telecommunications and Web/Internet by building upon common TCP/IP-based technologies.

- bridging the conceptual gap between Telecommunications and Web/Internet by abstracting from their individual conceptual specifics through the application of SOA concepts for Web-Telecom Converged service and application design and development.

This extension is conceptually illustrated in figure 7.1.

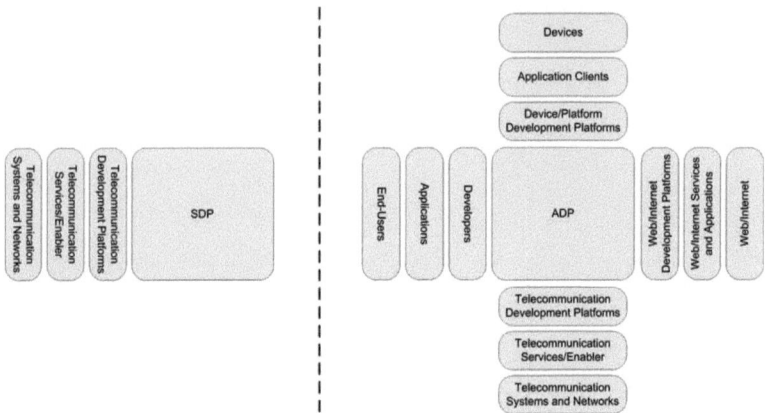

Figure 7.1: From Service Delivery Platform to Application Delivery Platform

On the left, the SDP focuses on the Telecommunications domain. It imports/manages Telecommunication Enabler-based Telecommunication services that were augmented, upgraded or refined on modern Telecommunication development platforms. Once imported, it provides and delivers these services to any authorized consumer that is outside of the platform.

On the right, the ADP extends the SDP concept by adding the domains of end-users, devices and Web/Internet. The ADP still imports/manages the Telecommunication services, but provides and delivers them on the platform to the other domains. In the end-users domain, developers use the ADP to implement their innovative Web-Telecom Converged application ideas for the end-users. In the devices domain, device/platform manufacturers provide mature development environments for developers to implement clients for their Web-Telecom Converged applications. In the Web/Internet domain, the ADP imports Web/Internet-based services using their APIs provided by their programmable Web/Internet development platforms.

The ADP covers a large portion of Web-Telecom Convergence. In figure 7.2, figure 2.14 from section 2.8.3 is adapted to illustrate this.

The ADP covers a complete Web-Telecom Converged distributed application from the services it uses from Telecommunications and the Web/Internet, over the convergence of these services and the application business logic, to the application clients for the different platforms of the different devices of the end-users.

The concept C1 supports the fulfillment of the requirements R1.1, R1.2, R1.9, R1.10, R1.12, R2.4 and R2.6 illustrated in chapter 6.

7.1. Core Concepts of the Application Delivery Platform

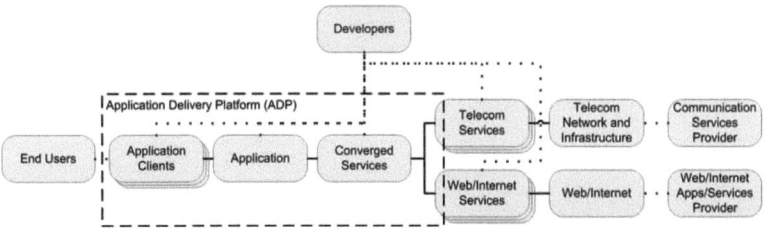

Figure 7.2: Web-Telecom Convergence ADP

7.1.2 C2 - Separation of Networks and Applications

As illustrated in section 4.1, traditional Telecommunication services were specified in flat architectures defining an, mostly specifically just for one service, unstructured system (e.g. GSM, UMTS) of various components and interfaces between them. All network protocols and service functionalities were woven directly into this flat system architecture without the use of any abstractions or layering. As a result the Telecommunication network and all services are inseparably coupled in a CSP's system. Thereby, in general, the applications on the devices that end-users use to access Telecommunication services are not able to access these services when the device is connected to another CSP's network. To overcome this in, at least, an international setting, "Roaming" concepts were added to the Telecommunication standards. Of course, due to the inseparable coupling, for every single new or updated Telecommunication service, a new Roaming concept has to be defined and standardized. This has further slowed down the development and innovation of Telecommunication services from an already very slow situation.

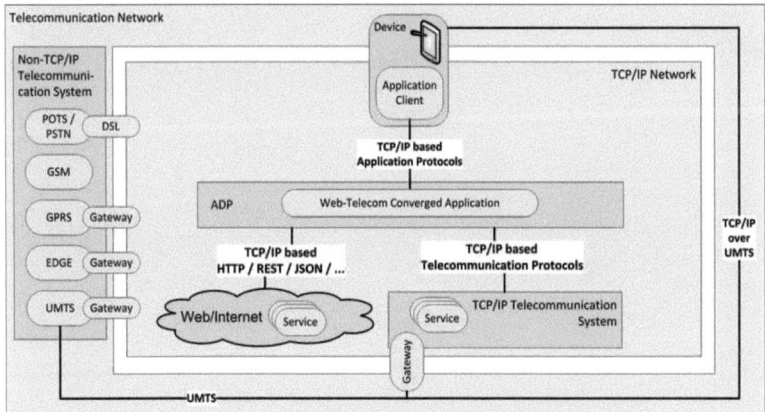

Figure 7.3: Separation of Networks and Application

As illustrated in figure 7.3, the ADP separates the end-users' devices' Telecommunication access network and its services from the application clients that end-users use to access a Web-Telecom

Converged application.

Traditionally, the Telecommunication networks and TCP/IP networks have been technologically separated. As the figure illustrates, several modern Telecommunication specifications such as TCP/IP Telecommunication systems and UMTS bridge this separation through gateways. The end-user device is connected to an UMTS mobile Telecommunication network, but in contrast to the traditional concept, this connection does not provide UMTS Telecommunication services to the device, but only a TCP/IP connection thought the UMTS gateway. The end-user uses the Application Client installed on the device, to access a Web-Telecom Converged application on the ADP.

The ADP manages the connections to the Web/Internet and TCP/IP Telecommunication services, which, through the gateway, include non-TCP/IP Telecommunication services. In contrast to the traditional concept, no Telecommunication services specific clients are embedded in the platform of the device. The ADP terminates all Telecommunication services related protocols and only application-specific protocols are routed from the ADP to the end-user device. Thereby, the device can use any Non-TCP/IP fixed and mobile Telecommunication network, provided by any CSP, to receive a TCP/IP connection, and can use that to utilize any Web-Telecom Converged application provided by any CSP or ASP. For the Web-Telecom Converged applications, the ADP provides access to Telecommunication network functionalities such as QoS reservations, bandwidth measurements, etc. so they can adapt themselves to the current status of the current network the device receives its TCP/IP connection from. This concept of networks and applications separation enables the exemplary Voice/Video Call scenario illustrated in figure 7.4.

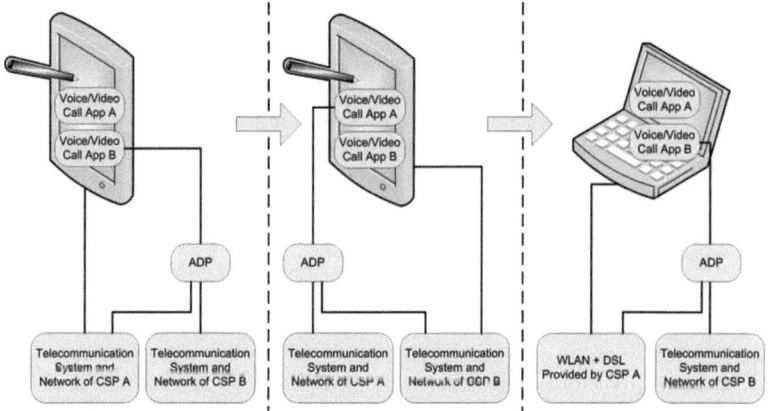

Figure 7.4: Networks and Applications Separated Scenario

In this scenario, an end-user wants to place a voice/video call, first, using his tablet, and later, using his laptop device. For both devices, CSP A and CSP B provide Voice/Video Call Apps (Web-Telecom Converged application clients) that are compatible with the devices' platforms, or are platform independent and Cross-Platform compatible. The ADP handles all cross-networks and cross-CSPs A4C and so, the end-user is constantly and automatically logged in into both Apps on all his devices.

In the first step, on the left, the end-user's tablet is connected to the Telecommunication network of CSP A. The end-user wants to place a voice call and has the choice between the two Apps. Due to the better price-per-minute for the number he is going to call, he chooses the App provided by CSP B to place the voice call. In the second step, in the middle, the end-user relocated and due to a better wireless signal, the end-user's device connects to the Telecommunication network of CSP B. The end-user wants place a video call to a different number, and, due to a better video quality, now chooses the App of CSP A to place the call. In the third step, on the right, the end-user moves from his tablet device to his laptop and wants to place a voice call. His laptop is connected to his private WLAN and DSL Web/Internet connection. He again has the choice between the two Apps and, due to the price, he again chooses the App provided by CSP B.

The example of the voice/video call in this scenario can be substituted by any application deployed, provided and delivered by the ADP. With the roll-out of EPC and LTE in future Telecommunication networks, a networks and applications separation is even further aided through the constant availability of an application-independent TCP/IP network connection on the LTE compliant end-user devices.

The concept C2 supports the fulfillment of the requirements R1.2, R1.7, R1.8, R1.9, R1.18, R2.2, R2.3 and R2.5 illustrated in chapter 6.

7.1.3 C3 - Layered Architecture

The ADP derives its layered architecture design from the SOA Service Layers concepts presented in section 2.2.5. As foundational basis, it defines the External Services Layer that includes the two sub-layers Web/Internet Services Layer and Telecommunication Services Layer. Those two represent the services provided by ASPs and CSPs that are imported into the ADP.

The ADP transforms the SOA Service Layers concepts of Application Service Layer and Business Service Layer into Shared Services and Web-Telecom Converged Application Services respectively. It provides means for orchestration on both of these layers, so the Orchestration Service Layer is duplicated and embedded in each of the two layers.

To deliver a Web-Telecom Converged application to end-users, the ADP defines a Client Layer that includes all application-specific adaptable clients for all supported device platforms.

The concept C3 consolidates concepts C3.1, C3.2, C3.3, C3.4 and C3.5 and so, supports the fulfillment of the requirements R1.1, R1.3, R1.5, R1.7, R1.8, R1.10, R1.12, R1.14, R1.17, R1.18, R2.1, R2.3, R2.4, R2.5 and R2.7 illustrated in chapter 6.

7.1.3.1 C3.1 - Web-Telecom Convergence on Lowest Platform Layer

Web-Telecom Convergence is the foundation for the whole ADP concept and must be the basis for every application that is deployed on, and delivered by the platform. To enable developers to implement Web-Telecom Converged application, details and complexities of the individual Web/Internet and especially Telecommunication services are abstracted on a low level of the platform. Experts for these individual services take care of the access, adaptation and import of the services into the ADP. The ADP manages, provides and shares these services so they are composed in Converged services and applications by developers on the platform.

Since the convergence layer is the foundation of all applications, it constitutes a single location, within the ADP, at which all management, maintenance and scaling for all services the applications use can be done centrally.

The concept C3.1 supports the fulfillment of the requirements R1.1, R1.3, R1.10, R1.12, R1.14, R1.17, R1.18, R2.5 and R2.7 illustrated in chapter 6.

7.1.3.2 C3.2 - Separation of Shared and Application Services Layers

The ADP fosters reuse of functionalities and services over application-specific and proprietary implementations. Therefore, it encourages developers to separate all functionalities that could be reused by other applications from their own application implementations and to deploy them onto Shared and Application Services layers.

- **Shared Services Layer** - It hosts and manages all services that are shared across all Web-Telecom Converged applications. This includes all Web-Telecom Convergence related services discussed in the previous section as well as Web/Internet and Telecommunication independent Business services that provide some functionality that can be valuable for many applications on the ADP.

    Since all applications on the platform are relying on these services, quality assurance and maintenance are exceptionally important. In order to make these factors explicit to developers, the ASP distinguishes between a Beta and a Live Services Layer.

    - **Beta Services Layer** - Hosts services that are typically early implementations of some functionality that are still in development and that must be further enhanced, maintained and tested by the whole developer community on the ADP. Services on this layer are deployed by the developers themselves and do not provide any quality guarantees or SLAs.
    - **Live Services Layer** - Hosts services that are stable versions of an implementation of some functionality and that provide certain quality guarantees and/or SLAs to the consumers. The ADP provider must define an inspection and testing process to certify the "Live" status of a service. Only the ADP provider deploys new or updated certified services on this layer.

- **Application Services Layer** - It hosts and manages all services a Web-Telecom Converged application uses to implement those application-specific parts of its business logic that are not provided by any Shared services and not implemented in the application clients. Services on this layer are only shared within their Web-Telecom Converged Application Service collection and not accessible from Application services of other applications or from any Shared services. The layer clearly separates the collections of Application services and provides management functionalities for the individual services.

Through the separation of Shared and Application Services Layers, developers can achieve a faster innovation cycle through re-using a growing collection of Shared services and so, less implementation effort for new applications.

Traditionally, Telecommunication services have been implementing explicitly high-quality standards [184], and end-users are expecting the same from future applications that are developed by third-party developers and delivered to them by the ADP. Through the certification, maintenance and quality assurances of Live Shared Services, Web-Telecom Converged applications can achieve an increased overall quality. Through the central location of problem/bug fixing, maintenance and updating of Shared Services, all Web-Telecom Converged application that use a Shared Services are always fixed, maintained and updated quickly at once.

The concept C3.2 supports the fulfillment of the requirements R1.1, R1.3, R1.7, R1.8, R1.10, R1.12, R1.17 and R2.7 illustrated in chapter 6.

7.1.3.3 C3.3 - The Introduction of the ISO/OSI Application Layer in Telecommunications

As introduced in sections above, traditionally, Telecommunication standardization defined a Telecommunication system always in combination with a fixed set of Telecommunication services that are tightly woven into the whole system architecture. The actual client applications on the devices that end-users use to utilize these Telecommunication services were typically out of scope of the standard. It was the device/platform vendors' responsibility to implement these application clients for their device platforms according to the Telecommunication standards. Thereby, on most device platforms, these client applications are deeply embedded into the platform and cannot be substituted by updated or improved versions. This hinders the development and distribution of innovative ideas and slows down the whole innovation cycle in the Telecommunication industry dramatically.

The Android platform provides an open device platform concept that allows, on the one hand, developers to develop concurrent versions of such Telecommunication service application clients, and, on the other hand, end-users to substitute the standard client application on their devices.

The ADP fosters the concept of open device platforms and defines a Client Layer that hosts and manages all application clients for all Web-Telecom Converged applications. The ADP defines application clients as the "Views" of a Web-Telecom Converged application. They are responsible for presenting all application data in a state-of-the-art form, for providing a GUI for the end-users and, since they are the only contact point to the end-users, for realizing an exceptional usability and user experience for the Web-Telecom Converged application. All data processing and business logic functionalities are completely out of scope of application clients and must be implemented in Application services on the Application Services Layer.

With the different concepts for mobile application development, evaluated in section 4.3, a variety of application client types can be distinguished.

- **Platform-Specific/Native Application Clients** - These application clients are implemented with device platform-specific implementation technologies, SDKs and APIs, and, as native software, can be executed only on the platform they were developed for. Examples are most of the current "Apps" that an end-user can find in the marketplaces of the modern smart phone platforms Android, iOS, Windows Phone 7 and Blackberry.

  The major advantage of native application clients is that they can use every technological feature of the platforms directly, and thereby, can always provide cutting edge technology innovation to the end-users. Since providing an application client for as many device platforms as possible is the goal of every Web-Telecom Converged application, the use of sophisticated technological platform features of one platform can lead to major problems when porting the client to other platforms. Thus, for the application client implementation, instead of exhausting every breakthrough feature of a single device platform, it is necessary to stick to the smallest possible set of common features of the platforms. A further challenge at developing an application client for an ADP compliant Web-Telecom Converged application is to keep it as thin and easily portable to other device platforms as possible, meaning to refrain from implementing any data processing and business logic and to stick solely to GUI and data presentation.

- **Platform-Abstracted/Independent Application Clients** - The idea of these application clients is to implement a software once and being able to execute it, without the need of porting or adapting, on many, ideally all, device platforms end-users use. Currently, there are two different types of platform-abstracted application clients.

- **Cross-Platform Native Application Clients** - These clients are implemented using a mobile cross-platform development framework that cross-compiles their, often platform-abstracted, source code into native software compatible with the selection of device platforms the individual framework supports. Most current frameworks aim at engaging Web/Internet developers in mobile application development, and therefore leverage state-of-the-art Web/Internet technologies such as HTML5 and JavaScript for their application development.

  The major advantage of this approach is that typically, these frameworks, in addition to Web/Internet standards, provide proprietary SDKs and APIs that bring the differences of the device platforms they support, especially their technological features, onto a common ground. Thereby, they typically provide more access to device platform features than current Mobile Web Application technologies.

  Their major disadvantages are that they are only partially compliant to standards, such as Web/Internet technology standards, and for a large part proprietary and incompatible with concurrent frameworks or technologies. The most popular frameworks support the major mobile device platforms Android, iOS, Blackberry, Windows Phone 7, but still, the framework needs to support the device platforms and applications need to be compiled for every platform separately. Thus, they do not enable truly platform independent application clients that can run seamlessly across all types of devices an end-user might use in the lifetime of a Web-Telecom Converged application.

- **Mobile Web Application Clients** - These clients are mobile web browser-based applications, implemented using state-of-the-art Web/Internet technologies and hosted and delivered by a Web/Internet technologies compliant web-server.

  Their major advantages are that they are, by default, compatible with all device platforms that provide an up-to-date Web/Internet technologies compliant web browser. Developers can implement them so that they adapt to device specifics, like screen size or user input options, dynamically and automatically while being delivered over the network.

  Their current disadvantages are that they are delivered over an HTTP connection and therefore not as reactive, graphically appealing and user friendly as native applications running on the devices. Their access to technological features of the device platform is limited by what current Web/Internet standards, and especially the mobile web browsers, provide. Currently, there is a strong impulse in the development of mature, rich and powerful Web/Internet technologies that is illustrated by the fast development of HTML5. In the near future, such new technologies can enable application clients that are at least as appealing and powerful as current native applications. Once these worldwide technology standards are adopted by all device/platform vendors, these technologies enable truly device platform independent application clients for Web-Telecom Converged applications.

The concept C3.3 supports the fulfillment of the requirements R1.1, R1.7, R1.8, R2.3, R2.5 and R2.6 illustrated in chapter 6.

7.1.3.4 C3.4 - QoS, AAA, SCIM and PEEM Layers

The ADP ensures a carrier grade QoS for all Live Services (see concept C3.2) as well as all high-quality Web-Telecom Converged applications that are delivered to end-users. It implements state-of-the-art QoS technologies [51] and protocols (e.g. Resource Reservation Protocol [252] (RSVP)), and accesses, leverages and manages the varying QoS features of the underly-

7.1. Core Concepts of the Application Delivery Platform

ing Telecommunication or data networks. It abstracts from their details and, through Shared Services, provides interfaces to them to all deployed services and applications.

The ADP provides state-of-the-art AAA functionalities to all services and applications on the platform. It implements a central user and group management service and allows coupling with existing AAA data sources, services and systems. These can be provided by the underlying Telecommunication or data networks as well as by imported services or applications from CSPs or ASPs.

The ADP includes a standardized Policy Evaluation Enforcement and Management [165] (PEEM) service (see section F.5.3.3) that manages, evaluates and enforces policies for every service or application interaction between the ADP layers in real-time. A policy is a formalized description that specifies how to manage and to provide a controllable access to services and applications.

The ADP implements the SCIM concept (see section F.5.3.2) as a service that resolves the dependencies and conflicts in the interactions between the Shared and Application Services that deliver the Web-Telecom Converged Application.

On the ADP, the PEEM and SCIM work in conjunction and figure 7.5 illustrates the concept of their combination.

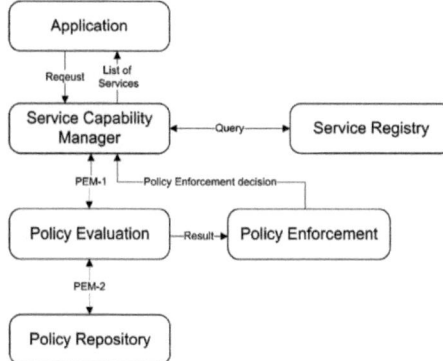

Figure 7.5: Service Capability Manager with Policy Evaluation [28]

For Web-Telecom Converged applications deployed on the ADP, by querying the Service Registry, the SCIM provides an interface to retrieve a List of Services that are available on the ADP. When an application initiates a Request to a service, the Request message data is forwarded to the Policy Evaluation.

The Policy Evaluation identifies the policies that are associated with the Request, retrieves them from the Policy Repository and evaluates their formalized descriptions. The policies are evaluated consecutively and the evaluation process continues as long as no policy is violated. The evaluation Result is defined as one of the three possible decisions Allow, Deny or Forward and is executed by the Policy Enforcement.

The Policy Enforcement is responsibility for executing the actions associated with the Result from the Policy Evaluation. It either allows a Request, denies a Request, modifies certain parameters of a Request message to meet policy conditions, or forwards a Request to a, by the policy, specified target. This might be either a specific service or a composed service possibly even executed by a workflow engine (see concept C6).

A Policy Management service provides an XCAP-based access to the Policy Repository and allows deployment, modification and removal of policies.

The concept C3.4 supports the fulfillment of the requirements R1.5, R2.4 and R2.6 illustrated in chapter 6.

7.1.4 C4 - Layered Telecommunication Standardization

A full separation of networks and applications enables the full potential and maximizes the speed of technology, service and end-user application innovation. The prime example for this is the Web/Internet, where the standardized generic underlying data networks and protocols such as TCP/IP and HTTP enable a completely open worldwide services and applications innovation platform.

The downside of such an environment is that all ASPs on the platform are driven by their individual business goals and success factors, which typically lead them to pursuing a maximization of their applications end-user base, while at the same time, locking them to their proprietary applications. As a result, most ASPs are not cooperating with any of their competitors and are even prohibiting any compatibility and interoperability of their services or applications. Thereby, end-users are unable to switch ASPs or to even connect to end-users that are subscribed to applications provided by another ASP. Prominent examples are that Skype end-users are unable to establish a communication channel to end-users using GoogleTalk, Apple FaceTime or any SIP standard compliant VoIP application, or that Facebook end-users are unable to share and interact with end-users on other social networks such as Google+, Orkut, Xing or LinkedIn.

Telecommunication networks are geographically fragmented by the CSPs that deployed and operate the networks. Technologically, the networks are standardized worldwide, fully interoperable and so, end-users can move with their devices from one CSP's network to another and still access their Telecommunication services and applications. Nevertheless, unfortunately through the declining, but still existing, excessive roaming costs CSPs charge from each other, in reality, this great concept is drastically constricted for end-users.

Telecommunication services and applications are developed and then standardized in conjunction with the Telecommunication system they are intended to be deployed on. Thereby, the level and speed of innovation is drastically limited compared to the Web/Internet. Nevertheless, for end-users, this worldwide compatibility and interoperability of all Telecommunication services and applications across all CSPs-based on a simple phone number is a huge advantage compared to Web/Internet applications.

The differences can be summarized in:

On the Web/Internet the network is technologically standardized and unified worldwide, but the applications are fragmented by ASPs business goals.

In Telecommunications, the network is fragmented by CSPs business goals, but the applications are technologically standardized and unified worldwide.

The guiding principle for Web-Telecom Convergence standardization is to find the narrow balance between retaining the interoperability advantages that Telecommunication standardization brings to end-users while providing a platform that maximizes the potential and speed of application innovation.

7.1. Core Concepts of the Application Delivery Platform

The ADP fosters this principle by proposing a shift from standardizing a whole Telecommunication system including all applications at once, to standardizing individual layers and applications in a layered ADP architecture. Concepts, technologies, components, services and even applications are standardized within the different layers independently. Clearly defined interfaces, protocols and technologies between the layers ensure full interoperability. Thereby, as long as those are standardized and stable, innovative (access) network layers can be standardized independent from innovative end-user applications on the layers above. Both can be standardized in parallel and through the focus on single layers, single applications within one layer, or even only single Shared Services standardization is completed faster. As a result, innovation cycles for Web-Telecom Converged application are shortened drastically, are not as short as on the Web/Internet, but provide innovative applications that are fully compatible and interoperable across all CSPs worldwide.

First developments in this direction can be seen in the Telecommunication industry at LTE, where the access and core networks were standardized independent from any specific application, at GSMA OneAPI, where technologies and interfaces to network functionalities are standardized worldwide, or at the Rich Communication Suite (RCS), where innovative applications are standardized on top of a generic TCP/IP network layer.

The concept C4 supports the fulfillment of the requirements R1.7, R1.8, R1.10, R1.18, R2.2, R2.3 and R2.7 illustrated in chapter 6.

7.1.5 C5 - Scopes and Types of ADP Services

The ADP defines certain scopes for its services that define how and from where these services can be accessed and consumed. Within these scopes, the ADP defines several types of services that define a categorization based on the type of task the service is providing to its service consumers. Figure 7.6 provides an overview about the scopes (light) and the types (dark).

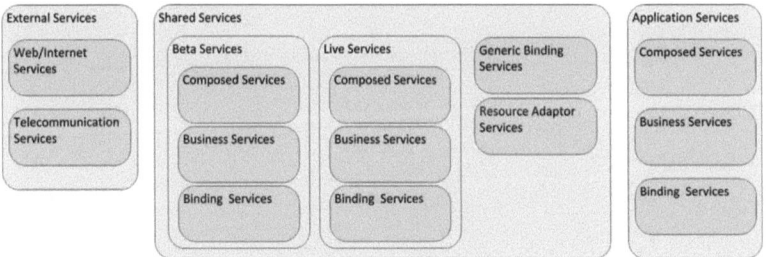

Figure 7.6: Scopes and Types of ADP Services

The ADP distinguishes the following scopes:

- **External Services** - Summarize all services that are hosted and provided by collaborating providers such as CSPs or ASPs outside of the ADP. Access and consumption details are controlled by, and have to be negotiated with these providers.

- **Shared Services** - As introduced in section 7.1.3.2, these services are shared within the ADP with all other Shared Services as well as all Application Services. Thereby, every service on the ADP can access and consume all Shared Services to compose them into new services, or to implement the business logic of a Web-Telecom Converged application.

- **Beta Services** - These services are still in active development and do not provide any quality or stability guarantees. All developers on the ADP can develop, maintain and deploy these services themselves.
- **Live Services** - These services completed a certification process that was designed by the ADP provider. These services are stable, tested and should provide some quality guarantees. Developers develop and maintain these services, submit them for certification and the ADP provider deploys them after they passed.

- **Application Services** - As introduced in section 7.1.3.2, these services represent a set of services that implement the business logic and data management of a Web-Telecom Converged application. They only implement application-specific functionality and so, are not relevant for any other services or applications on the ADP. Therefore, the sets of services of the applications are strictly separated from each other, and Application Services are only accessible from within the same set of an application.

The ADP distinguishes the following types:

- **Telecommunication Services** - These services are exposed by CSPs on their Inside-Out SDP solutions. They constitute Telecommunication end-user services such as Voice/Video Call, SMS, etc. as well as Telecommunication network services such as QoS management, A4C, etc. They provide Web/Internet technologies, typically TCP/IP,-based well-defined service interfaces to configure and consume them.

- **Web/Internet Services** - These services provide programmable access to certain functionalities and features of ASPs' Web/Internet applications. They are offered through Web/Internet technologies-based APIs, possibly including SDKs, hosted on ASPs' developer platforms.

- **Resource Adaptor Services** - To import External Services into the ADP, Resource Adaptor Services are used. They access the exposed interfaces of the CSPs' Telecommunication Services as well as the APIs of the ASPs' programmable Web/Internet Services to import their Telecommunications and Web/Internet functionalities. They manage and monitor the connections to the External Services and, due to their scope as Shared Service, generally map the External Services' interfaces, protocols and data to ADP internal interfaces that all services on the ADP can consume.

- **Business Services** - These services provide certain shared functionalities fully independent of External Services. They typically provide functionalities that were separated from Web-Telecom Converged business logic and generalized.

- **Composed Services** - These services combine Shared Services as well as, within a Web-Telecom Converged application, Application Services, to higher-level value-added services. When they combine Web/Internet and Telecommunication Resource Adaptor Services, they represent Web-Telecom Converged Services, the basis of Web-Telecom Convergence and the applications on the ADP.

- **Generic Binding Services** - On the ADP, service implementations are independent and separated from service interface and protocol standards and technologies. In order to provide a selection of interface and protocol options, Generic Binding Services implement their standards and technologies in generic Shared Services that can be reused by all services on the ADP.

7.1. Core Concepts of the Application Delivery Platform

- **Binding Services** - In order to provide interfaces based on specific interface and protocol technology standards, these services attach Shared and Application Services to the Generic Binding Services.

The concept C5 supports the fulfillment of the requirements R1.2, R1.4, R1.13 and R1.17 illustrated in chapter 6.

7.1.6 C6 - SOA Concepts-based Application Delivery Platform

The ADP applies SOA concepts end-to-end from the Telecommunication, Web/Internet and Converged services domains through the Web-Telecom Converged applications domain all the way to the client applications domain on the end-users device platforms. In addition, it takes into account the high state-of-the-art Telecommunication services and applications QoS standards [184], such as real-time performance and availability that end-users expect from Web-Telecom Converged applications. Therefore, the ADP is built upon a customized and extended carrier-grade SOA platform implementation.

From the general SOA and service definitions and concepts in sections 2.2 and 2.2.4 the following base concepts can be derived. These constitute the core of the ADP SOA environment and are, at least, provided by the underlying SOA platform implementation.

- **Service Creation and Service Repository**

    The ADP SOA is built upon popular, standardized and state-of-the-art software development technologies. It provides SDKs, tools, support and an active developer community and thereby, provides a familiar Service Creation and application development platform for third party developers.

    The ADP provides a carrier-grade Service Repository that hosts all Shared and Application services. Thereby, for beta testing, during service or application development, as well as for live deployment, at product launch, it allows third party developers to continuously deploy their services on a carrier-grade platform.

    All hosted services are exported, and so, made accessible for other services or applications, according to the Service Exposure concept illustrated below.

- **Service Execution**

    The ADP provides a Service Execution component that allows developers to continuously test and run their services on a carrier-grade platform. In conjunction with the Service Repository, this component supports, at least, the in figure 7.7 illustrated service execution cycle.

    In order to deploy a service, the software artifact (e.g. library, software bundle, class files) is installed on the ADP. The platform resolves all dependencies and hosts the services in the Service Repository. The Service Execution component can load it from there and start it. If the Starting procedure was successful, the service is Active as long as it is not stopped by the Service Execution component. Once the Stopping procedure was successful it is returned to the Service Repository. From there, the software artifact can be uninstalled and thereby, removed from the ADP.

- **Service Composition/Orchestration**

    The ADP enables developers to compose/orchestrate services of any type to more complex services of the same or any other type. To realize this, it differentiates between the following two approaches of Service Composition/Orchestration.

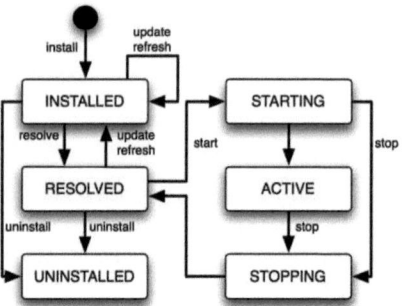

Figure 7.7: Service Execution Cycle [223]

- **Component/Source-Level Composition Approach**
  This approach is defined by a service model that is either based on a specific software development technology (e.g. Java in Open Services Gateway Initiative [177] (OSGi)) or abstracts from technologies (e.g. Web Services with SOAP). Services are hosted in a common Service Repository and developers can retrieve references to them using a global discovery functionality. These references can be used to include/import the interfaces to existing services into the implementation of new services, and to access, consume, and thereby, compose them on source-code level. The ADP's underlying SOA platform implementation provides, at least, a technology specific service model.

- **Workflow/Descriptive-Level Composition Approach**
  This approach abstracts from the underlying Service Execution sequence logic and promotes agility and reusability on a higher-level. It is defined by a (business) process model that allows specifying process states, transitions and service calls using a description language with a simple syntax. The following overview summarizes the most popular languages and technologies [134]:

    * **Business Process Execution Language (BPEL)** - Is designed as a specification for Web Services composition/orchestration that defines only the executable aspects of a workflow/process.
    * **Business Process Modeling Notation (BPMN)** - Is a standardized specification for workflows that provides interoperability between different design tools.
    * **VoiceXML/Call Control XML (CCXML)** - Is a Telecommunication domain specific composition/orchestration specification that is primarily designed for dialog-based Telecommunication systems and services.
    * **State Chart XML (SCXML)** - Is specified as an event-based state machine language that aims at providing a general-purpose composition/orchestration functionality.
    * **Yet Another Workflow Language (YAWL)** - Is a not standardized language including a graphical development tool and engine that also supports the modeling of human tasks.

  Project [134] identifies BPEL and State Chart XML [146] (SCXML) as the most suitable technologies for Telecommunication service composition. Therefore, the ADP's

7.1. Core Concepts of the Application Delivery Platform

underlying SOA platform implementation provides at least one of them for Web-Telecom Converged Service Composition/Orchestration. Figure 7.8 illustrates a performance comparison.

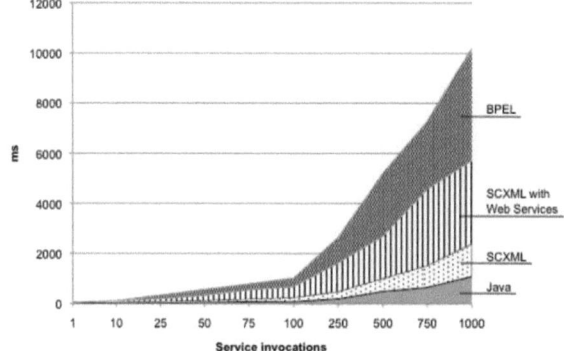

Figure 7.8: Performance Evaluation of BPEL and SCXML [134]

Even though BPEL is the common and widely accepted standard for SOA platforms, it has compatibility issues and low performance on platforms with heterogeneous network protocols. BPEL only supports composing/orchestrating Web Services. SCXML is suitable for composing/orchestrating hybrid real-time services in a simple and flexible way. For special applications, it is compatible with VoiceXML/CCXML services.

- **Service Exposure, Service Import and Service Monitoring**

    Service Exposure enables developers to provide access to generally technology and protocol independent Shared and Application services by defining technology and protocol dependent Binding Services. Thereby, other services or applications on the ADP can use these bindings to interface and consume the services. Details about SDP Telecommunication Service Exposure (Inside-Out) are provided in concept C7.

    Service Import provides a semi-automatic functionality to import Telecommunication and Web/Internet services as Shared Services onto the ADP. More details are provided in concept C8.

    Service Monitoring supervises the execution of all services on the ADP and provides real-time measurements, statistics and events to higher-level components such as SLA or QoS enforcement and management. More details are provided in concept C11.

To ensure an end-to-end SOA orientation of the platform and all deployed Web-Telecom Converged applications, the ADP architecture concepts govern an alignment to the SOA Manifesto principles (see section 2.2.1) as follows:

- **Business Value over Technical Strategy**

    The ADP is conceptualized as an open and as much as possible technology independent platform. The platform allows application developers to map business/application goals to services using implementation as well as service interface technologies of their choice.

- **Strategic Goals over Project Specific Benefits**

  The ADP's overall strategy defines a thorough SOA-based approach on platform as well as applications side. This encourages and also forces SOA design and architecture principles for Web-Telecom Converged applications hosted and deployed on the platform. In certain projects, this might lead to an overhead in the system architecture design phase but will lead to more reusable services on the platform and a maintainable and extendable application architecture.

- **Intrinsic Interoperability over Custom Integration**

  The ADP concept combines Web/Internet and Telecommunication services on a common platform using standards-based technologies that allow immediate interoperability. Applications follow SOA principles, are based on the same technologies as the imported services and so, are interoperable by definition.

- **Shared Services over Specific Purpose Implementations**

  The ADP encourages and incentivizes application developers to identify and encapsulate Shared Services from their Web-Telecom Converged applications during their SOA principles-based design and architecture work.

- **Flexibility over Optimization**

  The ADP platform concept enforces SOA design for all applications and services on the platform and does not allow any optimization shortcuts or deviations from these principles.

- **Evolutionary Refinement over Pursuit of Initial Perfection**

  The ADP platform defines applications as Application services and reusable services as Shared services. Through that, all applications as well as reusable services can be managed in a service life cycle that allows an evolution/update of all services on the platform over time.

The concept C6 supports the fulfillment of the requirements R1.1, R1.2, R1.3, R1.10, R1.12, R1.17, R2.4, R2.6 and R2.7 illustrated in chapter 6.

7.1.7 C7 - Inside-Out through Telecommunication Service Exposure

Inside-Out refers to the current trend that, in Open Innovation/Collaboration initiatives [151, 237], many CSPs are working on exposing selected Telecommunication and network services as reusable services to third party developers. Current Web-Telecom Convergence concepts and platforms (see section 4.2), research projects [109, 149, 28, 206, 198, 211], standardization bodies' (e.g. OMA) releases [168, 164, 161], and SDP vendor products [148, 8, 142, 156, 88] propose many mature solutions for this problem.

It can be expected that in a few years, most major CSPs will have an NGN implementation with some sort of Inside-Out solution in place. Telecommunication end-user services, such as Voice/Video Call, SMS, etc., as well as Telecommunication network services, such as Billing, Location, QoS management, A4C, etc., will be implemented based on modern Telecommunication standards, such as OMA Enablers [175], using TCP/IP-based concepts, such as ParlayX (see section 4.1.6), SOAP or REST.

The ADP leverages the availability of exposed Telecommunication services and encapsulates them conceptually in its Telecommunication Services Layer. Shared services access the services on this layer and import them into the Shared Services Layer.

7.1. Core Concepts of the Application Delivery Platform

The selection and availability of exposed Telecommunication will probably be determined or constrained by the fact if CSPs themselves or external providers provide the ADP to developers. CSPs will probably see the ADP as architectural extension of their SDP and define relaxed access restrictions. Thereby, the Shared services will have access to a large selection of Telecommunication services and functionalities. External providers will need to negotiate collaboration agreements/contracts with CSPs. Those will define the level of access to Telecommunication services and functionalities, and most probably will restrict access much stricter than in the CSP internal case.

The concept C7 supports the fulfillment of the requirements R1.1, R1.7, R1.8, R1.10, R1.12, R1.15, R1.18 and R2.6 illustrated in chapter 6.

7.1.8 C8 - Outside-In through Semi-Automatic Service Import

ASPs and CSPs provide a large selection of already available rich Web/Internet as well as Telecommunication services. Typical examples for Web/Internet services are Web 2.0 community services, photo libraries (e.g. Picasa, Flickr) or third party messaging services (e.g. GoogleTalk, Gmail). Typical examples for Telecommunication services are multimedia communication (e.g. Voice/Video Call, MMS) or network services (e.g. Location, Billing, QoS). For developers, it is a tremendous advantage to have the possibility to easily and flexibly access all these services on the ADP as Shared Services.

ASPs and CSPs describe their services in a non-standardized and non-structured manner, predominantly textually, in the form of HTML pages. They typically utilize REST or SOAP technologies to export their services' interfaces. Therefore, importing a large selection of these services, especially long-tail niche services (see section 3.1), manually, is too time consuming and costly for an ADP provider. To reduce effort, cost and time, the concept of a semi-automatic Service Import functionality was specified in the CDTM project [223] and incorporated into the ADP.

Figure 7.9 illustrates the overall design of the concept, including the semi-automatic service import process. A prototype implementation is presented together with the second iteration of the ADP prototype in section 8.2.3.1.

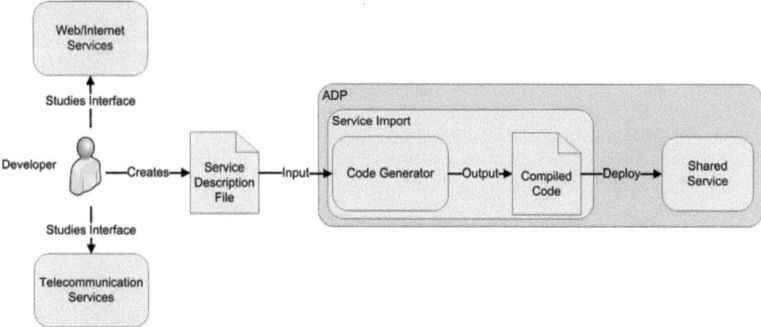

Figure 7.9: Semi-Automatic Service Import Concept (adapted from [223])

- The import process starts when a developer identifies a Web/Internet or Telecommunication service that he would like to include into his Web-Telecom Converged application on the ADP. He studies the interface descriptions and technical details of the service. These descriptions are typically textual information about the service protocol, service resource and mandatory/optional parameters including their names, types, value ranges and more.

- The developer creates an ADP Service Import compatible text-based Service Description File according to the interface details he previously studied. In [223], several service description languages were compared and evaluated. Web Application Description Language [180] (WADL) was identified as the most suitable language (see section B) and therefore, an ADP Service Import component needs to, at least, support this language. Since WADL is currently spreading fast on the Web/Internet, it can be assumed that in the future, developers do not need to write their WADL Service Description File themselves, but can retrieve it from the providing ASPs or CSPs for all their services automatically.

- The Service Description File is analyzed and processed by an ADP compatible Code Generator. This Code Generator automatically generates source code according to the implementation technology selected for the ADP. The generated source code links the service endpoints of the external Web/Internet or Telecommunication service with a generated ADP-internal Resource Adaptor implementation. The Resource Adapter provides ADP implementation technology-based access to the external service's functionalities on the ADP.

- The generated source code is compiled and packaged into a Shared Service that is compatible with the SOA environment selected for the ADP. This Shared Service exports the Resource Adaptor's interface and can be deployed on the ADP's Service Repository.

The concept C8 supports the fulfillment of the requirements R1.1, R1.7, R1.10, R1.12, R1.16 and R2.6 illustrated in chapter 6.

7.1.9 C9 - Internet of Services through a Collaboration of Platforms across Domains

To enable a seamless collaboration with other platforms, the ADP's SOA concepts are extended by the concept of an ESB on the Shared Services layer. As illustrated in section 2.3, ESBs provide means to flexibly connect them with each other across multiple deployments, companies, providers and domains. Hence, they are able to create a unified service platform across multiple ADP deployments. Thereby, developers on all collaborating ADPs are able to discover, access and utilize all Shared Services from all connected ADP deployments. This enables the creation of an open and worldwide Internet of Services that manages and provides state-of-the-art Web/Internet and Telecommunication services that are ready to be utilized in any future innovative Web-Telecom Converged applications.

The concept C9 supports the fulfillment of the requirement R2.7 illustrated in chapter 6.

7.1.10 C10 - Application Distribution

For the currently most successful mobile device platforms, the integration of a well designed and implemented Application Distribution concept, in form of the App Store at Apple or Android Market at Google, has become a major competitive advantage. To provide developers with powerful tools to distribute their Web-Telecom Converged applications to end-users, and to provide end-users with powerful tools to easily discover and install Web-Telecom Converged

7.1. Core Concepts of the Application Delivery Platform

applications on their devices, the ADP includes Application Distribution concepts aligned to the general Application Store concept illustrated in figure 7.10.

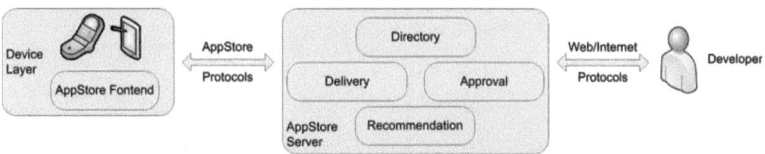

Figure 7.10: General Application Store Concept

An Application Store typically consists of two main components, a central server component (AppStore Server) that manages and hosts the Web-Telecom Converged applications, and an end-user client component (AppStore Frontend) that is available for, and ideally pre-installed on, all devices that are based on platforms the Web-Telecom Converged applications support.

Developers interact with the Application Store through a Web/Internet protocols-based interface, often an HTTP-based web application. This interface allows them to register and upload their applications onto the server component. There, the applications are analyzed, tested, and if successful, approved and added to the Directory of applications. Similar to the Live Services certification process discussed in concepts C3.2 and C5, the ADP provider is responsible for defining, implementing and enforcing an application approval process according to his business goals and customers.

End-users interact with the Application Store through native, in the future also platform-abstracted, client applications that are pre-installed on their devices. The client enables them to discover applications from the Directory through search, categories and Recommendation, to download the executable application resources onto their devices and to install those on the platform of the device. To improve the overall Recommendation system for all end-users, it encourages them to comment and rate applications they downloaded and installed. Since communication between the client and the server components is typically based on proprietary AppStore Protocols, the clients are dedicated and tied to one specific Application Store provider and do not support any form of meta-discovery across several application directories.

The concept C10 supports the fulfillment of the requirements R1.2, R1.8, R2.3, R2.5 and R2.6 illustrated in chapter 6.

7.1.11 C11 - Services and Applications Monitoring

Telecommunication services and applications are typically characterized by a high-quality [184], and all fixed and mobile Telecommunication standards heavily focus on, and satisfy, this important requirement. End-users are expecting the same quality from future Web-Telecom Converged applications that are developed by third-party developers and delivered to them through the ADP. Therefore, in addition to the definition and separation of Beta and Live Services discussed in concepts C3.2 and C5, the ADP includes a concept for real-time monitoring of deployed services and applications.

Services and Applications monitoring allows developers, the ADP provider and service consumers to define monitoring parameters, including their individual thresholds, in SLAs that are centrally stored on the ADP (e.g. as PEEM policies [28] - see section F.5.3.3). The underlying SOA platform implementation's components (see concept C6), especially Service Execution and Service

Exposure, provide probing and measurement interfaces that allow a real-time monitoring of these parameters and thus, the creation of quality statistics.

For the ADP providers SLA and QoS management and enforcement services and applications, the Services and Applications monitoring provides interfaces that provide real-time quality assessment information and that automatically trigger events in case of a breach of an SLA parameter threshold.

The concept C11 supports the fulfillment of the requirements R1.3, R1.6, R1.12, R1.14, R2.6 and R2.4 illustrated in chapter 6.

7.2 Logical Reference Architecture of the Application Delivery Platform

This section presents the logical reference architecture for the ADP that is illustrated in figure 7.11. The architecture takes the problems discussed in section 1.1 and the major stakeholder goals presented in chapter 3 into account, and combines them with the requirements summarized in chapter 6 as well as the core concepts introduced in section 7.1. It describes an end-to-end architecture concept for the delivery of Web-Telecom Converged Applications that ranges from reusable Web/Internet and Telecommunication services over Application Services to cross-platform end-user clients.

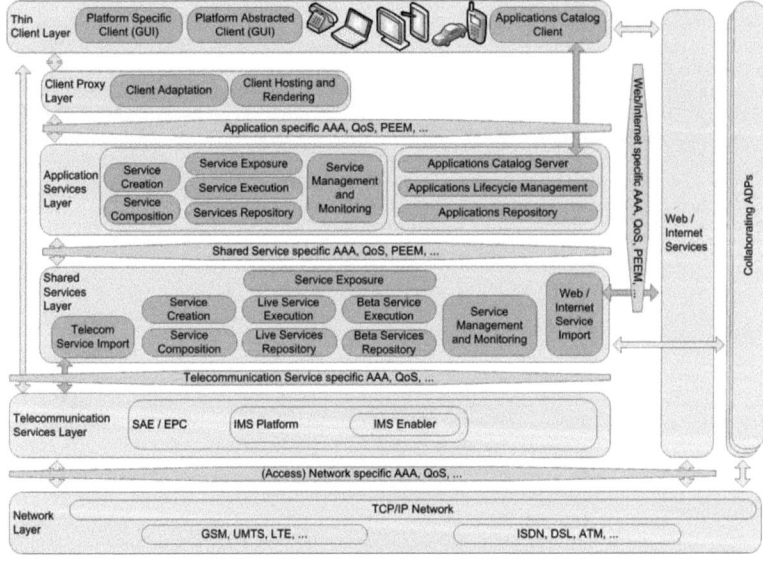

Figure 7.11: Logical ADP Reference Architecture

7.2.1 Network Layer

This layer is the foundation of all Telecommunication systems and Web/Internet infrastructures. It defines, standardizes and provides all means (e.g. protocols, data formats, interfaces, ...) for service and application signaling as well as service and application data transport. For end-user client device connectivity, it includes specifications and standards for mobile access network technologies such as GSM, UMTS and LTE as well as fixed access network technologies such as ISDN, DSL and WLAN.

7.2.2 Telecommunication Services Layer

Telecommunication systems based on GSM and UMTS are closed systems with limited/restricted access to, and no access from, TCP/IP-based networks such as the Web/Internet. Advanced Telecommunication system specifications such as LTE are more open, and so, the interoperability to and from TCP/IP networks is greatly improved. Due to most CSPs' business goals, Telecommunication service access is still mostly limited to end-user clients that reside within the network of the respective CSP. Nevertheless, the improved interoperability with TCP/IP removes most technical restrictions to access such Telecommunication services from future applications on TCP/IP-based networks.

Through recent Telecommunication concepts, specifications and standards such as Next Generation All-IP Networks, EPC, SAE, LTE and IMS, this layer represents a TCP/IP-based Telecommunication system architecture. This includes control and signaling capabilities for real-time Telecommunication and multimedia services such as Voice Call/Streaming, Video Call/Streaming, Text/Multimedia Messaging etc. IMS Enablers and SIP Application Servers provide means for Telecommunication system customization, Telecommunication services extensions, Web/Internet technologies-based Telecommunication services exposure as well as Telecommunication applications development. Thereby, this layer provides access to all TCP/IP-based Telecommunication services that are accessible from CSPs' Telecommunication networks.

7.2.3 Web/Internet Services Layer

Web/Internet services and applications are based on protocols that run directly on top of TCP/IP. Thereby, they provide and deliver their functionality in a universally accessible way for all end-user clients connected to the Web/Internet.

This layer provides access to all TCP/IP-based services and applications offered by ASPs on the Web/Internet. These services and applications use OSI Application Layer [97] protocols such as HTTP to provide access for end-user clients and to exchange/transfer service and application data. Reusable services use defacto Web/Internet service interface technology standards such as REST and data formats such as JSON to expose their functionalities to other services and applications on the Web/Internet.

7.2.4 Shared Services Layer

This layer hosts application-independent Shared Services that are specified and implemented by developers for developers, ready to be reused, and shared among all applications on the ADP. The ADP concept encourages and supports developers at identifying and extracting reusable business logic and functionalities from their applications, at encapsulating them in Shared Services, and so, at providing them to the whole developer community.

This layer distinguishes and physically separates the two scopes, Beta and Live, for all Shared Services. Beta Services are solely experimental or are still under active development/testing and service developers are working on enhancing them to the Live stage. Live Services are final and stable services that are managed and monitored by the ADP (provider) and that ensure a continuous high-quality.

This layer is the foundation of the concept of Web-Telecom Convergence. External Web/Internet and Telecommunication services are accessed, imported and wrapped by Resource Adapter Shared Services, and through the composition of these imported services, Web-Telecom Converged Composed Shared Services are created.

In detail, this layer defines the following components:

- **Service Creation** - This component provides functionalities, interfaces and tools for Shared Service identification, specification, development (SDKs, APIs, Protocol Stacks etc.), testing (IDEs, Simulators) and deployment (e.g. Developer Platform GUI) on the ADP. It supports the creation and deployment of a new and independent Shared Service from scratch, of a Shared Service from a Service Composition as well as of a Shared Service from a Service Import of an external Web/Internet or Telecommunication service.

- **Service Composition** - This component enables developers to compose services from already deployed Shared Services. It supports the two common approaches, Component/Source-Level Composition and Workflow/Descriptive-Level Composition. Thereby, the component provides the means to describe (workflow-based approach) or implement (component-based approach) Web-Telecom Converged Services by composing Resource Adapter Shared Services that import Web/Internet or Telecommunication services.

- **Live/Beta Services Repository** - These components host, physically separated, the packaged executable files and resources of all Shared Live and Beta Services on the ADP. For other ADP components such as Service Execution or Service Exposure, they provide access to the service packages as well as to the service and service interface descriptions and meta information.

- **Live/Beta Service Execution** - These components provide interfaces to, and manage, the whole service execution cycle of all Shared Live and Beta Services in conjunction with the Services Repositories. As illustrated in core concept C6, this includes at least service installation, resolving, starting, activating, stopping and uninstalling. The components physically separate the two different scopes of the Shared Services and apply suitable execution monitoring and management parameters and criteria accordingly.

- **Service Exposure** - This component provides Application Services Layer services with access to the Shared Beta and Live Services on this layer. It provides a shared collection of Generic Binding Services that implements a large selection of common Web/Internet technologies and protocols. Shared Service developers can implement Shared Service-specific Binding Services that leverage the Generic Binding Services to bind their Shared Services to their individual selection of technologies and protocols. Thereby, Application Services on the Application Services Layer can access the exposed Shared Services according to their specified interfaces through their bound interface technologies and protocols.

- **Service Management and Monitoring** - This component provides the developers and ADP provider with interfaces and functionalities to define, manage, monitor and analyze Shared Beta and Live Service Execution, QoS and SLA parameters and metrics such as scalability, availability, performance, exceptions, etc.

- **Web/Internet and Telecom Service Import** - These components provide functionalities to semi-automatically import Telecommunication as well as Web/Internet services into the ADP. They use textual descriptions of the external services' interfaces to generate Resource Adapter Shared Services. These generated services are deployed in the Services Repository and are from there, similar to all manually implemented or composed Shared Services, available for Service Execution, Service Composition and Service Exposure.

Developers can leverage the Web/Internet and Telecommunication Resource Adapter Shared Services to develop value-added composed Web-Telecom Converged Shared Services. These can then be reused on the Application Services Layer to implement innovative Web-Telecom Converged Applications.

7.2.5 Application Services Layer

The functionalities this layer provides are divided into two general parts. (i) This layer hosts the application-specific Application Services that implement application business logic and data management, and that are encouraged to reuse Shared Services from the Shared Services Layer. It strictly separates all deployed Web-Telecom Converged applications, hosts them physically separated and prohibits all access between Application Services across applications. (ii) For every Web-Telecom Converged application, this layer hosts version-managed application bundles that include all associated executable Application Services' files, all resources as well as end-user clients that are distributable and deployable on all device platforms the application supports. In addition to hosting, this layer provides functionalities that enable the distribution of Web-Telecom Converged application clients to the end-users' devices across all supported device platforms.

In detail, this layer consists of the following components:

- **Service Creation** - This component provides functionalities, interfaces and tools for Application Service specification, development (SDKs, APIs, Protocol Stacks etc.), testing (IDEs, Simulators) and deployment (e.g. Developer Platform GUI). It supports the creation and deployment of new Application Services from scratch as well as from Service Compositions, and provides tools and functionalities (e.g. service interface protocol/technology implementation, SDKs, APIs) to connect Application Services to exposed Shared Services on the Shared Services Layer.

- **Service Composition** - This component enables developers to compose Application Services from already deployed Application Services within one individual Web-Telecom Converged application. It supports the two common approaches, Component/Source-Level Composition and Workflow/Descriptive-Level Composition. Thereby, the component provides the means to describe (workflow-based approach) or implement (component-based approach) Composed Application Services.

- **Services Repository** - This component hosts, physically separated for each individual Web-Telecom Converged applications, the packaged executable files and resources of all Application Services for all applications deployed on the ADP. It provides access to the individual Application Service packages as well as to the service and service interface descriptions and meta information.

- **Service Execution** - This component provides interfaces to, and manages, the whole service execution cycle of all Application Services in conjunction with the Services Repository. As illustrated in core concept C6, this includes at least service installation, resolving, starting, activating, stopping and uninstalling. The component separates and executes the Application Services according to the Web-Telecom Converged application they belong to, and ensures that access between services within the same application is assisted, but across applications prohibited.

- **Service Exposure** - This component provides Thin Client Layer and Client Proxy Layer clients with access to the Application Services on this layer. It leverages the shared collection of Generic Binding Services that implements a large selection of common Web/Internet technologies and protocols from the Shared Services Layer. This enables developers to implement Application Service-specific Binding Services that bind their Application Services to selected technologies and protocols. Thereby, clients can access the exposed Application Services according to their specified interfaces through their bound interface technologies and protocols.

- **Service Management and Monitoring** - This component provides the developers and ADP provider with interfaces and functionalities to define, manage, monitor and analyze Application Service Execution, QoS and SLA parameters and metrics such as scalability, availability, performance, exceptions, etc.

  Service Management and Monitoring is tightly integrated into the Web-Telecom Converged application development and Application Services Creation processes. It is an essential part of the application certification process that approves an application to be deployed in the Applications Repository and to be distributed through the Applications Catalog.

- **Applications Repository** - This component hosts version-managed application bundles of all approved Web-Telecom Converged Applications. These include all associated executable Application Services' files, all resources as well as end-user clients for all supported device platforms.

  This component provides interfaces and functionalities to provide textual descriptions, descriptive multimedia resources and meta information about each application to other components such as the Applications Catalog. These descriptions are defined by the developers and/or ADP providers and help developers, the ADP provider or end-users to better understand the ideas and functionalities of all available Web-Telecom Converged applications.

- **Application Lifecycle Management** - In accordance to the concept defined in section 2.7, this component manages application lifecycle tasks such as development, version management, quality assurance, maintenance or distribution of new and updated versions of applications. It interfaces the Applications Repository component for application meta information such as versions, supported client platforms, etc. as well as the Applications Catalog component for application distribution, update management, etc. functionalities.

- **Applications Catalog** - This component gathers and summarizes descriptions and meta information such as application idea and functionality, client platforms support, versions and available updates for all approved Web-Telecom Converged applications on the ADP. From the gathered data, it builds and provides a browseable and searchable catalog that lists details about all applications.

  This component provides interfaces and functionalities to distribute the Web-Telecom Converged applications' clients, or their updates, to the end-users' client devices/platforms. Thereby, it enables the Client Layer Applications Catalog Client to download and install application clients, including their updates, from the Applications Repository application bundle onto the end-users' client devices.

  To realize a feedback channel for developers and ADP providers, this component provides bug-report, recommendation, user-ranking and user-commenting functionalities for all deployed Web-Telecom Converged applications.

7.2.6 Client Proxy Layer

This layer supports the ADP paradigm of thin platform-dependent or platform-independent clients on end-user devices. It supports the developers at keeping platform dependencies in end-user clients as small as possible while also keeping the business logic and data management implementations in the Application Services on the Application Services Layer device platform-independent. This layer provides the developers with server-side development components that can be used to adapt their platform-dependent clients to the specifics of the different device platforms as well as to develop platform-independent clients that can be rendered on all device platforms.

The Client Adaptation component provides adaptation support for platform-dependent thin clients. Since device platforms are very different in terms of screen sizes, processing capabilities, memory, battery power, user-interface technologies and concepts etc., this component allows developers to implement client adapters on server-side that adapt data, interactions, user-interfaces, etc. to the specifics of the different platforms.

The Client Hosting and Rendering component provides a hosting environment for platform-independent clients. Such clients are deployed on the server-side and only the GUI is transmitted to, and rendered on, the end-users' devices' platforms. Examples for that are clients developed using existing Web/Internet technologies such as HTML/AJAX rendered in a browser as well as upcoming Web/Internet technologies such as HTML5/BONDI etc. rendered in a browser, widget engine or similar. The component allows developers to deploy different platform-adapted versions of their clients as well as dynamically adapting clients that adapt to the different rendering engines on the different platforms automatically.

7.2.7 Thin Client Layer

This layer hosts and executes platform-dependent and renders (e.g. browser, widget engine) platform-independent Web-Telecom Converged Application clients on the end-users' devices. For client lifecycle management, it hosts the Applications Catalog client that allows end-users to, for example, discover, search, download, install, update, rank, comment and remove Web-Telecom Converged Application clients.

In addition, some end-user devices also run (mostly pre-installed by the device manufacturer or CSP) native and platform-dependent Telecommunication clients such as LTE or UMTS Voice/Video Call clients. These connect directly to the Telecommunication Services Layer and access Telecommunication control and signaling system components directly in order to implement real-time Telecommunication Services and Applications most efficiently.

7.3 Technical Architecture of the Application Delivery Platform

This section illustrates an exemplary technical architecture of the ADP. It makes technology and vendor decisions for layers and components of the logical reference architecture, and provides an overview about the components and platform services that must, at least, be deployed in order to fulfill the requirements and realize the core concepts from chapter 6 and section 7.1. A detailed specification or standardization proposal for all components, services, protocols, data formats and interfaces of an ADP is out of scope of this research project and may be part of future work.

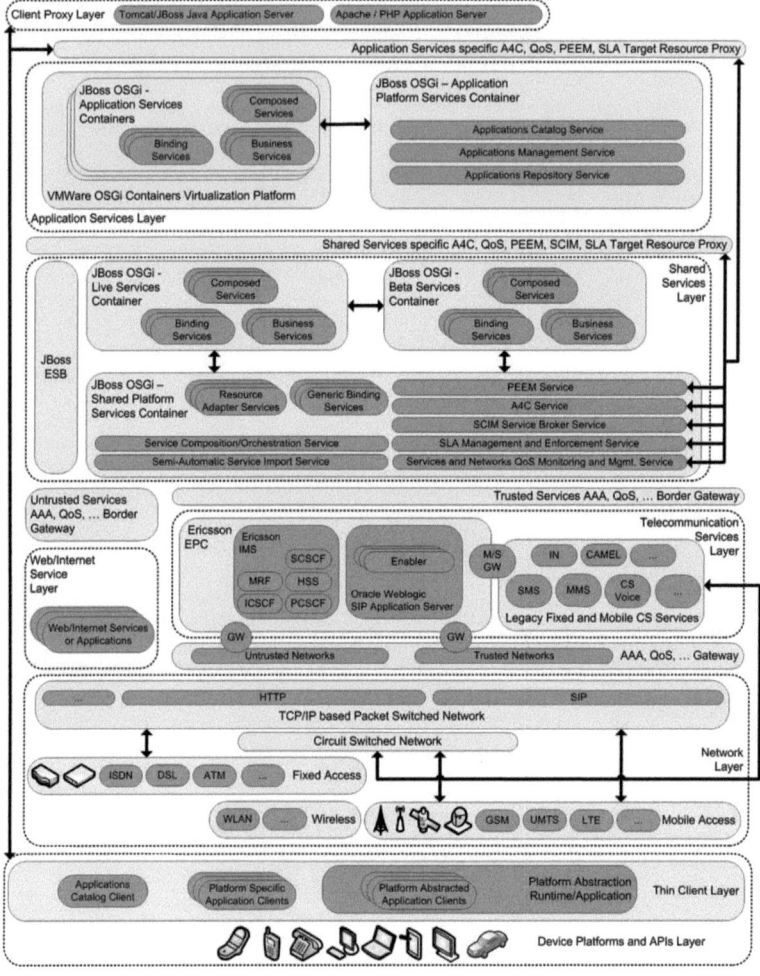

Figure 7.12: Technical ADP Architecture

The exemplary architecture is depicted in figure 7.12. Most interfaces and protocol links between components, services and layers are implicit. Generally, services within the same component, components on the same layer and layers, services and components above/below each other do have a TCP/IP (above the TCP/IP-based packet-switched Network) or Telecommunication (below the TCP/IP-based packet-switched Network) protocol-based link. Links between layers, services and components that are further spread out over the architecture are made explicit through line connections and explained in more detail below.

7.3.1 Device Platforms and APIs Layer

This Layer represents the different fixed and mobile devices, their various platforms and the platforms' APIs. The latter can be used by developers to develop Web-Telecom Converged application clients on the Thin Client Layer. This layer contains the following three different components.

- **Platform-Abstracted Application Clients** - These clients are developed with one of the mobile development frameworks compared and evaluated in section 4.3.2. Since they are platform abstracted, they need to be executed by a Platform Abstraction Runtime/Application such as a browser or virtual machine. For the, according to the comparison and evaluation, two most suitable frameworks, RhoMobile and PhoneGap, these are a Ruby virtual machine and a HTML5/JavaScript runtime respectively.

- **Platform-Specific Application Clients** - These clients are developed using platform-specific and native application development technologies and tools. The most popular platforms are compared and evaluated in section 4.3.1, which shows that the most suitable for native Web-Telecom Converged application clients are currently iOS and Android.

- **Applications Catalog Client** - This client connects to the Applications Catalog Service on the Application Services Layer's Application Platform Services Container using an ADP vendor implementation specific protocol. It is part of the realization of concept C10 from section 7.1, and is, at least, able to retrieve information about all available Web-Telecom Converged applications, transfer them to the device platform and install them.

7.3.2 Network Layer

This layer encapsulates all access and data transfer networks related to Web-Telecom Convergence. The Mobile Access Network provides GSM, UMTS and LTE technologies and protocols to connect mobile devices to the platform. It provides circuit-switched Network access for legacy mobile Telecommunication services such as Voice, SMS, etc. as well as packet-switched Network access to TCP/IP/SIP-based EPC and IMS Telecommunication services. The Fixed Access Network provides DSL, ISDN, etc. technologies to connect fixed, including WLAN, devices to the platform. It provides circuit-switched Network access for legacy fixed Telecommunication services such as Voice, ISDN services, etc. as well as packet-switched Network access to TCP/IP/SIP-based VoIP services as well as the Web/Internet.

7.3.3 Telecommunication Services Layer

This layer encapsulates all Web-Telecom Convergence related Telecommunication systems, components and services and is divided into the following two parts.

- **Evolved Packet Core** - The EPC builds the foundation for the IMS, which provides all packet-switched standard Telecommunication services, as well as for the SIP Application Server, which enables an extension of the IMS through Enablers. It provides and manages gateways to trusted (e.g. SIM-Card authenticated mobile access) as well as untrusted (e.g.

unauthenticated WLAN or DSL access) networks. These ensure AAA between the layers and QoS control, management and assurance on the Network Layer.

For the EPC and IMS implementations, the most wide-spread vendor product implementations by Ericsson were selected. The IMS must, at least, provide the three interconnected Call Session Control Functions (CSCFs), the user identities managing Home Subscriber Server (HSS) and the multimedia data processing Media Resource Function. For the AS the popular Oracle WebLogic product was selected, and the deployed Enablers provide accessible interfaces to the standard IMS Telecommunication services as well as to extended services. Thereby, they realize a part of core concept C7.

- **Legacy Fixed and Mobile Circuit-Switched Services** - These services are provided by currently deployed Telecommunication systems that are based on legacy Telecommunication standards and specifications. To access these services from the TCP/IP-based EPC Telecommunication platform, a Media Gateway and a Signaling Gateway are deployed in between them.

7.3.4 Web/Internet Services Layer

This layer encapsulates all programmable Web/Internet service and applications that provide an accessible TCP/IP-based API.

7.3.5 Shared Services Layer

This layer encapsulates the four components that enable services that are shared across the whole ADP, even across collaborating ADPs, according to the core concepts C1, C2, C3.2, C3.4, C5, C6, C7, C8, C9 and C11.

- **Enterprise Service Bus** - As illustrated in concept C9, the ESB enables a collaboration of ADPs worldwide. It connects the Shared Services Layers of cooperating ADPs transparently, and enables an immediate utilization of all Shared Services from all ADPs. For the ESB implementation the wide-spread and feature-rich commercial JBoss implementation was selected.

The Services Containers are based on JBoss OSGi product deployments that provide a broad foundation of SOA concepts. They realize a major part of the core concepts C1, C6 and C11.

- **Beta and Live Services Containers** - The two containers host Live and Beta Shared Services are linked through the common distributed OSGi technology. Thereby, Live and Beta Services are strictly physically separated, and different suitable management, monitoring, SLA and quality parameters can be applied independently. Both containers host Shared Services from concept C5 types Binding Services, Business Services and Composed Services.

- **Shared Platform Services Container** - This container hosts auxiliary Shared Services that implement ADP functionalities as well as universal Shared Services that implement functionalities that Live and Beta Services utilize. The container is linked to the Beta and Live Services Containers through the common distributed OSGi technology.

    – **Resource Adapter Services** - These universal Shared Services are generated and deployed by the Semi-Automatic Service Import Services and enable access to external

7.3. Technical Architecture of the Application Delivery Platform

Web/Internet and Telecommunication Services. They access the external services via their TCP/IP-based protocols and import them as technology and protocol binding independent services. Thereby, they realize parts of core concepts C7 and C3.1. Typical interface technologies that are supported are HTTP, REST, JSON, SOAP and SIP.

- **Generic Binding Services** - These universal Shared Services provide technology and protocol implementations that can be utilized by other Shared Services to bind themselves to a selected technology and/or protocol through a Binding Service. Thereby, they realize a part of core concept C7. Typical protocol implementations that are provided include HTTP, REST and SOAP.
- **Service Composition/Orchestration Service** - This auxiliary Shared Service provides component and workflow-based service composition functionalities according to core concept C6. If useful, with graphical composition tools for the ADP provider and developers.
- **Semi-Automatic Service Import Service** - This auxiliary Shared Service provides a Service Description Language (SDL)-based service import functionality according to core concept C8.

The Target Resource Proxy intercepts all requests from the Application Services Layer and forwards them for further processing to the five services: PEEM Service, A4C Service, SCIM Service Broker Service, SLA Management and Enforcement Service and Services and Networks QoS Monitoring and Management Service. Each service analysis and transforms the request according to its functionality, and if the request is processed successfully and permitted, it is forwarded to the target Shared Service.

- **PEEM Service** - This auxiliary Shared Service provides PEEM functionalities, as illustrated in section F.5.3.3, according to core concept C3.4.
- **A4C Service** - This auxiliary Shared Service provides A4C functionalities according to core concept C3.4.
- **SCIM Service Broker Service** - This auxiliary Shared Service provides SCIM functionalities, as illustrated in section F.5.3.2, according to core concept C3.4.
- **SLA Management and Enforcement Service** - This auxiliary Shared Service provides SLA functionalities according to core concept C11.
- **Services and Networks QoS Monitoring and Management Service** - This auxiliary Shared Service provides QoS and monitoring functionalities according to core concepts C3.4 and C11. It interfaces the Telecommunication Services and Web/Internet Services Layers to control, manage and assure QoS parameters for ADP services and applications.

7.3.6 Application Services Layer

This layer encapsulates the two components that enable ADP services that are specific to one Web-Telecom Converged application, according to the core concepts C1, C2, C3.2, C3.3, C3.4, C5, C6, C10 and C11. The arbitrary number of Services Containers are based on JBoss OSGi product deployments that provide a broad foundation of SOA concepts. They realize a major part of the core concepts C1, C6 and C11.

- **VMWare OSGi Containers Virtualization Platform** - This platform creates, executes and manages a virtualized JBoss OSGi Application Services Container for every

Web-Telecom Converged application on the ADP. All containers are physically separated and technologically not linked within the Virtualization Platform. Thereby, the ADP ensures that each Web-Telecom Converged application is executed and managed completely separated from all other applications, that no Application Service can be accesses from outside the individual application container and that the ADP is easily automatically scaleable. All virtualized containers host Application Services from concept C5 types Binding Services, Business Services and Composed Services.

- **Application Platform Services Container** - This container provides the three auxiliary services Applications Catalog Service, Applications Management Service and Applications Repository Service to realize application hosting, delivery and distribution according to core concepts C1, C2, C3.2, C3.3, C10 and C11.

  The Applications Catalog Service is linked to the Applications Catalog Client on the Thin Client Layer. It provides information about all available and device platform compatible applications in the Applications Repository, recommendation details for applications and the application client software implementation that is transferred to the device platforms.

  The Applications Management Service provides recommendation system functionalities, application certification functionalities, and manages the lifecycles of all applications according to requirement R1.2 and section 2.7. It accesses the application package in the Applications Repository to load all Application Services of an application, and passes them on to the corresponding Application Services Container that manages them. It loads the device platform compatible application client software implementation from the application package in the Applications Repository, and passes it on to the Applications Catalog Service that transfers it.

  The Applications Repository Service hosts for all certified Web-Telecom Converged applications all Application Services and client software implementations as application packages.

7.3.7 Client Proxy Layer

This layer enables developers to move device capabilities and device platforms specific rendering and adaption GUI logic onto the ADP. Thereby, it increases platform-abstraction and cross-platform compatibility of application clients according to core concepts C2, C3.3 and C10. Developers can implement their adaptive client GUI logic as Java Servlets and JSPs on Tomcat or as PHP components on Apache.

Chapter 8

Validation and Evaluation of the Application Delivery Platform Concept

This chapter presents the evaluation and validation of the ADP concepts. Initially, it assesses the level of fulfillment of the requirements within the ADP core concepts and the logical and technical architectures. Then, it presents two iterations of proof-of-concept ADP prototype implementations that each include a proof-of-concept Web-Telecom Converged application scenario implementation deployed on top. Finally, it assesses the level of implementation and validation of the ADP core concepts for the two iterations.

8.1 Requirements Assessment

This section presents an assessment of the level of fulfillment of the requirements that were introduced in chapter 6. Figure 8.1 illustrates three assessment views, (i) what core concepts from section 7.1 support the fulfillment of which requirement, (ii) to what level a requirement is fulfilled in the logical ADP reference architecture from section 7.2 or the technical ADP architecture from section 7.3, and (iii), as combination of (i) and (ii), to what level a requirement is fulfilled overall in this research work.

In the following, partially and not fulfilled requirements are discussed in more detail:

- **R1.4** - In the technical architecture, only one service container is defined to host and manage all Shared Services. Within this container, according to the logical architecture, design and implementation decisions for a separation of Beta and Live Services would need to be made by a vendor that would implement and provide an ADP product.

- **R1.5** - Concepts C3 and C3.4 as well as the logical and technical architectures cover security and policy enforcements of this requirement through an introduction of the officially standardized OMA PEEM (see also section F.5.3.3). In concept C6, a QoS-related evaluation of SOA concepts and technologies is discussed. Nevertheless, the architectures do not include any recent innovative QoS concepts, protocols or technologies, which would need to be included by an ADP vendor to create a viable product.

Concepts / Requirements	C1	C2	C3	C3.1	C3.2	C3.3	C3.4	C4	C5	C6	C7	C8	C9	C10	C11	Logical	Technical	Overall
R1.1	+		+	+	+	+					+	+	+			~	+	+
R1.2	+	+								+	+			+		+	+	+
R1.3				+	+	+					+				+	+	+	+
R1.4								+								+	~	~
R1.5			+			+										~	~	~
R1.6														+		-	~	-
R1.7		+	+		+	+		+			+	+				+	~	+
R1.8		+	+		+	+		+				+		+		+	+	+
R1.9	+	+														+	-	+
R1.10	+		+	+	+			+			+	+	+			~	+	+
R1.11																+	+	+
R1.12	+		+	+	+						+	+	+		+		+	+	+
R1.13								+								~	~	~
R1.14			+	+										+		+	+	+
R1.15										+						+	+	+
R1.16												+				+	~	~
R1.17			+	+	+				+	+						+	+	+
R1.18		+	+	+					+		+						+	+	+
R2.1			+													+	+	+
R2.2		+						+								~	-	~
R2.3		+	+			+	+						+			-	-	-
R2.4	+		+				+		+					+		~	+	~
R2.5			+	+	+								+			~	~	~
R2.6	+				+	+			+	+	+		+	+		~	~	~
R2.7			+	+	+			+		+				+		-	+	~

+ ... fulfilled
~ ... partially/limited fulfilled
- ... not fulfilled

Figure 8.1: Requirements Assessment

- **R1.6** - Monitoring and management of SLAs is essential for a carrier grade ADP. The logical architecture includes components for service management and monitoring on two layers. The technical architecture leverages the management and monitoring capabilities that the selected service containers provide. In order to implement a carrier grade ADP product, a vendor would need to extend these container capabilities with recent SLA management, monitoring and enforcement concepts and technologies.

- **R1.13** - The logical architecture provides a clear separation of the scopes External, Shared, Application, Beta and Live Services that were introduced in concept C5. Nevertheless, the logical and technical architectures do not provide a separation between the specified types of services. Therefore, to implement an ADP product, vendors would need to build a separation of service types into their individual choices of service container implementations.

- **R1.16** - The logical and technical architectures include a service import component that is defined to enable the (semi-)automatic import of external services. Nevertheless, for this research work, no existing concepts or technologies for service import were analyzed. Instead, the own concept C8 and a prototype implementation were developed within the internal project presented in [223]. For a carrier grade implementation of the ADP, vendors would need to evaluate, select and include stable and proven service import components.

- **R2.2** - Current Telecommunication standards previous to LTE, standardize a direct connection between the Telecommunication network and the standards-compliant, embedded and proprietary Telecommunication clients on the end-user device. The logical and technical architectures provide the possibility to fully separate the underlying networks from the applications, but they cannot force developers to omit this direct connection that bypasses all layers.

- **R2.3** - Current Telecommunication standards previous to LTE, standardize Telecommunication applications as whole systems that are utilized by standards-compliant, embedded and proprietary Telecommunication clients on the end-user device. Therefore, on current mobile platforms, third-party applications are currently treated differently than embedded pre-installed applications. The logical and technical architecture fully support platform-abstracted as well as platform-specific third-party application concepts and technologies.

- **R2.4** - Several concepts introduce certain aspects of performance and reliability considerations, but the logical and technical architectures do not include carrier grade components with these functionalities. Vendors would need to consider and evaluate performance and reliability aspects of their individual choices of carrier-grade components that they would be planning to leverage to implement their ADP products.

- **R2.5** - Through the Shared Services Layer, all Web-Telecom Converged applications can utilize end-user and group account management services from Telecommunication as well as Web/Internet services for implementing personalization features. Nevertheless, this research work does not evaluate recent sophisticated end-user context data management concepts and technologies and so, the logical and technical architectures do not define any dedicated context management components. A vendor would need to provide a state-of-the-art end-user context data management service as a Live Shared Service with an ADP product.

- **R2.6** - Enabling innovative applications to combine the newest Telecommunication as well as Web/Internet services, together with carrier grade SLA and QoS monitoring and enforcement provides a good basis for a great user experience. To ensure an exceptional user experience, the provider of an ADP platform needs to foster user experience governance within its developer community. There are many technical, but also usability and user-interface design aspects to an excellent user experience that cannot be covered by a logical or technical architecture.

- **R2.7** - The logical architecture defines a generic service-import component that can also be used for the conjunction of ADPs across domains. The technical architecture leverages the proven and defacto-standardized concept of an ESB (see section 2.3) to realize this functionality. This research work does not evaluate different recent concepts or technologies that allow publishing, discovering, accessing and composing services across domains.

8.2 Proof of Concept Prototypes

This section illustrates the results of the two-iteration process of ADP and Web-Telecom Converged application prototype development. In the first iteration, a basic ADP prototype including a Unified Address Book application prototype was implemented. In the second iteration, a Semi-Automatic Service Import prototype and an enhanced ADP prototype including a Social Notification Application prototype were implemented.

8.2.1 First Iteration Application Delivery Platform Prototype

The first ADP prototype architecture maps all central concepts and components of the logical reference architecture from section 7.2 to specific technologies, special purpose servers and ADP specific service, application or tool implementations. Illustration 8.2 provides an overview about the results.

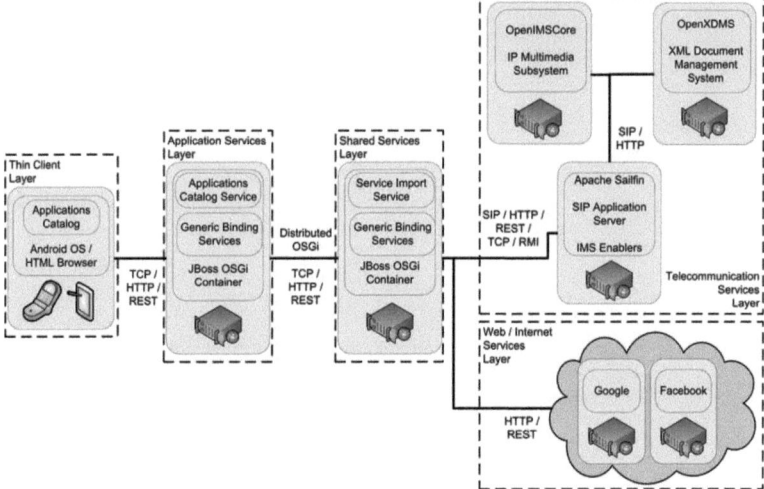

Figure 8.2: Prototype ADP Architecture

- **Telecommunication Services Layer** - This layer represents a future Telecommunication system solely based on TCP/IP technology. The central specification to provide multimedia services to end-users is the IMS and in order to use IMS capabilities in this prototype we chose the most widely used open source IMS implementation from Fraunhofer FOKUS, OpenIMS Core [73].

  In addition to the multimedia features for end-users IMS specifies additional functionalities such as a Network-based Address Book (NAB). This feature is specified as an application of an XML Document Management Server (XDMS) and in order to include this functionality in the ADP prototype, an OpenXDMS [104] is used.

  Finally, IMS also specifies a concept that allows developers to extend the core functionalities of an IMS through so called "Enablers". These are defined as SIP applications implemented and deployed on a SIP Application Server (AS). In the ADP prototype this feature is realized through an Apache Sailfin SIP AS.

- **Web/Internet Services** - In order to include services from the Web/Internet in the ADP prototype a simple HTTP and REST network gateway connection needs to be open and available. For the prototype described below, the Google Contacts service as well as the Facebook Friends-List service are used.

8.2. Proof of Concept Prototypes

- **Shared Services Layer** - In order to provide a lightweight and service interface technology independent service lifecycle management, OSGi was selected and in form of the JBoss OSGi Container implementation included in the ADP prototype.

  This layer takes care of importing/wrapping external services from the Web/Internet and Telecommunication domains. The basic functionality is provided by the "Service Import Service" deployed as OSGi service on this layer.

  Since OSGi is service interface technology independent, the ADP provides several "Generic Binding Service" OSGi services that can be used by Shared Service developers to bind their service interfaces to specific protocols. In the ADP prototype only one binding service for REST is implemented.

- **Application Services Layer** - This layer uses the same technical concept for service management as the Shared Services Layer - JBoss OSGi.

  Web-Telecom Converged end-user applications are deployed on this layer and the "Applications Catalog Service" OSGi service provides an overview over all applications available as well as over meta information, ratings, user feedback and details about client platform compatibility. Further, it manages versioning, installations and updates of application's thin clients on the different end-user client platforms.

  Similar to the Shared Services layer, this layer provides "Generic Binding Service" OSGi services to allow developers to bind service interfaces to protocols of their choice.

- **Thin Client Layer** - The ADP prototype provides an "Applications Catalog" client for the Android platform and so provides search, installation and updates of Web-Telecom Converged applications currently only on Android devices. Nevertheless, applications with a platform-abstracted GUI based on HTML or similar are of course accessible from all platforms with compatible browsers.

8.2.2 Unified Address Book Application Prototype

For the first Web-Telecom Converged application prototype implementation the scenario of a Unified Address Book (see section 5.1.1) was chosen. In this prototype it imports all end-user's contacts from two Web/Internet sources, Google Contacts and Facebook Fiends-List and one Telecommunication source, the IMS Network Address Book of the CSP. The application client is represented by a simple web browser that renders the HTML code returned by an Application Services layer service that accesses the Unified Contacts Service on the Shared Services layer. Figure 8.3 illustrates the service architecture of the prototype implementation.

- **External Services Layers** - These two layers provide the prototype with access to the contacts data. On the one hand, the Google API and Facebook API are used to retrieve the contacts from these Web/Internet services. On the other hand, the XDMS-based Network Address Book of the CSP's IMS is accessed to retrieve the contacts of the user that are stored centrally within the Telecommunication infrastructure.

- **Shared Services and Application Services Layers** - As the figure shows, most services of the application prototype are designed as Shared Services that can be reused by other applications in the future. All these services are deployed and managed on the Shared Services layer.

  The service that builds the connection to the end-user client converts the data from the Shared Services to client specific (in this case web browser) HTML. It is application-specific, cannot be reused by other applications and so, is deployed on the Application Services layer.

138 Chapter 8. Validation and Evaluation of the Application Delivery Platform Concept

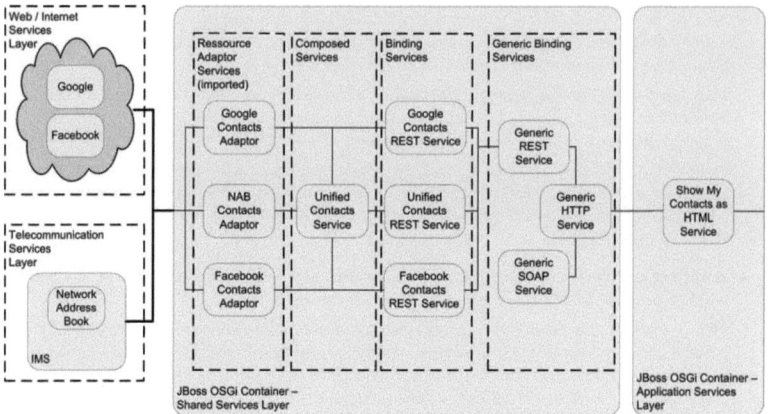

Figure 8.3: Converged Address Book Prototype Architecture

- **Resource Adaptor Services** - For each external data service one Resource Adaptor Service is deployed. This service takes care of mapping the external service data to an internal service interface that all services on the Shared Services layer can look up, reference and use.

- **Composed Services** - Declarative service composition such as with BPEL, iPOJO [12], SCXML etc. is not yet supported. The service composition is done within the composition service "Unified Contacts Service" on source code level using service container references to the Resource Adaptor Services that are composed.

- **Generic Binding Services** - Since all services on the Shared Services and also Application Services layers are interface protocol independent, services that provide a binding to certain protocols are available to be reused. For this prototype three different Generic Binding Services are available for the protocols HTTP, REST and SOAP. Every service on the platform can look them up, reference them and use them in order to bind its interface to a protocol.

- **Binding Services** - In order to keep all Shared Services interface protocol independent, protocol binding must not happen on source code level in the Shared Service but within an additional service that couples the interface of the Shared Service with a Generic Binding Service. This is done by the Binding Services. In the prototype only REST protocol Binding Services are implemented for the Google, Facebook and Unified Shared Services.

8.2.3 Second Iteration Application Delivery Platform Prototype

The second iteration of the ADP prototype is built upon the experience and learnings from the first iteration. It includes a prototype implementation of a Semi-Automatic Service Integration [223] that validates the Service Import concept C8. It solves service deployment issues of the first iteration by substituting the OSGi SOA foundation, and, by introducing Telecommunication

8.2. Proof of Concept Prototypes

multimedia services, it enhances the Telecommunication Services Layer to better match an actual CSP deployment [74].

8.2.3.1 Semi-Automatic Service Import

The concept C8 in section 7.1 illustrates a Service Description File and Code Generator-based approach for integrating external Telecommunication and Web/Internet services into the ADP. For the prototype implementation in the CDTM project [223], a simple XML-based SDL is derived from WADL, and the template-based code generation engine Apache Velocity is selected from an evaluation of four code generation technologies. Figure 8.4 illustrates the technical architecture of the prototype implementation.

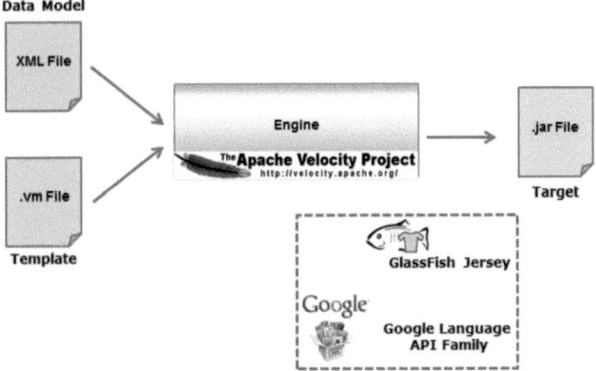

Figure 8.4: Semi-Automatic Service Import Prototype [223]

- **Data Model** - Is the textual description of the Telecommunication or Web/Internet service formulated according to the SDL specification.

- **Template** - Defines the mapping and transformation of the Data Model to Java source code, and from there, to a compiled ADP SOA compatible and deployable service. The template is formulated in a proprietary Apache Velocity specific template language and is illustrated in section D. Since the ADP prototype uses an OSGi foundation, the template is specifically tailored to generate OSGi compatible services.

- **Engine** - Is implemented based on Apache Velocity, parses the Data Model using the Simple API for XML (SAX) and generates Java source code. It compiles the code and leverages Maven, the Apache Felix Maven plugin and Apache Felix iPOJO to generate OSGi specific meta-data and to build a deployable OSGi bundle. The prototypical Engine implementation supports Telecommunication and Web/Internet services with REST interfaces and leverages the GlassFish Jersey framework in the generated source code to realize the interaction with them.

- **Target** - Is the final OSGi compatible .jar bundle that contains all compiled Java classes and resources.

The prototype implementation uses the Google Language API Family as Web/Internet service example.

Service Description Language (SDL) As introduced in concept C8 in section 7.1, the prototype SDL is derived as a simplified version of WADL that allows to describe a wide range of REST-based Telecommunication and Web/Internet services. It is self-sufficient and encapsulates all data and meta-data that are necessary for the Engine to generate source code. The SDL is a syntactic language, resource centric, and is defined by the XML Schema document illustrated in listing 8.1.

```xml
<?xml version="1.0" encoding="UTF-8"?>
<xs:element name="Content">
  <xs:complexType>
    <xs:sequence>
      <xs:element name="Class" maxOccurs="unbounded">
        <xs:complexType>
          <xs:sequence>
            <xs:element name="Parameter" type="xs:string" maxOccurs="unbounded"/>
              <xs:attribute name="name" type="xs:string" use="required"/>
              <xs:attribute name="type" type="xs:string" use="required"/>
              <xs:attribute name="value" type="xs:string" use="required"/>
          </xs:sequence>
          <xs:attribute name="name" type="xs:string" use="required"/>
        </xs:complexType>
      </xs:element>
    </xs:sequence>
  </xs:complexType>
</xs:element>
```

Listing 8.1: Prototypical ADP SDL [223]

The Content element can contain any number of Class elements, which represent imported service interfaces and are transformed to corresponding Java classes in the generated OSGi bundle. Each Class can contain any number of Parameter elements that must correspond to the interface specification of the REST service that is being described. Each Parameter has the three mandatory Attributes "name", "type" and "value" where "name" and "type" must correspond with the REST service and "value" allows to specify a predefined value. Listing 8.2 illustrates an exemplary Google Translate REST service description with the SDL.

```xml
<?xml version="1.0" encoding="UTF-8"?>
<Content>
  <Class name="Translate">
    <Parameter name="URI" type="String"
      value="https://ajax.googleapis.com/ajax/services/language"/>
    <Parameter name="q" type="String" value=""/>
    <Parameter name="v" type="String" value=""/>
    <Parameter name="langpair" type="String" value=""/>
  </Class>
</Content>
```

Listing 8.2: SDL Google Translate Example [223]

The service description describes a Translate Class with the four Parameters "URI", "q", "v" and "langpair" that are defined by the REST service specification of the Google Translate service. The "URI" specifies the location of the resource, the "q" the string that needs to be translated, the "v" the version of the service that should be used and the "langpair" the source and destination languages for the translation.

8.2. Proof of Concept Prototypes

8.2.3.2 Application Delivery Platform

The second iteration ADP prototype implements the logical reference architecture illustrated in section 7.2, applies learnings and experience, and solves problems from the first iteration. The final prototype architecture is illustrated in figure 8.5.

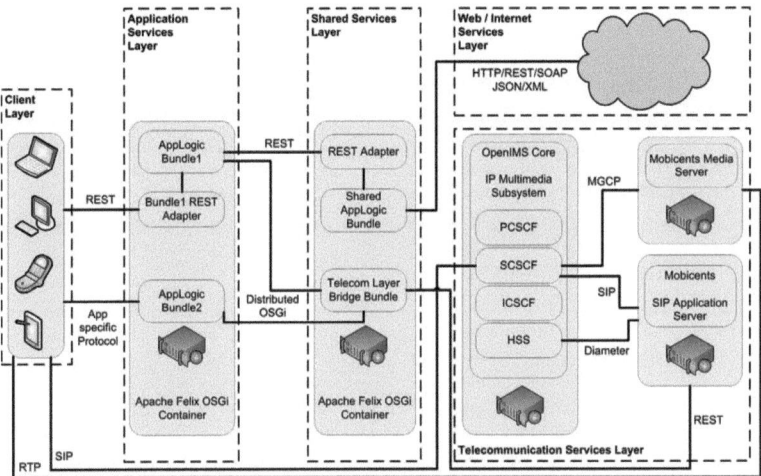

Figure 8.5: Second Iteration ADP Prototype (adapted from [74])

The prototype implementation is deployed on five independent virtual servers, where two run the Application Services and Shared Services Layers, and three the, by multimedia capabilities enhanced, Telecommunication Services Layer.

- **Client Layer** - Defines end-user devices, their mobile platforms as well as platform-specific and platform-abstracted Web-Telecom Converged application clients (see section 7.1.3.3) deployed on them. The clients implement standardized HTTP and REST as well as proprietary and application-specific protocols and technologies to connect to the Application Services on the Application Services Layer. In addition, according to current Telecommunication standards and specifications, there still are a direct SIP connection from the IMS as well as a direct Real Time Transport Protocol (RTP) (see section F.2) connection from the Media Server to the Telecommunication clients that implement the IMS and RTP standards. These clients are mostly pre-installed on the platforms and use SIP to set an IMS multimedia audio/video session up and RTP to exchange multimedia data between multiple clients and the controlling/multiplexing Media Server.

- **Application Services Layer** - Is realized through an Apache Felix OSGi container deployment that is enhanced by a selection of Generic Binding Services (HTTP, REST ...). In figure 8.5 two possible strategies for the implementation of Application Services that implement the application logic of a Web-Telecom Converged application, are illustrated.

  Bundle 1 connects to its clients as well as Shared Services mostly through standardized REST interfaces. It leverages the REST Generic Binding Service to provide a Bundle

1 REST Adapter service interface that the clients can use to connect. It connects to the Shared AppLogic Bundle through the REST Adapter service interface this provides. Only to the Telecom Layer Bridge Shared Service, Bundle 1 connects through the non-standardized Distributed OSGi feature of the platform.

Bundle 2 does not leverage any standardized technologies, but implements an application-specific protocol that its clients need to support in order to connect. To connect to the Telecom Layer Bridge Shared Service, it leverages the non-standardized Distributed OSGi feature of the platform.

- **Shared Services Layer** - Is realized through an Apache Felix OSGi container deployment that is enhanced by a selection of Generic Binding Services (HTTP, REST ...).

  The Shared AppLogic Bundle service leverages the REST Generic Binding Service to provide a REST Adapter service interface that Application Services can use to connect. It uses REST or SOAP to import Web/Internet Service functionalities.

  The Telecom Layer Bridge Shared Service does not leverage any Generic Binding Service, but simply relies on the Distributed OSGi feature to enable other service to connect to it. It uses REST to import Telecommunication Service functionalities.

- **Telecommunication Services Layer** - Consists of the three components IMS, SIP Application Server and Media Server.

  The IMS is realized through an OpenIMSCore deployment that provides standards compliant test-bed implementations of the interconnected P-, I- and S-CSCFs as well as the end-user identity and authentication managing HSS (see section F.5.2).

  The SIP AS is realized through a JBoss Mobicents SIP Application Server and hosts the REST interfaces to the Telecommunication Services that are provided by the Telecommunication Services Layer. It interfaces the IMS platform, which implements the Telecommunication Services, through SIP and Diameter.

  The Media Server is realized through a JBoss Mobicents Media Server that manages, controls, routes and multiplexes multiple RTP and Real Time Streaming Protocol (RTSP) (see section F.2) multimedia data streams of multiple IMS sessions. It is controlled by the IMS through a Media Gateway Control Protocol (MGCP) interface (see section F.1.5) and exchanges multimedia data with client applications through RTP streams.

- **Web/Internet Services Layer** - Represents all Web/Internet Services that are accessible through REST or SOAP interfaces and so, can be imported through Resource Adapter Services (e.g. the Shared AppLogic Bundle) as Shared Services into the ADP.

8.2.4 Social Notification Application Prototype

To validate the concepts and functionalities of the deployed ADP prototype and according to the scenario presented in 5.1.2, in the CDTM project [74], a prototype of a Social Notification Application (SNApp) was developed and deployed on top of the ADP prototype.

8.2.4.1 Motivation and Goals

Over the last decade, social networking has been growing rapidly and applications/platforms have become extremely popular. Today, basic social networking functionalities such as sharing, commenting and building a circle of friends, cannot only be found in the large social network applications Facebook and Google+, but also in regular Web/Internet applications like YouTube

8.2. Proof of Concept Prototypes

or Flickr as well as upcoming smaller-scale applications. As a result of this high level of social networking across multiple applications and platforms, end-users are overloaded by the amount of news, events and updates from their networking partners that they have to manually filter and process.

SNApp's goal is to reduce this overload by gathering social networking information from the different platforms an end-user is active on, and selectively actively notifying him about only those news, events and updates that are relevant for him. SNApp provides a Web/Internet technologies-based application that enables end-users to manage personal filter criteria for social network news, updates and events together with their preferred notification channel(s) TextMessage, E-Mail or automated Audio Phone Call. Thereby, end-users can precisely filter what social network information they would like to receive from whom on what communication channel. All unwanted information is automatically filtered out. In addition to notifying, for every received social network information, SNApp enables end-users to quickly respond via the communication channels SMS, MMS, Voice/Video Phone Call, E-Mail, SNApp's mobile application or SNApp's Web/Internet applications. Section E illustrates a typical SNApp social network information push sequence.

8.2.4.2 Component Architecture

The layered logical reference architecture of the ADP, illustrated in section 7.2, dictates most of the layout of the distributed component architecture of SNApp. Figure 8.6 illustrates the distribution of the collection of SNApp services onto the Shared, Application, Web/Internet, Telecommunication and Client Services Layers. In addition, it illustrates the Database and IMS components the application leverages.

- **Web/Internet Services Layer** - Represents all social network applications and platforms that provide an accessible and programmable interface. This is ideally based on standardized Web/Internet technologies such as REST or SOAP. The prototype implementation of SNApp accesses only the main functionalities of the Facebook application.

- **Telecommunication Services Layer** - Consists of the three components IMS Core, SIP Application Server (AS) and Media Server. The IMS provides the SIP-based standard Telecommunication services TextMessage, MultimediaMessage and Voice/Video Call. The SIP AS hosts the Message and PhoneCall Services that are implemented as SIP Servlets, access the IMS Telecommunication services and expose/provide them as REST interfaces to the Shared and Application Services. The PhoneCall Service needs to transform the notification information text data into audio data that can be streamed to an end-users Telecommunication client. It uses the Text-to-Speech Service on the Media Server to transform the text data and streams the resulting audio data to the client via RTP.

- **Shared Services Layer** - Contains all services that are implemented generic, without any SNApp application specifics, and shared/accessible by all future applications on the ADP. In addition to the shared E-Mail Service, Generic Persistence Service, Facebook Service, TextMessage Service and AudioNotification Service that implement certain functionalities an application can utilize, the Generic Binding Service "Generic REST Service" enables Shared Services to bind to the REST technology to be accessible from the Application Services Layer via REST. In the prototype implementation, only the Facebook Service is bound to REST via the Facebook-Service REST Adapter Binding Service.

- **Application Services Layer** - Contains all services that are SNApp specific and that are not accessible by any future applications on the ADP. The Application Services SNApp

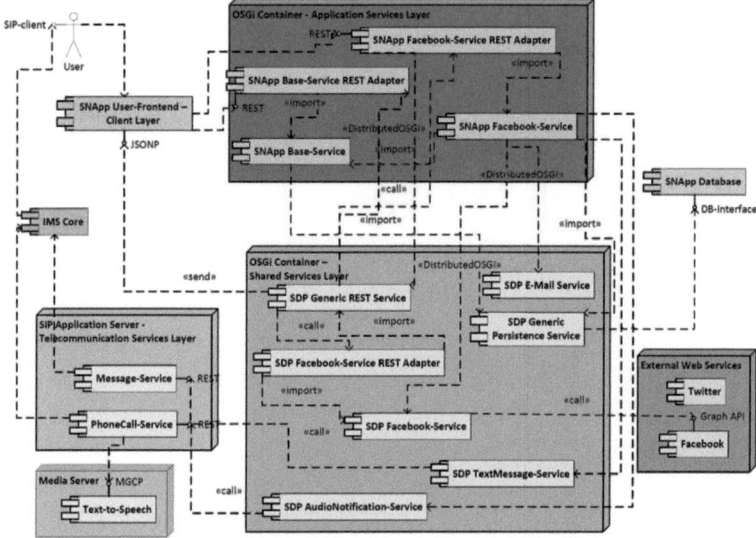

Figure 8.6: SNApp Distributed Component Architecture [74]

Facebook Service and SNApp Base Service implement the SNApp application prototype features and are bound to REST interfaces through their individual REST Binding Services (REST Adapters) which utilize the Generic Binding Service "Generic REST Service" on the Shared Services Layer.

- **Client Layer** - Contains the Web/Internet technologies-based as well as the Android platform-specific applications that access the SNApp Application Services via the REST interfaces those provide.

8.3 Core Concepts Assessment

This section presents an assessment of the level of implementation and validation of the ADP core concepts that were introduced in section 7.1. Figure 8.7 illustrates two assessment views, (i) to what level a concept is implementation and validation in the first iteration ADP prototype, and (ii) to what level a concept is implementation and validation in the second iteration ADP prototype.

- **C2** - Due to the fact that the prototype is based on the current mobile Telecommunication standard UMTS, and not the future standard LTE, there still is a direct Telecommunication protocol connection from the core Telecommunication network to a Telecommunication client on the end-users mobile devices. With LTE, the mobile device will have a generic and universal TCP/IP connection that can be used to connect to the ADP directly. Then,

8.3. Core Concepts Assessment

Concepts / Prototypes	C1	C2	C3	C3.1	C3.2	C3.3	C3.4	C4	C5	C6	C7	C8	C9	C10	C11
Iteration 1	+	+	+	+	~	+	-	+	+	~	~	-	-	-	~
Iteration 2	+	~	+	+	~	+	-	+	~	~	~	+	-	-	~

Figure 8.7: Concepts Assessment

the ADP will be able to terminate all Telecommunication protocols from the IMS and Media Server for the end-users device.

- **C3.2** - Since the prototype ADP is only hosting one Web-Telecom Converged application, there is no technical and physical separation of the different applications on the Application Services Layer. The prototype runs all Application Services in the same services container and does not create separate container instances for applications. The prototype does not distinguish between Beta and Live Services. A physical separation of these two types needs to be realized in a commercial product implementation of the ADP.

- **C3.4** - The ADP prototype does not implement or leverage and PEEM, SCIM or QoS standards or components. AAA is implemented application-specific by an Application Service and IMS user management and authentication is kept separated from ADP or application AAA.

- **C5** - The Web-Telecom Converged application architecture of the second iteration does not structure the implemented services into the types Composed Service, Business Service, Binding Service or Generic Binding Services. Since none of the services can be considered Live Services, there is no distinction between Beta and Live Services in the architecture or on the ADP deployment.

- **C6** - The selected OSGi platforms provide a suitable SOA foundation for the ADP prototypes that include Service Creation/Repository, Service Execution, basic Service Composition and Service Exposure. The ADP prototypes provide a component-based composition of services and both Web-Telecom Converged applications leverage this in some of their Shared and Application Services. The prototypes do not include any workflow-based composition or orchestration standards or components.

- **C7** - The ADP prototypes provide an IMS Telecommunication Services exposure through the SIP Application Servers in the Telecommunication Layers. On the AS, services access the Telecommunication functionalities in the IMS and provide REST interfaces to Shared and Application Services. The ADP prototypes do not implement any large-scale ParlayX or OMA Enabler interfaces, standards or specifications.

- **C8** - The first iteration ADP prototype does not provide any support, tools or automatism to import external functionalities as Shared Services into the ADP. It supports Service Import only through manual code-level implementation within a Resource Adapter Shared Service. The second iteration prototype provides a tool to semi-automatically import external REST-based Web/Internet and Telecommunication Services into the platform by describing their interfaces textually.

- **C9** - The ADP prototypes do not include ESB components within their Shared Services Layers.

- **C10** - The ADP prototypes do not include any application store prototype components implementations.

- **C11** - The OSGi platforms provide a basic service management and monitoring foundation including a Web/Internet-based user-interface. The platforms provide programmable interfaces to service status and real-time service monitoring functionalities, but the ADP prototypes do not implement any processing or evaluation of the provided data. The ADP prototypes do not implement any SLA management, monitoring or enforcement standards, concepts or specifications.

Chapter 9

Conclusion and Future Work

This research work identified and analyzed current problems within the Telecommunication industry and proposed as solution the design of an ADP that extends existing SDPs, Web-Telecom Convergence and SOA concepts in Telecommunications. The work analyzed the Web-Telecom Convergence related goals of the major stakeholders, combined these with an evaluation of existing Web-Telecom Convergence and Mobile Application Development concepts, and illustrated how the requirements for an ADP can be derived from that. From the requirements, eleven core concepts for an ADP design were created, and from these, a logical reference architecture and an exemplary technical architecture for an ADP were developed.

The ADP concepts and architectures were validated and evaluated in two iterations of ADP prototype implementations that each included the implementation and deployment of an exemplary Web-Telecom Converged application prototype on top of the platform. The application prototype implementations showed that the use of an ADP enhances the architecture, and so, maintainability of future applications as well as that it reduces the development time of new applications by leveraging a growing pool of powerful Shared Services. The assessments of the requirements and core concepts showed that the ADP is a feasible concept that is able to fulfill many of the requirements and goals, and so, provides great advantages for all major stakeholders.

Future work may include the extension of the ADP prototype through a set of imported Telecommunication and Web/Internet services. Especially real-time Telecommunication features such as Voice/Video and Conference Call or Instant Messaging features from the Web/Internet. This will allow an extended investigation of real-time concepts and requirements. In addition to services, upcoming client platforms such as smartphones, laptops, PCs, tablets and IPTVs may be included in future Web-Telecom Converged application scenario prototype implementations.

Future work may include enhancements of the QoS, SLA, Monitoring and AAA concepts through a thorough evaluation of existing proposals and standards in this area.

Future work may include a prototypical implementation of the application store concept as well as enhance the concept to a Meta-Store concept that realizes interfaces to the existing distribution channels of the different platforms (e.g. Apple App Store, Android Market, etc.).

Future work may investigate workflow-based service composition and orchestration concepts, standards and solutions including an integration, and evaluation of the usefulness, of graphical composition tools.

From the core concepts, logical reference architecture and exemplary technical architecture developed in this research work, future work may derive and create a precise specification/standard for all components, services, protocols, data formats and interfaces of the ADP.

In the future, a commercial ADP product could be implemented by a Telecommunication or Application Server vendor, and be deployed by a CSP, a CSP's subsidiary focusing on innovation and developer integration, or an independent Telecommunication or Web/Internet provider. In order to deploy an ADP implementation successfully the provider needs to adopt the mindset of Web/Internet service providers and fulfill all non-technical organizational, business and governance related stakeholder goals that are out of scope of the technical requirements and concepts of the ADP.

The provider needs to allow Beta Services and Applications development and distribution in short and unrestricted prototyping development cycles. It needs to attract a maximum of application developers by conveying an open and innovative mindset with a maximum of openness, flexibility and support, and a minimum of bureaucracy, binding contracts and costs.

The provider needs to successfully convey and advertise to developers the advantages of using an ADP, as a hosted and managed Web-Telecom Converged Application environment that provides access to a huge number of ready-to-use stable services. Further, it needs to offer incentives and tools for platform contributions, especially on the Shared Services Layer, and needs to manage all Shared Services and premium Live Applications with the highest possible quality.

An ADP deployment will only be successfully if application developers fulfill all non-technical end-user goals that are out of scope of the technical requirements and concepts of the ADP. Developer need to see the advantages and abide by the Web-Telecom Converged Application architecture the ADP defines and governs. They need to be supported at identifying and distinguishing Shared from Application Services. They need to adopt an open source community mindset and share their services in the whole ADP community in order to allow a collective and constant maintenance of Shared Services and Applications.

Appendix A

Web-Telecom Convergence Concepts and Platforms Evaluation Details

A.1 Business Requirements

These business goals drive every implementation of a Web-Telecom Convergence Platform architecture implementation (adapted from [125]):

- Improve market position - With the implementation of a modern platform, the telecommunication operator aims for expanding market share in operating markets, entering new markets and reducing time to markets of new products.

- Generation of new revenue streams - With the convergence of different networks, the telecommunication operator is able to generate new revenue streams from new entertainment services, advertising and content services.

- Transforming business models - Today, 40% of the operators that have deployed a platform expect it to allow them to transform their business models and to drive new revenues from third party application and services. The new business models need to include revenue splitting with third party service providers.

- Reduce Total cost of Ownership - Total cost of ownership describes the total cost of an information technology product over its lifecycle.

    It comprises of the following points:

    - Reduce cost of development - Additionally to the cost of development, the operator is required to manage flexible sourcing alternatives. Therefore, the system should be based on open standards to increase interoperability and portability.
    - Reduce cost of deployment, operations and maintenance - Especially the ease of installation and the ease of repair as well as the increase in flexibility and configuration possibility is important to the telecommunication operator.

– Reduce cost of retirement - Dealing with legacy is one of the most important aspects of a platform. From the business perspective it means to either to retire older systems, find a smooth transition to follow on systems and in the end to replace legacy systems/moving to a new system.

- Improve capability and quality of system - Business requires an increase in performance, reliability and availability of the system with new software architecture. Security, safety scalability, extensibility as well as internationalization possibly of the system are necessary.
- Support improved business processes - The software architecture is supposed to support distributed development and maintain jobs of workforce on legacy system.
- Widening the range of service sources - To produce a large number of services and applications, one of the most important goals for a platform is to attract as much third-party content and as many service providers as possible.
- Globalization - Many CSPs operate in various countries and therefore, the platform must be specified so that it can be deployed in different countries and regions to save costs and to interconnect platform.
- Resolving vendor lock-in - Legacy platform usually fails in time-consuming service creation and lacks of service portability, soaring service OPEX throughout the operation. Even annual maintenance fees of these legacy systems can surpass total cost of new service platform. Therefore, the telecommunication operator needs to gain financial and technological freedom in choosing the best of breed solutions provided by vendors.

A.2 Architectural Services

Service Creation Environment

- Managing usage of internal reusable service building blocks
    - Development tools to assists easy service building blocks development
    - High level features, which allow to efficiently reuse existing building blocks
    - Managing functionality for reusable service building blocks
    - Service publishing
    - Service composition
    - Service discovery
    - SLA agreement
    - Service repository
- Designing orchestration of services
    - GUI enabling orchestration of service components and integrating
    - External services without having to develop low-level code
    - Tools on mock-up of service composition
    - Enabling mapping of service requirements to service Logic
- Service testing
- Managing functionalities and reporting capabilities for third-party developers

Service Execution Environment

- Homogeneous end-to-end service lifecycle management
- Service discovery and service description

A.2. Architectural Services

- Service deployment
- Service orchestration
  - Creation of new business processes
  - Control of workflow regulation of services
  - Service composition from multiple service enablers
  - Binding component between service repositories offering description of available services
- Deliver mobile content/messaging
- Delivery of voice and data services
- Service fulfillment
- Tracing and log services

Service Control Environment

- Security
  - Authentication, authorization, auditing
  - Service capability access control
  - Network access and protection
  - Privacy and integrity
- Service control and monitoring
  - Monitoring and enforcement of Service Level Agreement (SLA)
  - Service access
  - Service profile management
  - Service monitoring
  - Network overlay service controlling
- User and roles management
  - User access
  - User profile management
  - Participant roles and authorization management
  - Addition and removal of participants
  - Support of participant interaction
  - Subscriber management
  - Single-sign on
- Policy management
  - Policy evaluation
  - Policy enforcement
  - Event handling
  - Key management
  - ID federation
- Other
  - Traffic control of each component, priority control and flow control

Service Broker

- Communication among diverse implementations of layers, platforms, service enablers and interfaces
- Management and monitoring of middleware
- Service interaction
- Resource delegation

- Service mobility to be exchanged throughout different devices
- Messaging bus transmitting the messages among components of the SDP
- Interconnecting internal application and service enabler

Interfaces

- Facilitating rapid OSS/BSS integration
- Integration with various, legacy systems
- Provision of open API platform
- Interface with external application and third-party service providers
- Network and device independence

Enablers

- Reusable service component, which can be composed to more advanced VAS
- Facilitate development, deployment and operation of services
- Expose simple standardized API, abstracting from underlying network
- Capabilities
- Hiding non-relevant programming support details and provide a high level method of describing services
- Standardized interfaces linking application to network elements

A.3 Quality Subfactors

Interoperability

- Device and network independence
- Industry standards to enable current and future technologies
- Enable integration of legacy systems
- Enable "write once runs anywhere" principle
- Multi-Vendor products support
- Interface with IMS and use IMS capability

Reliability

- Carrier-grade or near carrier-grade level of reliability
- Consistent and stable environment
- Service reliability
- Failure management

Availability

- Tolerant to system failures and overload
- Capable of quickly solving and isolating problems

Usability

- Enable non-experts to use platform
- Abstract from network and telecommunication knowledge
- Rapid development of services

Security

- Secure access to network resources and service enabler
- Data integrity
- Confidentiality
- Authentication
- Authorization
- Encryption
- Enablement of interoperability between different security domains
- Secure communication between cross-organizational services and to third party application/service providers
- Trust building procedure for external services
- Support of different certifiers and different trust models

Performance

- Perform near real-time
- Low latency, thus high throughout should not affect performance
- Addressing high volume of data and transaction

Scalability

- Addressing the needs of different networks and future technologies
- No loss of performance with increase in number of users and numbers of transactions

Appendix B

Service Description Languages Evaluation

Figure B.1 sums up the service description language evaluation results from the CDTM project [223]. The evaluation uses the following criteria:

- **The Officially Formulated Purpose** - Strategies of generality, simple service description or combinations.
- **The Orientation** - Resource-centric, interface-description focused or combined.
- **The Fundament** - Base technology/language.
- **The W3C Membership** - Standardized W3C recommendation.
- **The Stateless Feature Requirement** - Specified orientation of statefulness or statelessness.
- **The HTTP authentication** - Is, and if, how well is authentication specified?
- **The Schema Language** - What language is used, and is it standardized?
- **The Description Type** - Syntactic or semantic descriptions?
- **The Specific Operations** - Are GET, PUT, POST, DELETE supported? Are arbitrary user-defined operations possible?

Languages such as WADL, WRDL or RIDDL are syntactic and resource-centric, but not standardized. WRDL and RIDDL do not specify any stateless feature requirements, and allowing user-defined arbitrary operations adds to the complexity of the languages. The WADL specification contains numerous elements, which are not relevant for an ADP service import and lead to description documents that are complex and so, difficult to read and understand by developers.

Nevertheless, for the definition of the ADP's Outside-In concept, WADL is the most suitable description language and is defined as the language that must, at least, be supported by an ADP Service Import component. For the implementation of the semi-automatic service import prototype, a simplified version of the language is derived, implemented and supported by the Service Import component.

	WADL	WSDL 2.0	RIDDL	WRDL	WDL	SMEX-D	NSDL	RESEDEL	USDL
Officially formulated purpose	Offer a machine-readable description of HTTP-based web applications	Provide a general model for describing web services	Be a flexible, extensible, and as simple as possible description language	Describe the runtime behavior of the services	Reuse some of the WSDL features, but first define operations, and only then associate them with resources	Provide simple descriptions of a wide range of Web service message exchanges, both REST- and SOAP-based	Enable programmers to use Web services transparently, achieve some level of interoperability with standardized interfaces, in a simple fashion	Design a hybrid of SMEX-D and NSDL	Aim at aligning business services by unifying them using a common description format, complementing existing standards
Orientation	Resource-centric	Interface-centric	Resource-centric	Resource-centric	Interface-centric	Resource- and interface-centric	Not specified	Not specified	Not specified
Fundament	XML	XML	XML	XML	XML	XML	XML	XML	WSDL, WordNet OWL Ontology
W3C Membership	W3C Member submission - pending	W3C Recommendation (June 2007)	No	No	No	No	No	No	Part of the W3C Incubator Group until September 2011
Stateless feature requirement	Does not provide for any of the stateful features of HTTP	Supports HTTP cookies	Not specified	Not specified	Supports HTTP cookies	Provides stateful features	Not specified	Not specified	Not specified
HTTP authentication	Not supported	Supported	Not supported	Not specified	Supported	Not specified	Not specified	Not specified	Not specified
Schema language	W3C XML Schema and RELAX NG	W3C XML Schema	RELAX NG	Not specified	Not specified	RELAX NG, W3C XML Schema and Schematron	RELAX NG	RELAX NG	OWL Ontology-based
Description type	Syntactic	Syntactic	Syntactic	Syntactic	Syntactic	Syntactic	Syntactic	Syntactic	Semantic
Specific operations	GET, PUT, POST, DELETE	GET, PUT, POST, DELETE	GET, PUT, POST, DELETE, and arbitrary ones defined by the user	GET, PUT, POST, DELETE and arbitrary ones defined by the user	GET, PUT, POST, DELETE	Not specified	GET, PUT, POST, DELETE	GET, PUT, POST, DELETE	Find, create, delete, update

Figure B.1: Service Description Language Comparison Results [223]

Appendix C

Mobile Application Development Technologies Evaluation Details

C.1 Mobile Platforms

Table C.1: Mobile Platforms Comparison Details [121]

Categories	Criteria	Sub-Criteria	iOS	Android	Windows Phone7
Application Development					
	Development Workflow Support		2	1	1
	Developer Community and Support		1	1	1
	Development Environment				
		IDE	2	2	1
		Operating System for Development	0	2	1
		Cost of Development Tools	0	2	1
		SDK			
		Emulator	2	1	1
	Learning Curve		0	2	1
	Hardware Capabilities				
		GPS	1	1	1
		WLAN	1	1	1
		Bluetooth	1	1	1
		Gyro	1	1	1
		Accelerometer	1	1	1
		Compass	1	1	1
		HSDPA	1	1	1
		UMTS	1	1	1
		LTE	0	1	1
		WIMAX	0	1	1
		Audio Player, Recorder	1	1	1
		Video Player, Recorder	1	1	1
		Camera-Capture	1	1	1
		Screen Resolution, Multiple Screen	1	1	1
	Programming Language		0	2	1
Software Stack and Architecture					
	Cloud Computing		1	1	1
	API Capabilities				
		Web Service SOAP	1	2	1
		Web Service REST	1	1	1

Appendix C. Mobile Application Development Technologies Evaluation Details

			Access Database Servers	1	1	1
			Data Management Support	1	1	1
			Network Programming	1	1	1
			WI-FI	1	1	1
			Graphics - 2D	2	1	1
			Graphics - 3D	1	1	1
			Graphics API - Animation	2	0	1
			Video Formats	2	1	1
			USB Host	1	1	1
			Cloud Sync	1	1	1
			Game	0	0	1
			Face/Voice Recognition	1	1	0
			Gesture Recognition	1	1	1
			Barcode Reader	1	1	1
			Calendar	1	1	1
			Contacts	1	1	1
			Messaging	1	2	2
			VoIP	1	1	1
			Maps	1	2	0
			Photo Gallery	2	1	1
			NFC	0	1	0
		Memory Management and Process Management		1	1	1
		Multiple Screen		1	1	1
		Open Source		0	1	0
		User-Interfaces		2	1	1
		Web Browser		1	1	0
Capabilities and Constraints						
		Devices		1	1	0
		Ecosystem				
			App Store	1	1	1
			Supported Services	1	1	1
		Runtime Speed		2	1	1
Market Success and Issues						
		Fragmentation		2	1	1
		Mobile Platform Race		2	1	0

C.2 Cross-Platform Mobile Development Frameworks

Table C.2: Development Frameworks Comparison [121]

Categories	Criteria	Sub-Criteria	PhoneGap	Titanium	RhoMobile	WAC
Context						
	Open Source		1	2	2	2
	Cross-Platform		2	1	2	2
	Application Type		1	1	2	1
	Services					
		Data Storage	0	0	1	0
		Data Sync	0	0	1	0
Application Development	Debugger		1	1	1	1
	Build Process		2	1	2	1
	Test Process		1	1	1	2
	IDE					
		Emulator, Simulator	1	1	1	1
		Code Editing	1	1	1	1
		Cross Development Platforms	0	1	1	2
	Programming Language		HTML, Javascript	HTML, Javascript, Ruby, Python	HTML, JavaScript, Ruby	HTML, Javascript
	Community		2	1	2	0
	Learning Curve		1	1	0	1

Device API	Tutorials, Documentation		1	1	1	0
	Access to Mobile Platform		1	1	1	0
	Hardware Capabilities	GPS	1	1	1	1
		Bluetooth	0	0	1	0
		Accelerometer	1	1	1	1
		Compass	1	0	0	0
		NFC	0	0	1	0
		Proximity	0	1	1	0
		Audio	1	1	1	0
		Video	1	1	1	1
		Contacts	1	1	1	1
		Calendar	0	0	1	1
		Camera	1	1	1	0
		Barcode	0	1	1	0
		Native map	0	1	1	0
		Messaging	0	0	1	1
		Screen Resolution	1	1	1	0
		Screen Rotation	0	0	1	1
		Gesture	1	1	0	0
		Local Database	1	1	1	0
		File System	1	1	1	1
		Basic Sync	0	0	1	0
	Network API		0	0	0	1
	Extensibility		1	1	1	0
	Multiple Screen		1	1	0	0
Summary			14	16	20	9
Applications	Runtime		Platform Web Browser Engine, No Native UI	Native Code	Interpreter	Interpreter
	Type of Application		Hybrid Web App	Web App	Web App / Ruby App	Web App

Appendix D

Semi-Automatic Service Integration Prototype Template

```
1  #set( $implementation = "Impl" )
2  // Class $class.Name$implementation generated automatically
3  import java.util.*;
4  import com.sun.jersey.api.client.Client;
5  import com.sun.jersey.api.client.WebResource;
6  import com.sun.jersey.api.client.config.ClientConfig;
7  import com.sun.jersey.api.client.config.DefaultClientConfig;
8  import com.sun.jersey.core.util.MultivaluedMapImpl;
9  import javax.ws.rs.core.MultivaluedMap;
10 import org.json.simple.*;
11
12 public class $class.Name$implementation implements $class.Name {
13   #set( $uri = "URI" )
14   #set( $action = "Action" )
15   #foreach( $att in $class.Attributes )
16     #if ($att.Value!="")
17       private static String $class.Name$uri = "$att.Value";
18     #end
19
20     private $att.Type $att.Name;
21     public $att.Type get$utility.firstToUpperCase($att.Name)() {
22       return this.$att.Name;
23     }
24
25     public void set$utility.firstToUpperCase($att.Name)($att.Type $att.Name) {
26       this.$att.Name = $att.Name;
27     }
28
29     private static String $class.Name$action ( String... arguments) {
30       ClientConfig config = new DefaultClientConfig();
31       Client c = Client.create(config);
32       WebResource r = c.resource($class.Name$uri);
33       MultivaluedMap<String, String> params = new MultivaluedMapImpl();
34       if (arguments.length == $nr_atr - 1) {
35         for (int i = 0; i < arguments.length; i++) {
36           #foreach( $att in $class.Attributes )
37             #if ($att.Name != "URI")
38               params.add("$att.Name",arguments[i++]);
39             #end
40           #end
41         }
```

```
42      }else{
43         System.out.println("The number of arguments for the method
44            must be equal to the number of attributes in the
45            data model - 1 (the URI)");
46         String class_name = "$class.Name";
47         String response =
48            r.path(class_name.toLowerCase()).queryParams(params).get(String.class);
49         return response;
50      }
51   #end
52 }
```

Listing D.1: Prototype Code Generation Template

Appendix E

SNApp Exemplary Message Sequence of Facebook Support

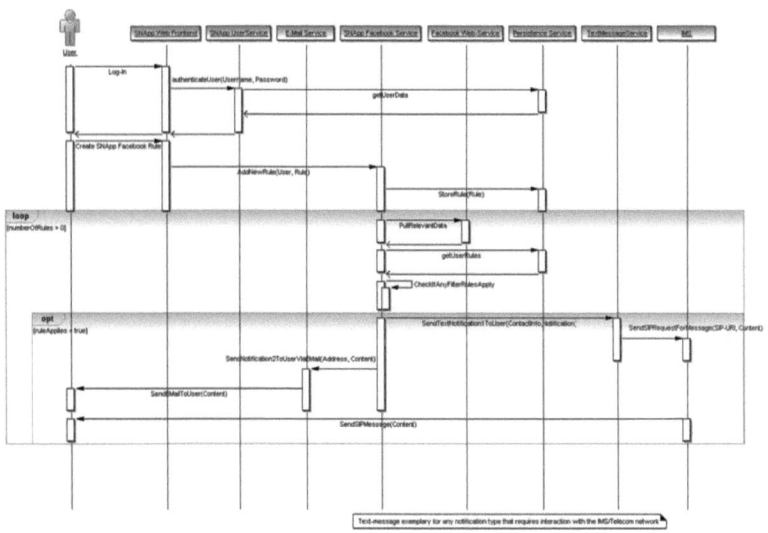

Figure E.1: SNApp Message Sequence [74]

Appendix F

Related Technologies, Standards and Specifications

This chapter describes the most important technology concepts that were used for the analysis, design and implementation of the ADP architecture and prototype. It gives an overview about the concepts in general and describes the most important technical details of every concept.

F.1 Internet and Telecommunication Protocols

This section describes the most important specifications and protocols in the area of mobile application development for VoIP systems. This includes transport and call-control protocols as well as specifications for server-side application development. It will be assumed that underlying basic protocols like IP, TCP and UDP are familiar. Information about them can be found in [53, page 161ff]

F.1.1 Hyper Text Transfer Protocol (HTTP)

HTTP is a text-based data transmission protocols for networks. It is mainly used to request and receive web pages and other Web/Internet related data and transfer that data to and from network devices such as web-servers and PCs with web browsers etc. HTTP is an application layer protocol and does not store or maintain any state information between requests, so an additional session manager needs to be implemented on top of HTTP if session information is important for an application.

HTTP is mostly used but not limited to transfer Hypertext encoded in HTML. Through its possible request extensions, additional header information and status codes it is possible to transfer any type of data as payload with HTTP.

Currently there are two versions of HTTP used, HTTP/1.0 and HTTP/1.1. Version 1.0 opens a new TCP connection for every request sent from a client to a server whereas version 1.1 is able to keep the TCP connection open while requests are sent to the same server. This eliminates a lot of useless TCP handshakes between client and server and increases the data transfer speed drastically. In addition to that HTTP/1.1 introduced new request methods that allow clients to delete files, request parameters or send data to the server in order to, for example, alter web pages or store files on the server.

HTTP Requests

The following list describes all HTTP request methods available in version 1.1:

- **GET** - The most common method to request content from the server.
- **POST** - Can be used to send additional data, such as form information or files, to the server when requesting content from the server. GET would also be able to send URL encoded parameters to the server, but POST is specifically designed for that, POST encodes the data in the request payload and allows a much larger amount of data to be sent.
- **HEAD** - Requests just header information without payload content from the server. This can be used to check validity of content in a cache or similar.
- **PUT** - Allows clients to put (store) files to a defined URL on the server. In the beginning of the Web/Internet this method was heavily uses, now new technologies such as WebDAV made it almost obsolete.
- **DELETE** - Allows clients to delete files at the specified URL. Similar to PUT, this feature is not used anymore and some new web-servers don't implement it.
- **TRACE** - Instructs the server to return the request as received. Can be used to debug connections and check if a request was altered on the way to the server.
- **OPTIONS** - Returns a list of all methods the server supports.
- **CONNECT** - Is used to open SSL tunnels with proxy servers.

The following listing F.1 shows a sample HTTP/1.1 request:

```
GET / HTTP/1.1
Accept: */*
Accept-Language: de
Accept-Encoding: gzip, deflate
User-Agent: Mozilla/4.0
Host: www.google.com
Connection: Keep-Alive
Cookie: PREF=ID=231f345654
```

Listing F.1: HTTP GET Request

The GET request line defines the absolute address of the server resource the client wants to retrieve. In this case it's just "/", which stands for the root folder and the server needs to have a standard configuration for what to return if just a folder and no specific file is requested. Normally the server returns an "index.html", "index.htm" or "index.php" document.

The request line is followed by Accept-Headers that define what types of data the client is able to accept as response. In this case they define what language the client prefers, what compression codecs the client can decompress and that the client accepts all MIME types. The host information defines what host the absolute address above references too and User-Agent defines what client is sending the request. Connection defines if the TCP connection should be kept open after this request and the Cookie information can be used as a session tracking mechanism or to store web site information on the client-side.

HTTP Response

Every HTTP request sent to a server is answered by a HTTP response sent back to the client. Every response contains a status code that defines the outcome of the request. In addition to that, every successful response contains the requested content as payload.

Status codes from the same type are combined in five code families and the following list shows an overview of these families:

- **1XX** - Information. Informs the client that the server is still processing the request and that processing might take longer than normal. Such a request is necessary since after a certain time-out most clients assume the request was not successful and present an error message.

- **2XX** - Success. The request was processed successfully and the response data is sent with response.

- **3XX** - Redirect. The requested resource was moved to a different location and the client needs to request the resource again from the new location. The Location-Header field of the response tells the client where to find the requested resource now.

- **4XX** - Client Error. Request processing was not successful due to an error caused by the client. This can be for example a 404 response that defines that the client requests an unknown resource or a 403 response that defines that the resource is restricted and the client is not allowed to retrieve it.

- **5XX** - Server Error. The request could not be processed due to an error caused by the server software. For example a 501 response informs the client that the server does not have all features (programs or additional files) to process the request.

The following listing F.2 shows the HTTP response to the GET request shown above:

```
1  HTTP/1.1 302 Found
2  Location: http://www.google.at/
3  Cache-Control: private
4  Content-Type: text/html
5  Server: gws
6  Transfer-Encoding: chunked
7  Content-Encoding: gzip
8  Date: Sun, 21 Oct 2007 11:54:42 GMT
```

Listing F.2: HTTP 302 Redirect Response

In this case the Google server sends a 302 Redirect response and informs the client to request the resource from a different location: "http://www.google.at/". So the client (in this case a Firefox web browser) sends another GET request to the other host.

The following listing F.3 shows the HTTP/1.1 200 OK response from the second GET request:

```
1  HTTP/1.1 200 OK
2  Cache-Control: private
3  Content-Type: text/html; charset=UTF-8
4  Content-Encoding: gzip
```

```
5  Server: gws
6  Content-Length: 1945
7  Date: Sun, 21 Oct 2007 11:54:42 GMT
8
9  <html><head><meta http-equiv="content-type" content="text/html; charset=UTF-8"><
       title>Google</title><style>body,td,a,p,.h{font-family:arial,sans-serif}.h{font
       -size:20px}.h{color:#3366cc}.q{color:#00c}.ts td{padding:0}.ts{border-
       collapse:collapse}</style>
10  .....
11  </script>
12  </head><body bgcolor=#ffffff text=#000000 link=#0000cc vlink=#551a8b alink=#ff0000
       onload="sf();if(document.images){new Image().src='/images/nav_logo3.png'}"
       topmargin=3 marginheight=3><div align=right id=guser style="font-size:84%;
       padding:0 0 4px" width=100%>
13  ...
14  </center></body></html>
```

Listing F.3: HTTP 200 OK Response

This response informs the client that the request was processed successful, includes a lot of meta information about the server and resource in the headers and contains the requested HTML web site as payload.

F.1.2 Session Initiation Protocol (SIP)

SIP is an Internet Engineering Task Force (IETF) application-layer signaling and control protocol specified in Request for Comment (RFC) 2543. It is used to establish, maintain, manage, alter and terminate multimedia sessions, which are used in IP telephony, audio and video conferences and other similar applications involving audio and video data transmission/streaming.

SIP is a text-based protocol with a message syntax and header fields comparable to HTTP. SIP messages are sent over TCP or UDP with possibly multiple messages carried in a single TCP connection or UDP datagram. Since SIP messages can grow very large, which can be a problem over low bandwidth mobile device radio links, some new specifications propose compressions such as DEFLATE to be used with SIP. These proposals are defined in the Signaling Compression [183] (SigComp) and Extended Operations [85] specifications.

SIP can be used to establish sessions and carry session descriptions in order to negotiate session parameters and details such as codecs etc. between end-points. It supports unicast and multicast sessions as well as point-to-point and multi-point calls. Connections can be established, maintained and terminated using the following five SIP facets:

- **User Location** - Defines how and where to contact a user a client wants to call. Involves client software (can be multiple ones for one physical user) SIP registrations at Registrar Servers and "DNS-like" resolving of SIP addresses in order to build a connection between the users clients.

- **User Capability** - Defines compatible codecs and communication parameters for the audio/video session.

- **User Availability** - Defines state information for the different devices a physical user is registered with. (e.g. offline, online, unavailable, available, busy, etc.)

- **Call Setup** - Defines signaling messages for call/session setup and communication parameter negotiations.

- **Call Handling** - Defines signaling messages for altering session parameters, moving sessions between registered devices, adding clients to a conference session/call, terminating sessions etc.

SIP can be used in conjunction with other signaling protocols, such as H.323, RTSP, RTCP etc., but it does not depend on any of these protocols.

Specifications, technologies and systems around VoIP are still being developed and extended and will require additional signaling capabilities in the future. The extensibility of SIP enables such development of incremental functionality. SIP message headers are versatile and one can register additional features with the Internet Assigned Numbers Authority (IANA). SIP's message flexibility enables developers to construct advanced telephony applications and services.

SIP Requests

The start line, often referred to as request line, distinguishes SIP requests from responses and contains three components: a method name, a request-URI and the protocol version. They appear in that order and are separated by a single space character. The request line itself terminates with a carriage return-line feed pair (CRLF):

- **Method** - indicates the type of request. Six are defined in the basic SIP specification [RFC3261]: the INVITE request, CANCEL request, ACK request and BYE request are used for session creation, modification and termination. The REGISTER request is used to register a certain user's contact information, and the OPTIONS request is used to query servers for their capabilities. Other methods have been created as an extension to the standard.
- **Request-URI** - is a SIP or a SIPS URI that identifies the requested resource.
- **Protocol version** - the current SIP version is 2.0. All standard compliant requests must include this version information in the form of: "SIP/2.0".

SIP Responses

The start line, often referred to as request line, distinguishes SIP responses from requests and contains three components: the protocol version, status code and reason phrase. They appear in that order and are separated by a single space character. The status line itself terminates with a CRLF pair:

- **Protocol version** - this is identical to the protocol version in the request line.
- **Status code** - the status code is a three-digit code that identifies the nature of the response. It indicates the outcome of the request.
- **Reason phrase** - this is a free text field providing a short description of the status code meant for human users/readers.

Status codes are classified into six classes (classes 2xx to 6xx are final responses):

- **1XX** - provisional/informational responses. They indicate that the request was received and the recipient is continuing to process the request.
- **2Xx** - success responses. The request was successfully received, understood and accepted.

- **3XX** - redirection responses. Further action needs to be taken by the requester in order to complete the request.
- **4XX** - client error responses. The request contains a syntax error. It can also indicate that the server cannot fulfill the request.
- **5XX** - server error responses. The server failed to fulfill a valid request. It is the fault of the server.
- **6XX** - global failure responses. The request cannot be fulfilled at any server. The server responding with this response class needs to have definitive information about the user.

The "xx" are two digits that indicate the exact nature of the response: for example, a "180" provisional response indicates ringing by the remote end, while a "181" provisional response indicates that a call is being forwarded.

Header

Every message contains a header with mandatory and optional fields that describe communication, session and connection details. Message headers specify the calling party, called party, route and message type of a call. Header fields also indicate message body characteristics and end with a CRLF pair. The headers section of a SIP message terminates with a CRLF as well.

The four groups of message headers are as follows:

- **General headers** - Apply to requests and responses.
- **Entity headers** - Define information about the message body type and length.
- **Request headers** - Enable clients to include additional request information.
- **Response headers** - Enable servers to include additional response information.

For more information about SIP requests and responses or the different header types and fields see [190] or [53, page 254ff].

The format of the header fields is as follows:

$$Header\text{-}name:\ header\text{-}value$$

Some headers are mandatory in every SIP request and response. Those headers and their formats are listed below:

- **To header** - To: SIP-URI(;parameters)
- **From header** - From: SIP-URI(;parameters)
- **Call-ID header** - Call-ID: unique-id
- **CSeq header** - CSeq: digit method
- **Via header** - Via: SIP/2.0/[transport-protocol] sent-by(;parameters)
- **Max-Forwards header** - Max-Forwards: digit
- **Contact header** - Contact: SIP-URI(;parameters)

F.1. Internet and Telecommunication Protocols

The Contact header is mandatory for requests that create dialogs, the Max-Forwards header is typically set to 70. Note that the brackets around "parameters" indicate that they are optional and not part of the header syntax. The transport protocol for the Via header is the User Datagram Protocol (UDP), Transmission Control Protocol (TCP) or Transport Layer Security (TLS).

Body
The message body (payload) can carry any text-based information, while the request method and the response status code determine how the body should be interpreted. When describing a session, the SIP message body is typically a Session Description Protocol (SDP - see section F.1.3 on page 173) message.

In addition to messages and headers, SIP also defines three important main system components: user agents, network servers and SIP addresses. The following three sections give a short overview about these components.

User Agents
User agents are client applications that contain both a user-agent client (UAC) and a user-agent server (UAS) also known as client and server.

- **UAC** - Initiates SIP requests and acts as the user's calling agent.

- **UAS** - Receives requests and returns responses on behalf of the user. The server acts as the user-called agent.

Typically SIP Softphones for PCs or mobile devices are full scale user agents and implement all functions of a UAC and UAS as defined above.

Network Servers
SIP defines four different basic types of servers for its infrastructure, registrar server, proxy server, redirect server and location server. These servers are able to provide all necessary session setup, maintenance, management and termination functionality for a SIP multimedia infrastructure. Additional functionalities and services such as billing, QoS etc. require additional servers.

- **Registrar Server** - Accepts REGISTER requests and is used to store explicit binding between a user's address of record (SIP address) and the address of the host (e.g. phone, mobile phone, PC) where the user is currently residing or wishing to receive requests on.

  Every UAC needs to register to a registrar server. Normally this is done at start-up of the UAC, e.g. when the SIP Softphone is started on the PC. The Registrar server authenticates and manages all UAC registrations by checking user credentials at the Home Location Register (HLR)/ Home Subscriber Server (HSS) and supervising registration timeouts etc. For most servers the registration timeout is around three minutes and all clients need to send (re-)registrations within three minutes of the last (re-)registration, otherwise the server assumes the client is disconnected and deletes the registration.

- **Proxy Server** - Acts on behalf of other clients, is the first connection point for a client within a SIP infrastructure and contains both client and server functionality. A proxy server interprets and rewrites request headers before it passes them on to other servers. If the receiving UAC is member of a different domain, it also resolves SIP address domain information in order to find the right next proxy or server the message needs to be forwarded to. Rewriting the headers identifies the proxy as initiator of the request and ensures that replies follow the same path back to the proxy instead of directly to the client. A forking proxy server can also send a request to a number of locations at the same. Forking can be parallel or sequential.

There are three proxy server types:

- Dialog-statefull proxy - a proxy is dialog-statefull if it retains the state for a dialog from the initiating request (INVITE request) to the terminating request (BYE request).
- Transaction-statefull proxy - maintains client and server transaction-state machines during the processing of a request.
- Stateless proxy - forwards every request it receives downstream and every response it receives upstream.

Figure F.1 on page 172 shows the SIP signaling exchange for an INVITE (call/session setup) request message using a proxy server.

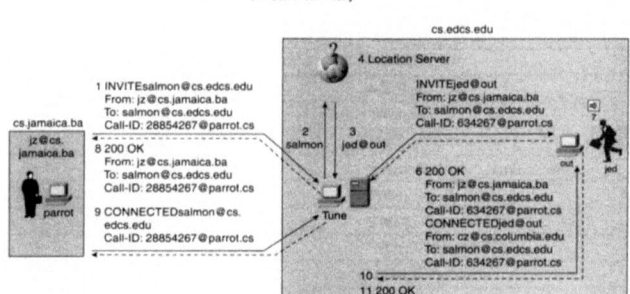

Figure F.1: SIP communication exchange for INVITE (call/session setup) request message using a proxy server
[53, page 258]

- **Redirect server** - Accepts SIP requests and sends a redirect response back to the client containing the address of the next server. Redirect servers do not accept calls, nor do they process or forward SIP requests, they just inform clients about different connection endpoints to use. Figure F.2 on page 173 shows the SIP signaling exchange for the INVITE (call/session setup) request message using a redirect server.
- **Location Server** - keeps track of the location of users.

SIP Addresses

SIP addresses, also called SIP Universal Resource Locators (URLs), are similar to e-mail addresses, defined in the form of *user@host*. The user portion of the address can be a user name or telephone number and the host portion can be a domain name or network address. You can identify a user's SIP URL by his or her e-mail address. To determine that an address is a SIP address and not an e-mail (mostly implicit protocol descriptor "mailto:") address most applications need to have the protocol descriptor "sip:" in front of an address.

The following two examples show possible SIP addresses/URLs:

sip:christian@menkens.at

sip:456687838@213.34.2.171

F.1. Internet and Telecommunication Protocols

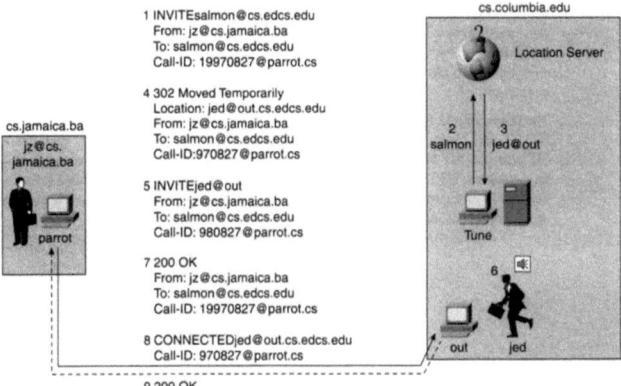

Figure F.2: SIP communication exchange for INVITE (call/session setup) request message using a redirect server
[53, page 259]

The first address defines a user "christian" in the domain "menkens.at" which requires a proxy server outside the domain "menkens.at" to resolve the domain name and forward a request for this address to the resolved proxy server in the other domain.

The second address defines a phone number at the SIP server "213.34.2.171". Since the IP is given, the proxy does not need to resolve a domain and is able to send a request right away. Since a phone number is given as user, the receiving server will contact a SIP-to-PSTN gateway in order to establish a phone call to this number.

For more information about SIP see [190] or [53, page 251ff].

F.1.3 Session Description Protocol (SDP)

The Session Description Protocol (SDP) is used to describe general multimedia sessions such as audio or video streaming from a server to a client, but also VoIP multimedia session between two or more VoIP phones, devices or applications.

In the case of one way streaming from media server to client, the SDP describes the media the client wants to receive (audio, video, etc.) including codecs, bit-rate etc. In this case SDP is added to the DESCRIBE response as mentioned above.

In the case of a VoIP session setup, SDP is used to negotiate parameters between then endpoints in order to find compatibilities that can be used to start a media streaming session. These negotiations can include several messages that all include all compatible parameters both sides agreed on so far.

An SDP description consist of a number of simple text lines in the form of Type=Value pairs.

Type is always exactly one character and case sensitive. The following list describes some of the most important types of SDP (* marked ones are optional).

```
Session description
    v= protocol version
    o= owner/creator and session identifier
    s= session name
    i=* session information

    u=* URI of description
    e=* email address
    p=* phone number
    c=* connection information
    b=* bandwidth information

    <Block with one or more time descriptions>

    z=* time zone adjustments
    k=* encryption key
    a=* zero or more session attribute lines

    <Block with zero or more media descriptions>

Time description
    t=* time the session is active
    r=* zero or more repeat times

Media description
    m= media name and transport address
    i=* media title
    c=* connection information
        - optional if included at session level
    b=* bandwidth information
    k=* encryption key
    a=* zero or more media attribute lines
```

F.1.4 Diameter

Diameter [40] is an authentication, authorization and accounting (AAA) protocol developed by the Internet Engineering Task Force (IETF). Diameter is used to provide AAA services for a range of access technologies. Instead of building the protocol from scratch, Diameter is loosely based on the Remote Authentication Dial-In User Service (RADIUS) [187], which has previously been used to provide AAA services for dial-up and terminal server access environments. As basic foundation for the Diameter specification, the AAA Working Group first gathered requirements for AAA services as they apply to network access from different interest groups.

The final Diameter protocol is actually split into two parts: the Diameter base protocol and the Diameter applications. The base protocol is needed for delivering Diameter data units, negotiating capabilities, handling errors and providing for extensibility. A Diameter application defines application-specific functions and data units. Each Diameter application is specified

separately. Currently, in addition to the base protocol, a few Diameter applications have been
defined and some are in the process of being defined:

- Mobile IP
- NASREQ
- Extensible Authentication Protocol (EAP)
- Diameter credit control
- Diameter SIP application

The Diameter base protocol uses both the Transmission Control Protocol (TCP) and the Stream
Control Transmission Protocol (SCTP) as transport. However, SCTP is the preferred choice,
mostly due to the connection oriented relationship that exists between Diameter peers. It is
beneficial to be able to categorize several independent streams to a single SCTP association,
instead of keeping all streams open as independent TCP connections. Both Internet Protocol
Security (IPsec) and Transport Layer Security (TLS) are used for securing the connections.

Protocol components
Diameter is a peer-to-peer protocol, so any Diameter node can initiate a request. Diameter has
three different types of network nodes: servers, agents and clients.

A Diameter server services client requests within a realm, according to the used Diameter application and handles authentication, accounting and authorization requests for this particular
domain, or realm. All Diameter messages are routed according to the network access identifier
(NAI) of a particular user.

A Diameter agent provides value-added services for clients and servers that include either relay,
proxy, redirect or translation services.

Clients are generally the user or edge devices of a network that perform access control and originate AAA requests. Typically, the Diameter client is a network access server (NAS) that performs
AAA services for a particular access technology. The NAS needs to authenticate the terminals
that are attached to a network before allocating network resources for them: for example, a Wireless Local Area Network access point may need to ascertain the user's identity before allowing
access.

F.1.5 Simple Gateway Control Protocol (SGCP) and Media Gateway Control Protocol (MGCP)

Simple Gateway Control Protocol (SGCP) and MGCP are gateway control protocols designed
to support gateways that have external intelligence (external call-control elements). Therefore,
their use is prevalent in large trunking gateways and residential gateways. The following two
sections give a short overview about these two protocols.

Simple Gateway Control Protocol
SGCP enables call-control elements to control connections between trunking, residential and
access-type VoIP gateways. Although these gateways target different market segments, all of
them convert time-division multiplexing (TDM) voice into packet voice. Call-control elements
are generally referred to as Media Gateway Controllers (MGCs) or call agents.

SGCP assumes an architecture whose call-control intelligence is outside of the gateway and is handled by call agents. In this model, one or more call agents can participate in constructing a call. Synchronization among these call agents is assumed and is not covered by SGCP.

SGCP is used to establish, maintain and disconnect calls across an Internet Protocol (IP) network. This is accomplished by controlling the required connections between desired and corresponding endpoints. Authorization of calls and connections is outside of the scope of this protocol. SGCP does not contain a security mechanism for unauthorized call setup or interference but the specification states that it is expected that all transactions are carried over secure Web/Internet connections.

SGCP request and response messages are sent to IP addresses of specific endpoints using UDP and packet losses or delays are handled by repeating requests.

The basic constructs of SGCP are endpoints and connections. Connections exist in either point-to-point or multi-point form and groups of connections constitute a call, which is set up for one or more call agents. Endpoints are sources or sinks of data that physically or logically exist within an entity. Physical endpoints can be trunk circuits connecting gateways or phone switches whereas logical endpoints can be announcements stored in audio devices etc.

For more information about SGCP see [15] and
[53, page 263ff].

Media Gateway Control Protocol
MGCP controls VoIP through external call-control elements. The first version of MGCP was based on the fusion of SGCP and the Internet Protocol Device Control (IPDC). Therefore, the differences between MGCP and SGCP are largely due to functionality inspired by IPDC.

MGCP utilizes the same connection model as SGCP, where the basic constructs are endpoints and connections, but enables connections to be established over several types of bearer networks like:

- IP Networks - Transmission of audio over TCP/IP networks using RTP and UDP.

- ATM Networks - Audio transmission over an ATM network using ATM adaption Layer 2 (AAAL2) or another adaption layer.

- Internal Connections - Transmission of packets across TDM backplane or bus of the gateway.

Similar to SGCP messages, MGCP messages are transmitted across the packet network over UDP but they can piggyback other messages. MGCP enables several messages to be sent to the same gateway in one UDP packet. These piggyback messages should be processed as if they were received as several simultaneous messages.

In MGCP a formal wildcard structure, which was inspired by IPDC, was introduced. Call agents can use wildcard convention when sending commands to gateways.

For more information about MGCP see [102] and
[53, page 273ff].

Summary
SGCP and MGCP are vital components used during the transition from a network whose components are in one monolithic platform to a network whose components are distributed. SGCP and MGCP form the basis for call agents and gateways to communicate. This is one of the keys to a distributed packet network. Currently dozens of vendors have written to the MGCP standard

and the MGCP is a simple and powerful protocol that will be the basis for packet-based voice networks for many years to come.

F.2 Multimedia Streaming Protocols

This section presents and describes some important streaming protocols used in VoIP Telecommunication applications and services. Figure F.3 on page 177 shows the packet-switched streaming protocol stack that 3GPP has agreed on for 3G mobile networks. It shows how all important streaming protocols like RTSP, RTP and Real Time Control Protocol (RTCP) work together with the session description and transport protocols SDP and HTTP as well as how they build on TCP/IP/UDP for packet transport.

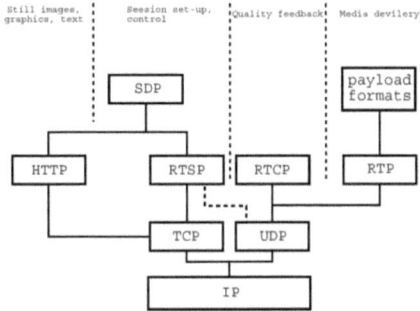

Figure F.3: 3GPP Packet-Switched Multimedia Streaming Protocol Stack [199, page 13]

F.2.1 Real Time Streaming Protocol (RTSP)

RTSP is used for establishment and control of time-synchronized streams of continuous media such as audio and video. One could think of RTSP as a remote control for media servers. In order to define the interaction between RTSP servers and clients flexible, the protocol does not define a notion of a connection. Instead a RTSP server maintains a session identifier associated with media streams and their states. This leads to the possibility that, during a session and as long as the session identifier is included and valid, a client could use any reliable transport protocols such as TCP to send RTSP requests to a RTSP server.

Multimedia streams controlled by RTSP are not limited to use any specific transport protocol to deliver the media, which makes RTSP a very general and extensible protocol. However since most applications and development frameworks use the RTP to transport time-sensitive data, RTP is the media transport protocol that is most commonly used with RTSP.

RTSP is a text-based protocol and has inherited its design and architecture from HTTP/1.1. Due to that RTSP messages are easy to read and understand with simple text editing tools and so applications that work with RTSP are easy to debug and maintain. Although RTSP has similarities to HTTP there are some important aspects that differ:

- RTSP uses a session concept that is comparable to server-side session concepts known from J2EE or PHP.
- Contrary to HTTP, RTSP servers manage and maintain states based on the client sessions.
- RTSP requests can originate from client and server.
- RTSP request URIs are always absolute paths to the referenced resource.

Since RTSP is an UTF-8 text protocol it is vulnerable to bit errors and should not be used with transport protocols that do not have any error correction mechanism implemented. Figure F.4 on page 178 shows the general structure of a RTSP message.

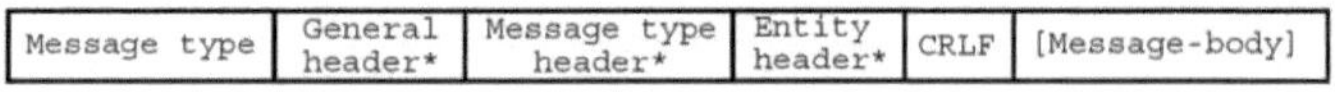

```
| Message type | General header* | Message type header* | Entity header* | CRLF | [Message-body] |
```

Figure F.4: General RTSP Message Structure
[199, page 14]

- **Message Type** - Determines if the message is a request or response message
- **Headers** - *General Header*, *Message Type Header* and *Entity Header* are optional and normally used to add meta information, such as *Content Length* within the *Entity Header*, to the RTSP message.
- **CRLF** - Every line of the RTSP message is terminated by *Carriage Return* and *Line Feed* symbols.
- **Message Body** - *Content Length* long message body text containing additional information, commands and parameters.

RTSP Request Messages

An RTSP Request puts a *Request Line* in the *Message Type* part of the general RTSP message as first line of the message. Figure F.5 on page 178 shows such a *Request Line* with all its components.

Figure F.5: RTSP Request Line
[199, page 14]

The *Request Line* contains a *Method* field that determines what type of request the message defines, a *Request URI* that references the resource this message is for as well as the *RTSP Version* of the message that is used.

The following list shows an overview about some (not all) of the most important *Request Methods*:

- DESCRIBE
- SETUP

F.2. Multimedia Streaming Protocols

- PLAY
- PAUSE
- TEARDOWN

See the RTSP example sequence below for more details on these methods.

Listing F.4 presents a simple SETUP Request originating from a client.

```
1  SETUP rtsp://193.0.0.2:554/file.3gp/trackID=4 RTSP/1.0
2  CSeq: 2
3  Transport: RTP/AVP;unicast;client_port=6974-6975
4  User-Agent: RealPlayer10.5
```

Listing F.4: RTSP SETUP Request

A SETUP Request defines the transport mechanism/protocol for the streaming media as well as acceptable transport parameters for the client (e.g. Ports, Protocol, etc.) in the *Transport Header*. Since RTP will be used as streaming protocol two ports are necessary. The even port number will be used for data transport and the odd port number for RTCP control data.

RTSP Response Messages

Response Messages always follow Request Messages and are never sent without an associated Request Message sent first. An RTSP Response Message puts a *Status Line* in the *Message Type* part of the general RTSP message. Figure F.6 on page 179 shows the general structure of a RTSP *Status Line*.

| RTSP-Version | WS | Status-Code | WS | Reason-Phase | CRLF |

Figure F.6: RTSP Response Status Line
[199, page 15]

The first part defines what Version of the RTSP protocol is used, after a white-space, the second part defines the numeric status code for the response and after another white-space the third part contains the, with the status code associated, textual description, the so-called *Reason-Phrase*.

There are a lot of different status codes for all states, errors and success responses RTSP supports. All status codes are divided into five general groups:

- **1XX** - Informal
- **2XX** - Success
- **3XX** - Redirection
- **4XX** - Client Error
- **5XX** - Server Error

Listing F.5 presents a simple SETUP response that is answering to the previously, in listing F.4 on page 179, shown SETUP request.

```
1  RTSP/1.0 200 OK
2  CSeq: 2
3  Session: 539445775480508750
4  Transport: RTP/AVP;unicast;source=193.0.0.2;client_port=6974-6975
5  server_port=6970-6971;ssrc=0F0F0E42
```

Listing F.5: RTSP SETUP Response

The server response contains transport parameters for both, client and server, and includes a SSRC (synchronization source) and session ID in order to assign further messages to the session that is built by this SETUP sequence.

RTSP Example Sequence

In order to get an impression of how RTSP works together with other protocols in the streaming protocol suite, this section discusses the simple RTSP sequence shown in figure F.7 on page 180.

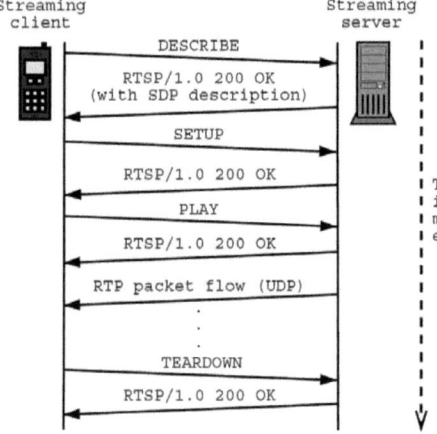

Figure F.7: Streaming Sequence using RTSP, RTP and SDP
[199, page 17]

- **Describe** - The DESCRIBE request retrieves detailed information and a description of a presentation or media resource.
- **200 OK** - The response to a DESCRIBE request contains detailed SDP (Session Description Protocol) (see section F.1.3 on page 173) information about the resource in the message body.
- **Setup** - The SETUP request specifies the transport mechanism that should be used for streaming the media resource.
- **200 OK** - The response to a SETUP request contains transport parameters for server and client as well as SSRC and session ID.

- **Play** - The PLAY request informs the server that the client is ready to receive streaming data and streaming should be started.
- **200 OK** - The response to a PLAY request can but must not contain an RTP info line that defines RTP parameters of the media resource and server.
- **RTP** - RTP data packets are transmitted from server to client using UDP.
- **Teardown** - The TEARDOWN request stops the RTP server stream and the server frees its resources.
- **200 OK** - The response to a TEARDOWN request normally only contains *Status Line* with no body content.

F.2.2 Real Time Transport Protocol (RTP)

RTP is the standard for transmitting real-time and delay-sensitive traffic across packet-based networks. Since simplicity and speed and not reliability are the most important factors for RTP it uses UDP in contrast to TCP as underlying transport protocol. RTP consists of a data and a control part, later called RTCP (see section F.2.3 on page 182 for more information). The data part of RTP is a thin protocol that provides support for applications with real-time properties including timing reconstruction, loss detection and content identification. RTP itself does not ensure timely delivery or any other quality-of-service (QoS) guarantees and relies on underlying protocols, network management, network architecture and infrastructure to ensure that.

RTP gives receiving stations additional information that is not available in connectionless UDP/IP streams, so typically VoIP and streaming media applications and services use RTP on top of UDP. RTP streaming data is carried with an RTP/UDP/IP packet header. This real time transport header is shown in Figure F.8 on page 181

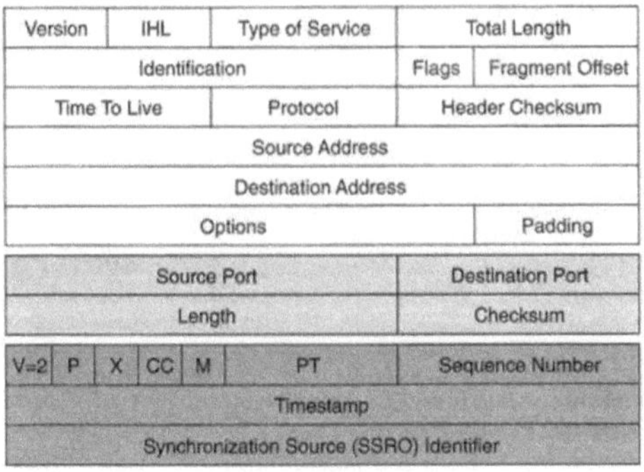

Version	IHL	Type of Service	Total Length	
Identification			Flags	Fragment Offset
Time To Live		Protocol	Header Checksum	
Source Address				
Destination Address				
Options				Padding
Source Port			Destination Port	
Length			Checksum	
V=2	P	X	CC	M	PT	Sequence Number
Timestamp				
Synchronization Source (SSRC) Identifier				

Figure F.8: Real Time transport header (IP/UDP/RTP)
[53, page 182]

- **V (2 bit)** - Version.
- **P (1 bit)** - Padding. Defines if RTP packet has padding octets at the end (bit set to 1). Last byte of payload defines the number of padding octets in the packet.
- **X (1 bit)** - Extension. Defines if the fixed header is extended by a header extension.
- **CC (4 bit)** - CSRC Count. Contains the number of CSRC identifiers that are part of the RTP header. The CSCR follows the fixed header.
- **M (1 bit)** - Marker. How to interpret this marker is defined by a profile. E.g. events like frame boundaries can be marked this way.
- **PT (7 bit)** - Payload Type. Holds information about the kind of payload the RTP packet contains. This can be any media codec such as AMR, PCM, MP3 etc.
- **Sequence-Number (16 bit)** - This number increments by one for each packet sent by the server. Normally this number is initialized with a random number in order to make the protocol more robust against attacks.
- **Timestamp (32 bit)** - Reflects the sampling frequency of the first octet of data in the payload. Its initial value is also random and it increments linearly and monotonically over time.
- **SSRO (0-15 items, 32 bit each)** - Contributing Source Identifiers. Identifies the contributing sources for the payload contained in the specific RTP package.

The list above shows the two most important additional bits of information RTP adds to UDP/IP, Sequence-Number and Timestamp. RTP-based applications use the Sequence-Number to determine whether the packets are arriving in order, to order them and use the Timestamp to determine the inter-arrival packet time.

Further information about the protocol and its usage can be found at [101] or in [53, page 181ff].

F.2.3 RTP Control Protocol (RTCP)

RTCP is used as a control protocol while streaming data using RTP. RTCP is used to monitor the quality-of-service (QoS) within a streaming session between client and server and it offers Quality of Service (QoS) feedback from receivers. In addition to that, it can be used to gather and distribute information about streaming session members and their streaming parameters.

RTCP allows to monitor important streaming parameters such as delay, bandwidth quality in order to build statistics about the streaming session. This allows the system and server to customize streaming parameters such as bit-rate, codec, image size etc. to specific members of a streaming session in order to deliver the best media stream possible for the current connection.

RTCP also includes source identification, synchronization of different media streams and support for gateways, such as audio/video bridges and multicast-to-multicast translators.

Further information on the protocol and its usage can be found at [101] or in [53, page 181ff].

F.3 Voice-over-IP (VoIP)

The term Voice-over-IP (VoIP) stands in general for transmitting voice information/data in digital form in discrete packets using TCP/IP rather than using traditional circuit-switched protocols

F.3. Voice-over-IP (VoIP)

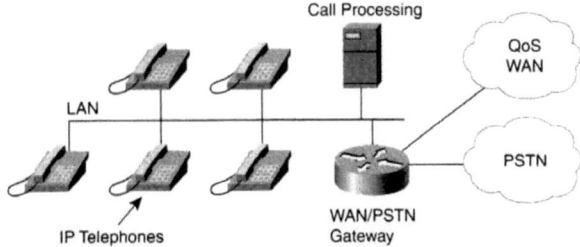

Figure F.9: Basic Voice-over-IP PBX system
[53, page 148]

over the PSTN. But actually VoIP describes much more, it involves technical standards that were either developed specifically for VoIP, like the protocols SIP, H.232 and IAX, or are used by VoIP systems to transport voice over data networks, like the protocols User Datagram Protocol (UDP), RTP and RTSP. See sections F.1 on page 165 and F.2 on page 177 for a detailed description of the most important VoIP and Media Applications related protocols and standards.

The term VoIP also involves different kinds of available systems that use VoIP to connect their users. There are systems that offer PC to PC voice and video communication like MSN Messenger or Skype but there are also large scale systems that substitute existing Private Branch Exchanges (PBX) like the Open-Source VoIP PBX Asterisk [18], the Cisco CallManager VoIP system [45] or systems based on the 3GPP specification of the IMS [213] which is mainly targeted towards Telecommunication companies, mobile phone carriers and service providers. Figure F.9 on page 183 shows a simple VoIP PBX system with a call processing server such as Asterisk, Cisco CallManager or IMS Server.

As the major advantage of VoIP and Web/Internet telephony, the fact that it reduces or avoids the tolls charged by ordinary telephone service companies is often mentioned, but there are more benefits of VoIP [53, page 129ff]:

- For enterprise networks consolidating voice and data networks might mean they can order fewer circuits from the PSTN.

- An IP infrastructure requires fewer additions, moves and changes than a traditional voice or data network.

  For example many large companies determined that it costs several hundred dollars just to move a telephone today (this is due to such factors as labor costs and the costs of reconfiguring the switch). Such costs are not incurred in an IP infrastructure because technologies like Dynamic Host Configuration Protocol (DHCP) configure the devices automatically independent from the current physical location.

- An enterprise has the ability to have one Information Services (IS) department that supports both voice and data networks.

- Common infrastructure tools like physical ports for services such as voice mail are no longer needed. In a circuit-switched voice network, voice mail is sold based on the number of mailboxes and number of physical ports needed to support simultaneous users. With VoIP, physical circuit-switched ports are not necessary. The voice mail servers only need to have an IP connection (Ethernet, Asynchronous Transfer Mode (ATM), ISDN, DSL, etc.).

Appendix F. Related Technologies, Standards and Specifications

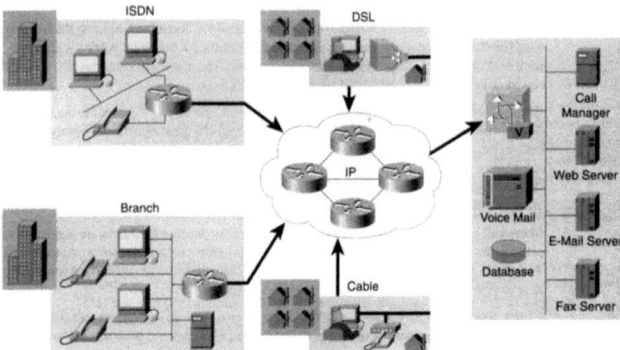

Figure F.10: Fully integrated Voice-over-IP system with different locations connected via various technologies like DSL, ISDN, etc.

[53, page 132]

- VoIP enables the use of standard-based platforms (such as PCs and UNIX machines) instead of proprietary hardware from a specific vendor.
- VoIP helps to integrate different systems in an enterprise. For example voice-mail, e-mail, fax and web can be integrated so that voice-mail or fax messages are sent to the e-mail mailbox or web account of the user.

Figure F.10 on page 184 shows a fully integrated enterprise VoIP system of a random example company. This company has two locations that are connected to the Web/Internet via ISDN as well as two free agents at their homes using DSL and Cable to connection their equipment to the Internet. All of these locations have full access to all VoIP Services of the company, such as telephony, voice-mail, e-mail, company specific multimedia applications etc. by using an TCP/IP-based network.

Many companies strive to change into a new network, whereby voice is an application on top of a data network. Several reasons for that are
[53, page 19ff]:

- Data has overtaken voice as primary traffic on many networks built for voice.

    Data is now running on top of networks that were built to carry voice efficiently. Data has different characteristics such as a variable use of bandwidth and a need for higher bandwidth.

    Soon, voice networks will run on top of networks built with a data-centric approach. Traffic will then be differentiated based upon application instead of physical circuits. New technologies (such as Fast Ethernet, Gigabit Ethernet and Optical Networking) will be used to deploy the high-speed networks that need to carry all this additional data.

- The PSTN cannot create and deploy features and new applications quickly enough.

    With increased competition due to deregulation in many Telecommunication markets, the Telecommunication service companies are looking for ways to keep their existing clientele.

The primary method for keeping customers is by enticing them through new services and media applications.

The current "not-full-IP" infrastructure allows only equipment vendors to develop applications for their specific proprietary equipment, so it is very difficult for a company to meet all the needs of the customers. A more open infrastructure and platform, by which many vendors can provide applications, enables more creative solutions and applications to be developed.

- Data/Voice/Video (D/V/V) cannot converge on the PSTN as currently built.

  With only an analog line to most homes, you cannot have data access, phone access and video access across one 56-kbps modem. High-speed broadband access, such as digital subscriber line (DSL), cable or high-speed wireless is needed to enable this convergence. In the backbone of the PSTN the convergence has already started.

- The architecture of the PSTN is not flexible enough to carry data.

  Because the bearer channels (B channels and T1 circuits), call-control (SS7 and Q.931) and service logic (applications) are tightly bounded in one closed platform it is not possible to make minor changes that might improve audio quality.

  New platform and infrastructure specifications such as the IMS, mentioned above, break this tightly bounded structure of the PSTN of today and allow an easy integration of all sorts of data services and media applications.

It is also important to note that circuit-switched calls require a permanent 64-kbps dedicated circuit between the two devices. Whether the caller or the person called is talking or not, this 64-kbps connection cannot be used by any other party. This means that this bandwidth cannot be used for any other purpose and the Telecommunication service company must bill the parties for consuming the whole resource. This leads to many reserved but unused connections that cost a lot of money for carriers and customers and results in a very bad utilization of the whole PSTN infrastructure.

Data networking, on the other hand, has the capability to use bandwidth only when it is required. This difference, although seemingly small, is a major benefit of packet-based voice and data networking (VoIP).

F.4 Mobile Web/Internet Access Network Technologies

Since the concepts of this research work need to support different mobile Web/Internet access networks such as GPRS [215], EDGE [215], 3G [216], LTE [147] and WLAN, this chapter will briefly summarize their most important facts.

Figure F.11 on page 186 presents a very simplified view of a mobile network architecture with 3G and GSM/GPRS/EDGE access networks. One can see that UMTS Terrestrial Radio Access Network (UTRAN) and GSM Base Station Subsystem (BSS) share the same GPRS backbone to transmit data. This GPRS backbone network is protected by a firewall with (sometimes) included NAT translation and is connected to the Web/Internet to access Web/Internet services such as streaming audio and video services etc.

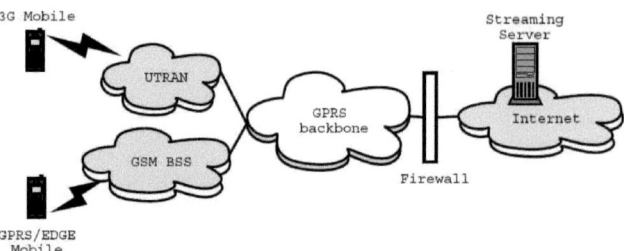

Figure F.11: Typical Mobile Network Architecture
[199, page 12]

F.4.1 General Packet Radio Service (GPRS)

GPRS is an additional component to the existing GSM specification. GPRS enables packet-switched communication and the use of packet-switched protocols for transmitting data on the GSM mobile network.

GPRS was generally introduced because the GSM network was not suited to handle packet-switched data in an efficient way. Two main components build GPRS, Coding Schemes (up to four different schemes) and Time Slots (up to eight different schemes).

Theoretically GPRS consists of four different channel coding schemes: CS-1, CS-2, CS-3, CS-4 and all of these schemes have different properties. CS-1 hast the most efficient error correction and is best suited to be used when the connection quality of the radio link is poor or interferences are high. CS-4 has no error correction at all and should only be used when the radio link is perfect and does not experience any interferences. Today, mobile networks mostly use only CS-1 and CS-2 and only these protocols are implemented by most device vendors.

GPRS allows several mobile stations (usually mobile phones/devices) to share the same frequency by dividing it into different time slots. Due to the packet-switched characteristics of GPRS the allocation of the available time slots may vary from one instant to the next (e.g. it may have eight time slots at one time and four at the next transmission attempt). This allows multiple users to share the same transmission medium by using only the part of the bandwidth they require. This can lead to problems when dealing with real-time transmission where applications and devices try to have a steady and consistent bit rate all the time.

The main features of GPRS are speed, immediacy and better use and utilization of network resources. By using multiple time slots simultaneously and more efficient algorithms for channel coding, GPRS can achieve higher data rates than GSM. Immediacy means that no "dial-up" connection procedure needs to be used to start packet-switched transmission, as it is standard in circuit-switched data networks. Instead the data is transferred in packets and routed individually, which means that there is no need to establish connections between network nodes. So the data can be transferred almost immediately to the mobile station.

In addition to the advantaged mentioned above, this also makes billing for carriers more flexible. The carrier is able to bill an end-user based on the data transferred instead of "dial-up" connection time. GPRS is also able to use unused circuit-switched time slots for packet-switched data transfer, which leads to a much better utilization of the network for the carrier.

F.4. Mobile Web/Internet Access Network Technologies

Coding Scheme	CS-1	CS-2	CS-3	CS-4
Data Rate with 1 time slot	9.05 kbps	13.4 kbps	15.6 kbps	21.4 kbps
Maximum Data Rate with 8 time lots	72.4 kbps	107.2 kbps	124.8 kbps	171.2 kbps

Table F.1: GPRS Data Rates

In theory GPRS can transfer data with a speed of up to 171.2 kbps by using all eight time slots and a channel coding with almost no error correction (best connection and least interference only). Figure F.1 shows GPRS data rates for using one and eight time slots.

F.4.2 Enhanced Data Rates for GSM Evolution (EDGE)

EDGE is an enhancement specification for the GSM and GPRS mobile network that improves the air link between a mobile station such as a mobile phone and a base station. By using EDGE carriers can increase the speed of both, packet-switched and circuit-switched data transmission.

EDGE allows more simultaneous users to share the same time slots and so it helps to improve and enhance the network capacity. In addition to that EDGE is able to share time slots with conventional GPRS networks, which improves the utilization of carrier radio resources.

Both, EDGE and GSM/GPRS operate on the same frequency but they use two different radio channel modulations as well as different protocols on top of that. EDGE also uses the usually more efficient 8 Phase Shift Keying (8PSK) whereas GSM/GPRS uses Gaussian Minimum Shift Keying (GMSK).

EDGE uses 9 different coding schemes, MSC-1 to MSC-9. The first four are comparable to the GSM/GPRS coding schemes and use the less efficient GMSK radio channel modulation. They are tailored for bad radio link connections and conditions with a lot of interferences. The last five schemes use the newly introduced 8PSK, offer a higher data rate and are tailored for better radio link connections with fewer interferences.

The first four schemes achieve data rates from 8.8 kbps to 17.6 kbps whereas the last five schemes achieve rates from 22.4 kbps to 59 kbps per time slot. EDGE achieves its theoretical maximum data rate of 473.6 kbps when using eight time slots simultaneously.

F.4.3 Universal Mobile Telecommunications System (UMTS)

3G [216] is the third generation of mobile phone standards and technologies, after 2G (GSM and additions). It is based on the International Telecommunication Union (ITU) family of standards under the International Mobile Telecommunications program, "IMT-2000". 3G technologies enable network operators to offer users a wider range of more advanced services while achieving greater network capacity through improved spectral efficiency. Services include wide-area wireless voice telephony and broadband wireless data, all in a mobile environment. UMTS is one of the 3G cell phone technologies and is standardized by the 3GPP.

UMTS is not an upgrade of GSM/GPRS anymore, it is a completely new specification and technology and is illustrated in figure F.12. UMTS uses Wideband Code Division Multiple Access (WCDMA), which lets all connected devices share the same frequency and separates them only using unique hash codes during data transmission. This means WCDMA does not need the concept of time slots etc. anymore.

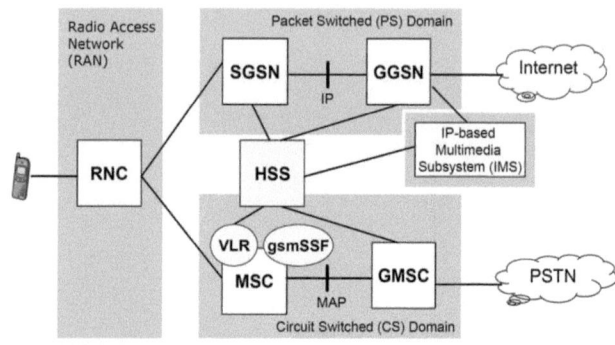

Figure F.12: UMTS Service Architecture with IMS
[110]

Due to this new access technology UMTS needs a different base station sub system, which is called UTRAN and more and enhanced base station hardware. Nevertheless, UMTS and GPRS use both the same core network and so UMTS mobile and base stations are also backward compatible with GSM/GPRS and mobile stations can use GSM/GPRS if no UMTS connection is available. Furthermore, base stations can serve mobile stations that do not support UMTS with a GSM/GPRS connection.

The theoretical maximum data rate of UMTS is at 384 kbps for circuit-switched connections, voice and video calls and 2 Mbps for packet-switched data connections.

The UMTS specification defines four different QoS (Quality of Service) classes:

- **Conversational Class** - For real-time services like voice and video call as well as real-time games etc.

- **Streaming Class** - For streaming of multimedia content to and from the mobile station.

- **Interactive Class** - For web browsing and non-real-time applications.

- **Background Class** - For downloading of e-mails, messages, news etc. in the background.

Data classified in Class 1 or Class 2 will be transmitted as real-time traffic over real-time connections using the WCDMA radio link and these classes are specified for high response time and high throughput. Class 3 and Class 4 transmit data as scheduled non real-time packet data with lower response time and less throughput.

3G Enhancements [78]

High Speed Downlink Packet Access (HSDPA) is a 3G mobile telephony communications protocol in the High-Speed Packet Access (HSPA) family, which allows networks based on UMTS to have higher data transfer speeds and capacities. Current HSDPA deployments support down-link speeds of 1.8, 3.6, 7.2 and 14.4 Mbps. HSDPA has been specified in the 3GPP release 5. It introduced new basic functions and is aimed to achieve peak data rates of 14.4 Mbps. Newly introduced are the High Speed Downlink Shared Channels (HS-DSCH), the adaptive modulation QPSK and 16QAM and the High Speed Medium Access protocol (MAC-HS) in base station.

High Speed Uplink Packet Access (HSUPA) is a 3G mobile telephony protocol in the HSPA family with up-link speeds of up to 5.76 Mbps. The specifications for HSUPA are included in UMTS release 6 standard published by 3GPP.

High Speed OFDM Packet Access (HSOPA) is a proposed part of 3GPP upgrade path for UMTS. HSOPA is also often referred to as Super 3G. If adopted, HSOPA succeeds HSDPA and HSUPA technologies specified in 3GPP releases 5 and 6. Unlike HSDPA or HSUPA, HSOPA is an entirely new air interface system, unrelated to and incompatible with WCDMA. It introduces antenna array technologies such as beam-forming and Multiple Input Multiple Output (MIMO) communications.

F.4.4 Long Term Evolution (LTE)

LTE constitutes the 3GPP WCDMA successor of UMTS, HSDPA, HSUPA and HSPA+ and is specified in 3GPP Release 8. The official LTE working group formed by Nortel Networks was created in 2004 and their main goal was to bring the major advantages of the Orthogonal Frequency Division Multiplexing (OFDM) technology that was already leveraged in WLAN standards, to mobile Telecommunication networks.

In contrast to HSDPA, HSUPA and HSPA+, LTE is not designed as an adaptive evolution of existing concepts and technologies into an existing UMTS mobile Telecommunication network. LTE introduces a new technology for the wireless link layer that is incompatible with GSM and UMTS and so, requires the deployment of completely new mobile Telecommunication network equipment.

LTE is specifically optimized for packet-based data services. It reduces latency and defines a Telecommunication network architecture that ensures that all data traffic passes a minimum number of network components. In an UMTS/HSPA network, an end-user device connects to the Web/Internet through the four 3G components Gateway GPRS Support Node (GGSN), Service GPRS Support Node (SGSN), Radio Network Controller (RNC) and base station (NodeB). In an LTE network, the base station (eNodeB) is directly connected to the Web/Internet gateway (Serving SAE Gateway) that connects the mobile Telecommunication networks to outside data networks (see section F.5.1).

The major technical advantages of LTE over HSPA are:

- The available bandwidth is increased by a factor of 10
  - Downlink typical up to 100Mbit/s - theoretical limit is 326,4Mbit/s.
  - Uplink up to 50Mbit/s - theoretical limit is 86,4Mbit/s.
- The network latency is reduced by a factor of 2 to 3: round trip below 10ms; delay below 200ms.
- The spectrum efficiency is increased by a factor of 2 to 4.

The thereby enabled major features of LTE are:

- Optimized for packet-switched instead of circuit-switched traffic.
- Increased focus on personal and device mobility as well as related security aspects.
- Increased energy efficiency for end-user devices.
- Flexible frequency utilization between 1.25MHz and 20MHz.
- Increased flexibility in wireless network topology planning: optimal performance in 5km cells; reduced performance with cells of up to 100km possible.
- Fewer interferences on the wireless link through enhanced Orthogonal Frequency Division Multiple Access (OFDMA) channel scheduling.
- Completely TCP/IP-based environment.
- Operation in parallel to other 3GPP standards such as GSM and UMTS possible.
- Reduction of Telecommunication network components.
- Higher data transmission rates through
    - Increased spectrum efficiency and broader frequency bands.
    - Downlink modulation from 4PSK over 16QAM to 64QAM including MIMO in 2x2 and even 4x4 setups.

F.4.5 Wireless Local Area Network (WLAN) / Wireless Fidelity (Wi-Fi)

WLAN is the general term for Wireless Local Area Network, which means it is a technology to connect computers to build a local network without wires. The term WLAN covers a whole set of specification that are all part of the IEEE 802.11 set of standards. It was developed by the IEEE LAN/MAN Standards Committee (IEEE 802) in the 5 GHz and 2.4 GHz public spectrum bands.

The 802.11 family includes over-the-air modulation techniques that use the same basic protocol. The most popular ones are those defined by the 802.11b and 802.11g protocols, which are amendments to the original standard. 802.11a was the first wireless networking standard, but 802.11b was the first widely accepted one, followed by 802.11g and 802.11n.

Table F.2 on page 191 shows an overview about current and upcoming WLAN standards. One can see that the currently common standard 802.11g achieves a maximum data rate of up to 54 Mbps, which is much higher than any current UMTS/(3G) technology deployed. Unfortunately this data rate is only achieved if the distance between mobile and base station is less than 140 meters, which means WLAN is obviously not a technology designed for wide range mobile networks.

Nevertheless, some municipals such as New York, Toronto and others are planning to and have already started to build a WLAN that covers the whole city including all districts and boroughs. Compared to wide range mobile networks such as UMTS or the newly introduced specifications around WIMAX [96], WLAN requires a lot more (but already quite cheap) base stations and equipment, but when completed, offers a reliable high speed connection for mobile devices.

F.5 Mobile IP Core Network Technologies

This section provides summaries of the current state-of-the-art concepts and technologies for TCP/IP-based Telecommunication core networks. It presents the SAE/EPC and the, built upon,

F.5. Mobile IP Core Network Technologies

Protocol	Release Date	Op. Frequency	Data Rate (Max)	Range (Radius Indoor)	Range (Radius Outdoor)
Legacy	1997	2.4 GHz	2 Mbit/s	20 Meters	100 Meters
802.11a	1999	5 GHz	54 Mbit/s	35 Meters	120 Meters
802.11b	1999	2.4 GHz	11 Mbit/s	38 Meters	140 Meters
802.11g	2003	2.4 GHz	54 Mbit/s	38 Meters	140 Meters
802.11n	Sept 2008 (est.)	2.4 GHz and 5 GHz	248 Mbit/s	70 Meters	250 Meters
802.11y	March 2008 (est.)	3.7 GHz	54 Mbit/s	50 Meters	5000 Meters

Table F.2: WLAN Specifications

IMS specifications and provides an overview about three concepts that were designed to support the development of future TCP/IP Telecommunication applications.

F.5.1 System Architecture Evolution (SAE) and Evolved Packet Core (EPC)

The EPC supports a wide range of diverse Radio Access Networks (RANs) simultaneously. Thereby, it enables mobility, roaming and handovers between the different RANs as well as with other supported EPC, mobile or fixed networks.

The EPC is optimized for data traffic. It incorporates concepts to prevent loss of data and to ensure an overall transmission delay of less than 20ms, whereat, by the core network, only a maximum of 5ms can be consumed. The EPC ensures an interworking with legacy packet- and circuit-switched Telecommunication services and supports IPv4 as well as future IPv6-based Telecommunication services. Thereby, it connects networks and end-user devices across the different versions of TCP/IP.

The EPC defines a high level of QoS that specifies, for example that handovers must not entail any perceivable interferences, irrespective of if taking place between two packet-switched access networks, or between a packet- and a circuit-switched access network. To ensure an excellent seamless mobility between LTE, UMTS and GSM the EPC QoS concept is fully backwards compatible to previous 3GPP QoS concepts.

The EPC ensures the highest possible level of security and privacy and defines similar concepts to what previous mobile Telecommunication networks provide.

The EPC architecture is illustrated in figure F.13 and consists of the following major functional components.

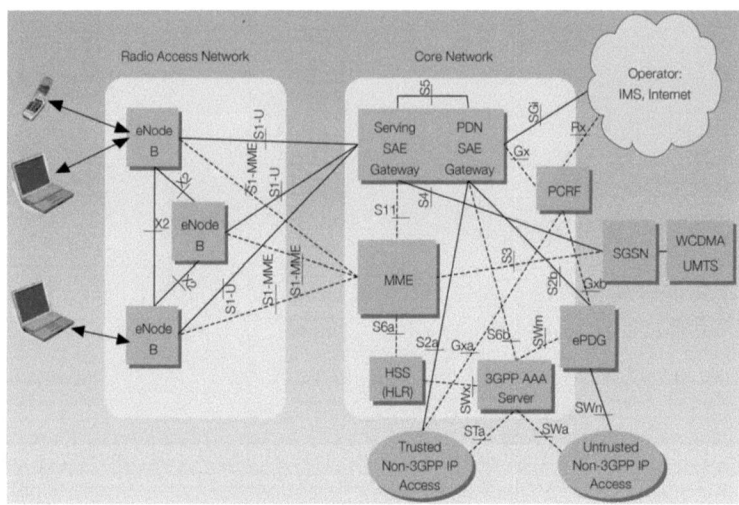

Figure F.13: SAE EPC Architecture [89]

- **Radio Access Network (RAN)**

    The RAN consists of the single node eNodeBs that interface with the end-user devices. An eNodeB hosts the PHYsical (PHY), Medium Access Control (MAC), Radio Link Control (RLC), and Packet Data Control Protocol (PDCP) layers. It offers Radio Resource Control (RRC) functionality corresponding to the control plane and implements many functionalities including encryption, admission control, scheduling, enforcement of negotiated QoS, cell information broadcast, ciphering/deciphering of data and compression/decompression of packet headers.

- **Serving SAE Gateway (SGW)**

    The SGW routes and forwards user data packets. During inter-eNodeB handovers, it acts as mobility anchor for the user plane. By terminating the S4 interface and relaying the traffic between 2G/3G systems and the SGSN, it acts as an anchor for mobility between LTE and other 3GPP technologies.

    For idle end-user devices, the SGW terminates the downlink data path and triggers when new data arrives. It manages and stores device contexts (e.g. parameters of the TCP/IP bearer service, network internal routing information) and performs replication of data traffic in case of lawful interception.

- **Mobility Management Entity (MME)**

    The MME is the key control node for the LTE access network. It is responsible for idle mode end-user device tracking, paging procedure and retransmissions, and is involved in the bearer activation/deactivation process. The MME is responsible for choosing an SGW for a device at (i) the initial attachment, and at (ii) intra-LTE handovers involving Core Network (CN) node relocation. Through interaction with the HSS, it is responsible for authenticating end-users and devices. It terminates the S6a interface towards the HSS for roaming devices.

The MME terminates the Non-Access Stratum (NAS) signaling. It is responsible for the generation and allocation of temporary identities to devices, checks the authorization of devices and enforces device roaming restrictions. The MME is the termination point for ciphering/integrity protection for NAS signaling, handles the security key management and supports lawful interception of signaling.

By terminating the S3 interface from the SGSN, it provides the control plane functionality for mobility between LTE and 2G/3G access networks.

- **Packet Data Network SAE Gateway (PDN GW)**

    The PDN GW is the point of exit and entry of end-user device data traffic and so, provides connectivity between devices and external Packet Data Networks (PDN). A device may have simultaneous connectivity with more than one PDN GW for accessing multiple PDNs. The PDN GW performs device or end-user-based policy enforcement, packet filtering, charging support, lawful interception and packet screening. It acts as anchor for mobility between 3GPP and non-3GPP technologies such as WiMAX and 3GPP2 (CDMA 1X and EvDO).

F.5.2 IP Multimedia Subsystem (IMS)

The IMS standard defines a set of specifications for offering mobile and fixed Voice over IP (VoIP) and multimedia services. The IMS standard was introduced by the 3GPP as a part of their Release 5. It supports multiple access types, including GSM, GPRS, EDGE, UMTS, WLAN and fixed broadband (e.g. DSL) access.

F.5.2.1 IMS Vision

In the move towards a converged network architecture, the IMS standard defines a generic Next Generation Networking (NGN) architecture. It is a set of specifications for offering mobile and fixed Voice over IP (VoIP) and multimedia services. The IMS standard was introduced by the 3GPP as a part of their standard in Release 5. The standard supports multiple access types, including GSM, GPRS, EDGE, WCDMA, UMTS, fixed broadband access and WLAN.

IMS truly merges the Web/Internet with the cellular world; it uses cellular technologies to provide ubiquitous access and Web/Internet technologies to provide appealing services. It enables the integration of different enabling services, such as presence [188], location [212], messaging [41], video, voice, picture and text into one application and supports charging and Quality of Service (QoS). IMS shortens application development time and supports standardized deployment and reuse of applications and services. IMS uses TCP/IP as its underlying network protocol and in IMS Release 5 the 3GPP has chosen the text-based SIP (see section 168 on page 168) as signaling protocol. This enables IMS applications to interact with any current and future Web/Internet service by defining standard interfaces over an IP-based infrastructure. In addition to that, SIP is based on a straightforward request-response interaction model making it simple and comprehensible for developers.

F.5.2.2 IMS Architecture

The IMS architecture is derived from the SIP system architecture and servers summarized in section F.1.2 on page 168. The 3GPP extended the SIP architecture, defined new and more in depth specified interfaces and added new important mandatory services and servers. In contrast to the SIP architecture, IMS is specified and tailored for large scale deployments at mobile phone carriers or Telecommunications companies and the specification includes all services and features such as roaming, charging/billing, QoS, subscriber services, etc. that are necessary for that.

Figure F.14 in page 194 shows the (simplified! - no charging or QoS) general architecture of the IMS as specified by 3GPP. The 3GPP only standardizes functions and not nodes, which means that the IMS architecture is a collection of standardized interfaces. Implementers are free to combine two or more functions into a single node or split a single function into two or more nodes.

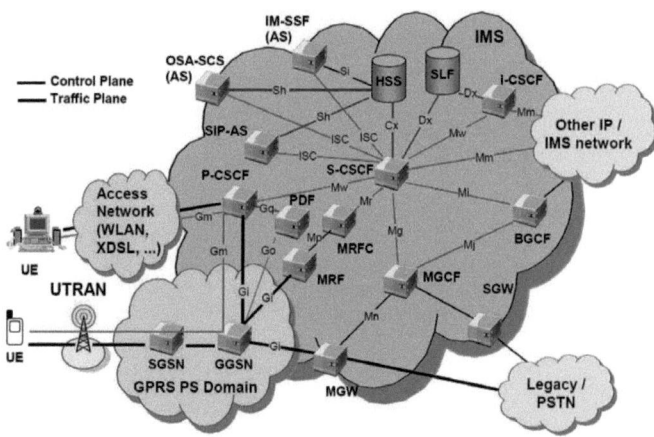

Figure F.14: Simplified IMS Architecture
[197, page 35]

The figure shows the most important interfaces of the IMS, which are typically defined as two- or three-letter codes. The IMS mobile terminals, called User Equipments (UE), are shown on the left and are attached to a packet network, such as GPRS, WLAN or DSL. The gray cloud in the center shows all nodes involved in the IP Multimedia (Core) Network Subsystem. These nodes are:

- One or more databases, called HSS and Subscriber Location Function (SLF).

- One or more SIP servers, collectively known as the CSCF. It comes in three variations: Proxy CSCF (P-CSCF), Serving CSCF (S-CSCF) and Interrogating CSCF (I-CSCF)

- One or more *Application Servers* (A/S) (see section F.5.3.1 on page 205).

- One or more *Media Resource Functions* (MRF). The MRF provides the ability to play announcements, mix media streams (e.g. during a multimedia conference), transcode between different codecs, etc. It is further divided into Media Resource Function Controller (MRFC) and Media Resource Function Processor (MRFP).

- One or more *Breakout Gateway Control Functions* (BGCF). The BGCF is essentially a SIP server that includes routing functionality based on telephone numbers. It is only used in sessions that are initiated by an IMS terminal and addressed to a user in a circuit-switched network, such as the PSTN or the PLMN. The main functionality of the BGCF is to select an appropriate network if a connection with the circuit-switched domain is requested as well as to select an appropriate PSTN/CS gateway if a connection, within the same network where the BGCF is located, is needed.

- One or more CS gateways. The CS gateway provides an interface towards a circuit-switched network, allowing IMS terminals to make and receive calls to and from the PSTN (or any other CS network). The CS gateway is decomposed into a Signaling Gateway (SGW), a Media Gateway Controller Function (MGCF) and a Media Gateway (MGW).

Home Subscriber Server (HSS) and Subscriber Location Function (SLF)

The HSS is the central repository for user-related information (like the HLR for the GSM network). Among other items, it contains location information (contact address of users' devices), security information (for authentication and authorization), user profile information (subscribed services, policies, ...) and the S-CSCF assigned to the user. A network may contain more than one HSS but all data related to a particular user is stored in a single HSS.

The SLF is a simple database that maps user addresses/identifications to HSSs. Networks with only one HSS do not need an SLF. Both the HSS and the SLF implement the Diameter protocol with an IMS-specific Diameter application so that other servers and services such as the S-CSCF, SIP A/S etc. within the system can access and alter the information.

Call Session Control Function (CSCF)

The CSCF, which is basically a SIP server, is one of the most essential functions in the IMS. The CSCF processes SIP signaling messages in the IMS. There are three different types of CSCFs in an IMS, Proxy, Interrogating and Serving CSCF. As mentioned earlier, depending on the vendor (e.g. Siemens, Ericsson) and implementation architecture, these CSCF types are split into three physical servers or combined into one or two servers.

Proxy CSCF (P-CSCF)

The P-CSCF is the first point of contact in the signaling plane between the IMS terminal (e.g. mobile phone, IMS phone, PC etc.) and the IMS network. From the SIP point of view, the P-CSCF acts as an outbound/inbound SIP proxy server.

The following list describes some of the most important P-CSCF features:

- It is automatically allocated to an IMS terminal during network connection configuration (e.g. DHCP, wireless connection establishment, etc.) and before IMS registration and does not change for the duration of the registration/connection of the device.

- It authenticates the user and asserts the identity of the user to the rest of the IMS network.

- It verifies the correctness of SIP requests sent by the IMS terminal.

- It may compresses/decompress the SIP messages
 (SigComp [183]).

- It may include a Policy Decision Function (PDF).

- It might generate charging information at a charging collection node.

The P-CSCF may either be located in the network currently visited by an IMS mobile terminal (roaming) or in the home network of the IMS terminal/user. In case the underlying packet network is based on GPRS/UMTS, the P-CSCF is always located in the same network where the GGSN is located and a carrier scale IMS network usually includes a number of P-CSCFs.

Interrogating CSCF (I-CSCF)

The I-CSCF is a SIP proxy located at the edge of an administrative domain and the address of the I-CSCF is listed in the DNS records of the domain. When a SIP server follows the standard SIP procedures to find the next SIP hop for a particular message, the SIP server obtains the address of an I-CSCF of the destination domain via DNS lookup.

The I-CSCF uses Diameter to interface the SLF and/or the HSS in order to locate the message recipient and routes the messages to the appropriate destination (typically the S-CSCF assigned to the recipient at registration). The I-CSCF is usually located in the home network but in case it is located in a visited network it may hide sensitive information about its domain (THIG). An IMS network will typically include a number of I-CSCFs in order to provide more than one connection points into the IMS domain.

Serving CSCF (S-CSCF)

The S-CSCF is the central node of the signaling plane and is essentially a standard SIP server with additional functionalities. It performs session control and acts as a SIP registrar, i.e. it maintains a binding between the user location (i.e. the IP address of the terminal the user is logged on) and the user's SIP address of record (public user identity).

The S-CSCF uses Diameter to interface the HSS and download the authentication vectors and user profiles of the served users in order to inform the HSS that this is the S-CSCF allocated to the user for the duration of the registration. All SIP signaling sent and received by the IMS terminal traverses the allocated S-CSCF and the S-CSCF inspects every SIP message and determines whether the SIP signaling should visit one or more application servers ("service triggers" defined as part of the user profile). The S-CSCF is always located in the home network.

Policy Decision Function (PDF)

The role of the PDF is to inform the GGSN about the characteristics of the session a user agent is authorized to establish at a particular time. The GGSN uses this information to install packet filters in its routing logic. If the user agent tries to do something unauthorized like sending media at an abundant data rate or to a different destination than the one indicated in the negotiations earlier, the packet filters discard the user agent's traffic.

In 3GPP IMS Release 6 the interfaces of the PDF are standardized. The IMS uses the COPS (Common Open Policy Service) protocol between the PDF and the GGSN (Go interface) and the DIAMETER protocol between the PDF and the P-CSCF.

F.5.2.3 Identification in IMS

In any network there must be a possibility to uniquely identify users and so in the PSTN, for example, users are identified by the assigned telephone number. In addition to that, when a service is provided, it is also necessary to identify the service as well as additional service parameters and information. In the PSTN services are specified by special numbers, typically indicated through a special prefix and so IMS also specifies a mechanism to identify services.

Public User Identities

The IMS identifies its users deterministically by typically one or more Public User Identities, which can be:

- a SIP URI (as defined in RFC 3261)

- a TEL URI (as defined in RFC 2806)

Public User Identities are "human readable" and are meant to be used as contact information on business cards etc. Within the IMS, Public User Identities are used to route SIP signaling and for the IMS what an MS-ISDN is for GSM.

When the Public User Identity is defined as a SIP URI, it typically has the form of *sip:firstname_lastname@operator.com*. Additionally, it is possible to include a telephone number in a SIP URI using the following format:
sip:+49-89-63676190@operator.com;user=phone. This format is needed due to the fact that SIP requires the URI to be a valid SIP URI for registration. So it is not possible to register a TEL URI in SIP directly.

When the Public User Identity is defined as a TEL URI, it typically has a form like *tel:+49-89-63676190*. Since PSTN numbers are represented by just digits, the TEL URIs are needed to make a call from an IMS terminal to a PSTN phone as well as to connect phone calls from PSTN subscribers to IMS users.

Private User Identities

The IMS assigns a Private User Identity to every IMS subscriber at the IMS home network. In contrast to Public User Identities, Private User Identities are not SIP URIs or TEL URIs. Instead they are defined in the format of a Network Access Identifier (NAI) such as *username@operator.com*.

Private User Identities are exclusively used for subscription identification and authentication purposes and never used for routing SIP messages. A Private User Identity performs a similar function in the IMS as an IMSI (International Mobile Subscriber Identity) does in a GSM network. Typically users do not need to know their Private User Identity and similar to the IMSI, it could be stored in a smart card such as a phone SIM card.

The Relation between Public and Private User IDs

In earlier version of the IMS specification, operators would assign one or more Public User Identities and one Private User Identity to each user in their network. In the case of GSM/UMTS the smart card (SIM) stores one Private User Identity and at least one Public User Identity. In contrast to that, in IMS the HSS stores the Private User Identity and a collection of Public User Identities issued to that user.

In 3GPP Release 6 an IMS subscriber is not only issued one but a number of Private User Identities. This is necessary when using a mobile network such as UMTS and more than one mobile device. As mentioned above, with UMTS only one Private User Identity is stored on the SIM card, but users may have more than one phone and more than one SIM card that they use in different terminals. Figure F.15 on page 198 shows this relationship between subscriber, Private and Public User Identities.

F.5.2.4 Roaming

Roaming support has been a general requirement since the second generation of cellular networks and users have to be able to roam to different networks (e.g. a user visiting a foreign country).

Figure F.15: IMS Identification
[197, page 39]

It is important to get access to services regardless of the geographical location. Roaming makes it possible to use services even when not being registered at the home network. The IMS uses the same concept of home and visited network as GSM/UMTS does. Most of the IMS functions such as S-CSCF, HSS, etc. are located in the home network and the only function that can be either in the home or the visited network is the P-CSCF that provides the access to the system for a registered user agent.

There are three instances of roaming:

- **GPRS Roaming** - GPRS roaming means the capability to access the IMS when the visited network provides the RAN and SGSN and the home network provides the GGSN and IMS.

- **IMS Roaming** - The IMS roaming model refers to a network configuration, in which the visited network provides IP connectivity (e.g. RAN , SGSN, GGSN) and the IMS entry point (i.e. P-CSCF) and the home network provides the rest of the IMS functionalities. In this model it is necessary that the GGSN and the P-CSCF reside in the same network (in order to allow the P-CSCF to control the GGSN over the so-called Go interface). In addition to that, since the media plane has to traverse the GGSN, it is preferable to have both of them located in the visited network. The main benefit of this roaming model compared to the GPRS roaming model is optimum usage of user-plane resources.

- **IMS circuit-switched (CS) Roaming** - Roaming between the IMS and the CS CN domain refers to inter-domain roaming between IMS and CS. When a user is not registered or reachable in one domain a session can be routed to the other domain. It is important to note that both the CS CN domain and the IMS domain have their own services and cannot be used from another domain. Some services are similar and available in both domains (e.g., Voice over IP in IMS and speech telephony in CSCN).

Figure F.16 on page 199 shows a typical "IMS Roaming" scenario with two user agents both roaming in visited networks.

The mobile stations (MS) roam in the visited networks A and B and at first, both register at their home network using the SIP REGISTER method (red lines). Since the P-CSCF in the visited network is the first and main connection point to the IMS system every message traverses

F.5. Mobile IP Core Network Technologies

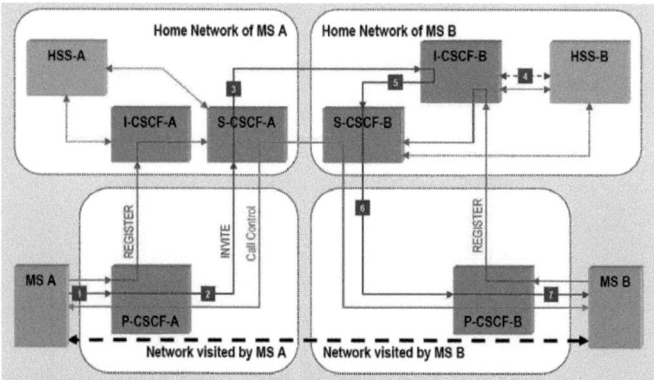

Figure F.16: IMS Roaming
[197, page 49]

this proxy and the proxy needs to route the message to the right destination. For first-time message transfers between domains, the proxy will always use the I-CSCF since this is the main connection point for inter domain traffic if the address of the, for this user, responsible S-CSCFs is not known. After more information about the target domain (users S-CSCF) was gathered the proxy can route messages straight to the S-CSCF. This is shown at the SIP INVITE sequence MS A starts in order to start an IMS session (blue line). After the session was established and the S-CSCFs for both mobile stations are known, all call control traffic can be routed between proxies, S-CSCFs and MSs.

Interworking with other networks
It is evident that the IMS will not be deployed all over the world at the same time. Moreover, people may not be able to switch terminals or subscriptions very rapidly. This will raise the issue of being able to reach people regardless of what kind of terminals they have, what contracts and subscriptions they use and where they live (what network is available). To be a new, successful communication network technology and architecture the IMS has to be able to connect to as many users as possible. Therefore, the IMS supports communication with PSTN, ISDN, mobile and Web/Internet users. Additionally, it is possible to support sessions with Web/Internet applications that have been developed outside the 3GPP community.

F.5.2.5   IMS Charging

From an operator or service provider perspective the ability to charge users is a must in any network. The IMS architecture allows different charging models to be used, which for example includes the possibility to charge just the calling party or to charge both the calling party (e.g. entirely on IMS session basis) and the called party (e.g. based on used resources such as time, transmitted data in bytes, etc. in the transport level). In IMS it is possible to use completely different charging schemes at the transport and IMS level. In addition to that, an operator might be interested in correlating charging information generated at transport and IMS (service and content) charging levels. This capability can be provided by utilizing a policy control reference point using the PDF.

IMS sessions may include multiple media components (e.g. audio and video) and it is required that the IMS provides a means for charging per media component. This allows charging one or both parties if new media components are added to a session. In addition to that, it is required that different IMS networks are able to exchange live charging information to be applied on a current session as well as exchange generated charging information of roaming users.

The IMS architecture supports both online and offline charging capabilities. Online charging is a charging process, in which the charging information affects a service in real time and therefore interacts with session/service control directly (e.g. pre-paid phone service). In practice, an operator could check the user's account before allowing the user to engage a session and stop a session when all credits are consumed.

Offline charging is a charging process, in which the charging information does not affect the service in real time but generates charging information after a session has ended. This is the traditional model, in which the charging information is collected over a particular period and, at the end of the period, the operator generates a bill for the subscriber.

F.5.2.6 IMS Enabling Services

IMS is specified as a SDP that allows easy integration of all sorts of services for its network users. Users use their IMS enabled clients (e.g. PC, mobile phones, etc.) to access these services and to communicate with each other. This leads to the fact that there are two general types of applications in an IMS:

- **Client-to-Client application** - is the most basic type of application in an IMS. Such an application does not take advantage of any IMS enabling service or application, but uses the IMS only as a SIP network that allows localizing (e.g. IP address) other users, routing SIP messages and setting up multimedia sessions between the client devices.

- **Enabling Service Application** - is an advanced type of application that uses the IMS network to access services and applications that run on application servers. These services allow the application to extend its own functionality with all features offered by these enabling services. Examples for these services are Presence, Messaging and Group Management, which are described in more detail below.

Typically every IMS-aware client application will take advantage of enabling services offered by the IMS network. Enabling services are reusable components on an IMS application server and new IMS applications can be developed by integrating existing and developing additional services. This speeds up the development process dramatically while ensuring better quality through extensively and often tested reusable services.

Figure F.17 on page 201 shows the typical IMS layer architecture.

At the bottom are the different IMS enabled fixed or mobile stations that access an IP network using different access technologies, such as UMTS for mobile networks or DSL for fixed networks. Using the Internet Protocol, these devices can access the IMS Common Service Control, which is basically the network of IMS core servers. On top of the core network, IMS developers can deploy enabling services using for example the Java SIP Servlet API on a SIP A/S. On the top layer, third party application developers or carrier internal developers can build end-user centric applications using the enabling services with additional application software/code.

Figure F.18 on page 201 shows how an enabling service is invoked by an IMS user application installed on a mobile terminal.

F.5. Mobile IP Core Network Technologies

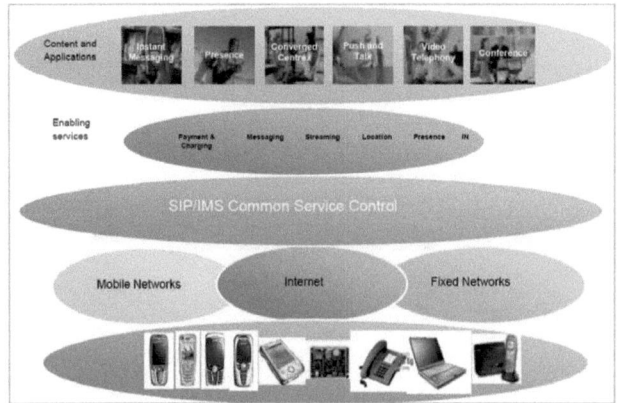

Figure F.17: IMS Layers
[197, page 13]

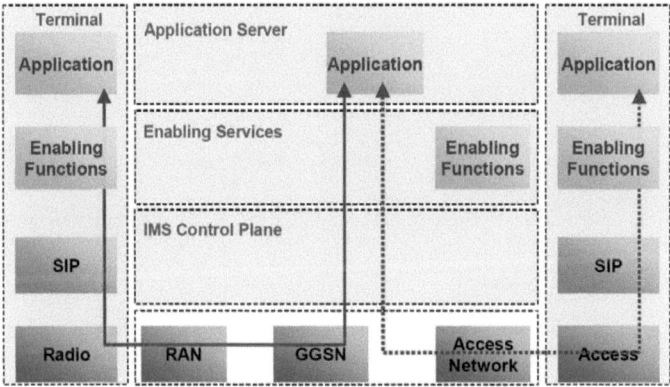

Figure F.18: IMS Enabling Services with SIP A/S
[197, page 27]

The application shown in the figure is composed of two parts, one installed on the mobile terminal, the other installed on a SIP A/S within the IMS network. When a user interacts with the mobile terminal, the application sends signaling and/or application-specific messages to the IMS network. These messages traverse all parts of the network, which includes the access network components such as RAN and GGSN, the IMS Control Plane (Core Servers such as CSCFs), enabling services offered by the IMS network that are also installed on SIP A/Ss and of course the part of the application that is installed on the SIP A/S within the IMS network that offers the application.

Presence

This subsection gives a simplistic high level overview about what presence is, and how it is used to publish and access presence information.

In essence, presence is the ability and willingness to be reached for communication and it consists of two things: it involves making my status available to others and the statuses of others available to me. A users presence information may be related to the current mobile network connection status, however it represents much more than just whether a user has network coverage or not, for example a user can also define a set of access rules to control access to his presence information.

Presence information may include (see also Figure F.19 on page 202):

- person and terminal availability
- communication preferences
- terminal capabilities
- current activity
- current mood
- location such as GPS data

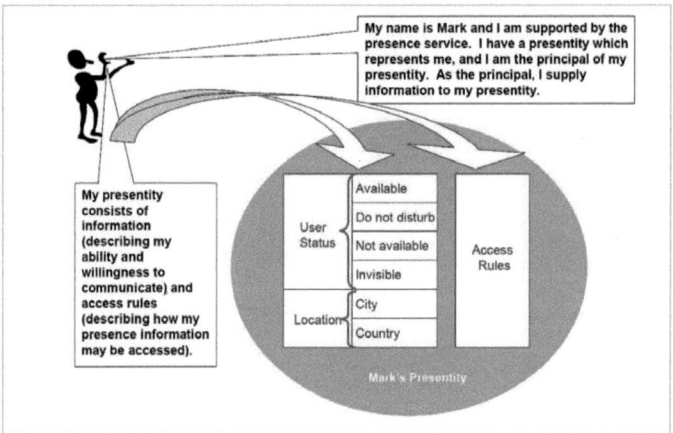

Figure F.19: IMS Presence Service
[197, page 21]

It is envisioned that presence will facilitate all mobile communication, not only instant messaging, which has been the main driver for presence. In the mobile environment presence information will be used as an indicator of the ability to engage in any session, including voice calls, video and gaming. All mobile communications will be presence-based. Presence-specific and presence-enhanced applications and services will be available in the near future. A typical example of a presence-specific application will be a dynamic, phonebook with embedded presence information, which will be the initial information the user sees before establishing communication. This information will affect facts like the choice of communication method, the content of the communication, timing etc.

SIP for Presence
SIP has been extended for presence and an event package called "presence" was added. When subscribing to such an event, a subscriber places the "presence" token in the Event header of the SIP message. Some additional definitions were specified to describe the subscriber and the notifier for the purpose of presence:

- **Presentity** - The presence entity is a resource that provides presence information to a presence service or server.

- **Watchers** - Are entities that request presence information about network resources such as services and users. There are two kinds of watchers, called fetchers and subscribers. A fetcher simply requests the current value of some presentity's presence information from the presence service. A special kind of fetcher is one that fetches information on a regular basis. This is called a poller. In contrast to that a subscriber requests notifications from the presence service of all changes in a presentity's presence information.

The 3GPP Release 6 specification defines two SIP entities for presence:

- **Presence agent (PA)** - capable of storing subscriptions and generating notifications (e.g. Presence Server).

- **Presence user agent (PUA)** - manipulates presence information for a presentity and publishes such presence information (e.g. User Terminal).

For presence information the SIP NOTIFY request message body carries the presence state information from the presence server to watching users. The state information is the presence state of a presentity and is encoded as XML (Extensible Markup Language) document with the Multipurpose Internet Mail Extension (MIME) type "application/pidf+xml" as defined in the Presence Information Data Format (PIDF) and can be extended with additional information elements if necessary. In order to upload presence information from the presentity to the presence server, the SIP PUBLISH method, with presence state information as payload, is used.

Presence Service Architecture in IMS
A user's presence information can be obtained from a multiplicity of entities in the IMS network. It could be a PUA located in a foreign network, a PUA at the terminal or a PUA located as an entity in the network. The presence server itself is an example of an IMS application server or server application. Watchers may be in the same home domain as the presentity or in a foreign domain.

Security and Access Control
To protect privacy and confidentiality, a presentity has full control over whether any group of watchers can access the published presence information. A presentity may give different watchers different levels of access. A presentity can control (per watcher) which parts of the presence information may be seen, may decide that specific watchers have restricted access and that some do not have any access at all. In addition to that a presentity may also define presence information and access rules so that different watchers are given different presence state information (e.g. One is told: not available, when at the same time others are told: available).

Messaging

In today's world, both in the wired and wireless networks, there are many different types of messaging services and applications available. Unfortunately, the most popular Web/Internet-based instant messaging services are usually based upon closed and proprietary protocols (e.g. ICQ, MSN, Skype), which made it impossible for different service providers to allow interoperable messaging between their respective users. In addition to that, most Web/Internet-based messaging services today do not take the wireless environment and the needs of operators to provide services that are commercially viable (e.g. providing support for charging, etc.) into consideration.

Typical characteristics of instant messaging are instant delivery of the messages to the targeted recipient(s) and interaction with presence information that allows users to see availability and status information. The expectations of messaging services in general differ in that some are designed to be used in what is perceived as 'real' time (e.g. ICQ Chat, Skype Chat, MSN Chat), whereas others are designed as a 'mailbox' service (e.g. E-Mail) where the messages are stored for later collection or delivery.

The IMS Messaging service incorporates one or more of the following messaging types:

Immediate Messaging

The sender expects immediate message delivery in (almost) real-time. Typically the sender is aware of the availability of the recipient(s) through the use of a Presence service before sending this type of message. If the recipient is not available the message may be discarded or deferred. An immediate message may be deferred by the recipient's network based on message filtering settings defined by the recipient or by the recipient's IMS service provider.

Immediate Messaging uses the SIP MESSAGE method for sending messages between peers. The sending IMS user agent simply generates a MESSAGE request, fills in the desired content (e.g. text, audio, video, images), populates the request URI with the recipients address and routes the message using the IMS core network to the receiving user agent.

Session-Based Messaging

Session-based messaging relates to a familiar paradigm of messaging already in use in the Internet, the Internet Relay Chat (IRC). In this mode of messaging users participate in sessions, in which the main media component often consists of short textual messages. As in any other session a message session has a well-defined lifetime (session setup till session closing). After the session was set up between the participants, media flows directly from peers to peers and only peers participating in the session are allowed to send or able to receive messages. A peer can be an end-user's user agent, or a messaging back-to-back user agent that manages a group chat or conference.

Session-based messaging forms a natural unison with conferencing as well. Using the conferencing functionality, session-based messaging can turn into a multi-party chat conference. In this mode it can enable applications similar to modern day voice conferences, which can include additional data channels that transfer audio, video, graphics, collaborative sketch boards, etc.

Deferred Delivery Messaging

The sender expects the network to deliver the message as soon as the recipient becomes available (store-and-forward delivery). The requirements for the "deferred delivery messaging" are basically the same as for the well-known Multimedia Messaging Service (MMS).

Typically, IMS messaging is direct and in almost real-time between user agents. So, for that to work, both agents need to be online during message exchange. For a deferred delivery it is necessary to include a virtual agent (back-to-back messaging server/SIP A/S) that accepts all messages for an offline user agent. This agent then forwards the stored messages, as soon as the recipient user agent registers with the IMS again.

Group Management

The IMS group management service provides an easy to use possibility to manage network-based groups that are personalized for every public user identification. The driver for specifying a generic group management service in IMS was twofold: the same group created by a user (or service provider) can be used in many services and the same group management functions can be utilized independent of the service being used.

IMS group management allows managing an (almost) unlimited number of groups per user, adding/removing other users (buddies) to/from a group, defining different roles and rights to members of a group, setting group level information and properties, etc. The IMS group management service is a generic capability that can be utilized in other IMS applications together with other enabling services in order to implement comprehensive new applications or services quickly. Some examples for services/applications that use the IMS group management service are:

- **Presence service** - The Presentity is in control of who is able to see his presence information. The control is carried out via access control lists that can be managed with the IMS group management. A watcher can subscribe to a list of presentities instead of subscribing to every single presentity, one by one. The list can be managed with IMS group management.

- **Chat** - The administrator of the chat is able to control users that are allowed to participate in the chat. The control is carried out via access control lists, which can be managed with IMS group management.

- **Messaging** - In messaging the server may be able to distribute the messages to several recipients based on the delivery list. The content of the delivery list can be managed with IMS group management.

F.5.3 IP Telecommunication Application Development

This section provides a summary of the three concepts that support future TCP/IP-based Telecommunication application development: SIP Application Servers, Service Capability Interaction Managers and Policy Evaluation Enforcement and Management.

F.5.3.1 SIP Application Server (SIP A/S)

A SIP A/S is a SIP-based server and an entity in the network that hosts a wide range of value-added multimedia services and provides these services to end-users. A SIP A/S could be used to provide presence, messaging and conferencing services.

An example of an application server that is being developed in 3GPP is the Voice Call Continuity Function (VCC Server). Depending on the actual service, the SIP A/S can operate in SIP proxy mode, SIP UA (user agent) mode or SIP B2BUA (back-to-back user agent) mode. A SIP A/S can be located in the home network or in an external third-party network. In addition to the SIP interface a SIP A/S may optionally provide an interface to the HSS that may be used to download or upload user related data that stored in the HSS. If located in the home network, it can query the HSS with the DIAMETER Sh interface (for a SIP A/S) or the Mobile Application Part (MAP) interface (for IM-SSF).

Figure F.20 on page 206 shows the three different types of Application Servers.

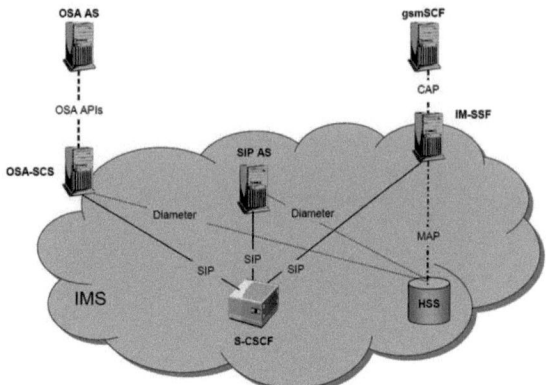

Figure F.20: Different SIP A/S types in an IMS SIP network
[197, page 40]

- **SIP A/S** - This is the native SIP A/S that hosts and executes IP multimedia services based on SIP. The Siemens IMS uses Ubiquity SIP application servers.

- **OSA-SCS** - This A/S provides a northbound interface to an OSA framework A/S and a southbound SIP interface to the S-CSCF.

- **IM-SSF** - an IP Multimedia Service Switching Function interfaces with Customized Applications for Mobile networks Enhanced Logic (CAMEL). This specialized A/S allows reusing CAMEL services that were developed for GSM.

Beyond SIP A/S: The Converged Applications Environment

The converged applications environment (Application Server Component Architecture for SIP) is based on the distributed Web/Internet architecture and is not dependent on any proprietary APIs and operating systems for connecting multiple servers. All control functions are based on simple SIP and HTTP message flows and the open architecture is especially suited for third-party service providers across IP networks or across the Internet.

Figure F.21 on page 207 shows the integration of communications with applications and transactions, as is required for mobile applications and services. The real-time communications part is emphasized here with the main communication servers logically clustered around the capability to exchange SIP and HTTP messages. The various components are loosely coupled, in the sense that once their functions have been invoked by simple call flows, the details of operation are left to each server, without affecting the operation of (but possible interaction with) other servers.

The following list describes some of the main types of communication servers:

- **General-Purpose SIP Server** - (in the center, with database access) acting as registrar, redirect server, and for admission control in conjunction with the AAA and location services, such as databases or ENUM. The redirect server can also implement private dialing plans for enterprise networks.

F.5. Mobile IP Core Network Technologies

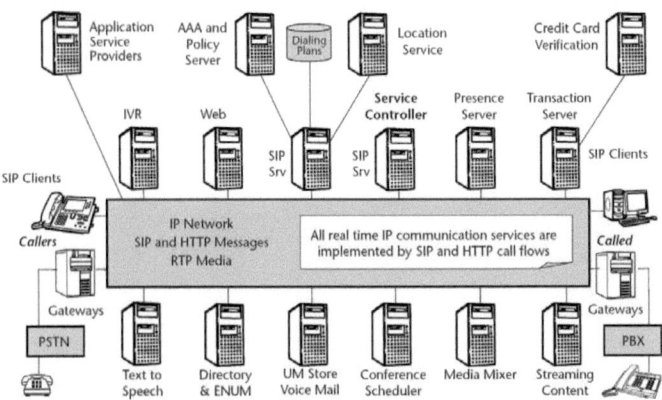

Figure F.21: Servers for communications, applications and transactions
[25, page 323]

- **Service Controller** - for delivery of services in conjunction with specialized communication servers. The service controller uses SIP third-party call control to orchestrate the interaction between the various servers.
- **Voice Portal** - using VoiceXML technology for voice control and voice browsing. This also acts as an interactive voice-response (IVR) server.
- **Web-Server** - for provisioning and control by end-users.
- **Presence-Server** - for extended user status information such as availability, mood, etc.
- **Text-to-Speech Server** - for the conversion of textual data into spoken audio files or streams.
- **Voice-Recognition-Server** - for the conversion of spoken audio data into computer processable natural language information.
- **Universal Messaging (UM) Server** - for unifying different channels and technologies of messaging systems.
- **Conference Scheduler** - for automated conference calls.
- **Media mixer for audio conferences** - for unifying audio streams from several sources and transmitting to conference participants.
- **Content server** - for streaming multimedia, such as stored presentations, shows, and so on.

In addition to servers for communications, other servers add additional services and functionality:

- **Transaction server** - for transactional processes such as bank or credit card transactions.
- **Application service providers** - such as productivity software. This allows for the integration of office applications (document editors, spreadsheets, presentations, databases) and personal information managers with real-time communications.

Other interesting applications for outsourcing, however, go beyond the generic services shown here:

- **Services of general interest** - such as travel and weather
- **Highly specialized services** - such as security by voice recognition or Public Key Infrastructure (PKI) systems
- **Virtual communities** - for business and nonprofit organizations

Service providers offering such an open and integrated environment for web, e-mail, and voice can be referred to as application infrastructure service providers.

F.5.3.2 Service Capability Interaction Manager (SCIM)

IMS services should not provide overlapping logic implementations that result in redundant code across several ASs. To avoid that, services are being broken down into the basic building blocks, called Service Capabilities (SC), that are needed to provide them. Such a decomposition of services requires the incorporation of service brokering and interaction management functionalities into the IMS architecture. A service broker manages the requests to access SCs of third party Application Services. An interaction manager resolves the dependencies and conflicts in the interactions between the SCs that deliver the complete service.

The 3GPP proposes the SCIM as an optional node in the IMS architecture. It is defined to perform interaction management and control functions. Figure F.22 shows the SCIM node below the SIP ASs in the IMS architecture.

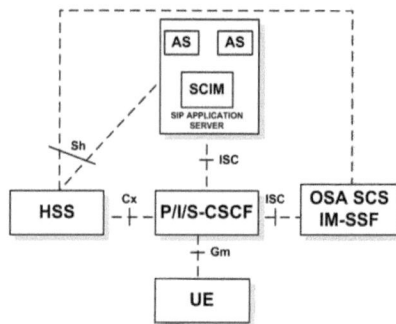

Figure F.22: SCIM in an IMS Architecture [225]

The SCIM constitutes a middleware that is co-located with SIP ASs that implement a certain service and so, are all required to fulfill the delivery of an initiated service request. In a typical multimedia telephony service that uses call barring, call forwarding and voicemail SCs, the SCIM needs to be able to prioritize the execution of these different SCs in an optimal way. Prioritizing voicemail above the others is, for example, inappropriate, since this will result in all calls being forwarded to voicemail. The chaining of SCs should be handled in a dynamic fashion, taking also non-SIP data such as, for example, intermediary execution results and external end-users context data into account.

Two general approaches for placing a SCIM between the service layer and the control layer of the IMS architecture are proposed:

1. **Centralized approach:** designing the SCIM as an intermediate AS between S-CSCF and SCs.

   The SCIM retrieves the end-user profile from the S-CSCF for each service the end-user is subscribed to and invokes the related SCs according to defined interaction rules. Managing all interactions centrally within the network may result in scalability issues for networks with large end-user bases.

2. **Distributed approach:** delegating interaction management functionalities of the SCIM to the S-CSCFs.

   Instead of implementing the SCIM as a centralized middleware for interaction management decisions, the interaction management tasks are integrated into the S-CSCFs. Coordination and cooperation between S-CSCFs provides a scalable solution to SC interaction management issues and enables an interaction at service level. Since each S-CSCF has already retrieved the end-user profiles of all subscribers during registration, the interface between SCIM and S-CSCF is less complex than in the previous approach.

The lack of an official SCIM specification by the 3GPP led to various different and proprietary proposals and solutions of interaction models by IMS researchers and vendors.

F.5.3.3 Policy Evaluation Enforcement and Management (PEEM)

An alternative approach for access brokering and orchestration of standardized OMA IMS enablers, such as Presence, XDM or Group Management, is specified in OMA's PEEM enabler.

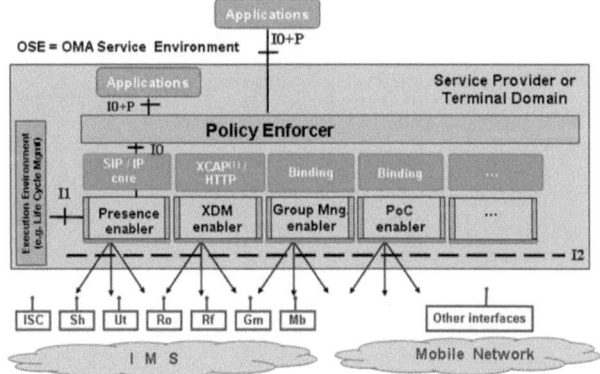

Figure F.23: OMA PEEM with IMS Enablers [165]

In the PEEM specification, policy management is viewed as a horizontal layer residing between the IMS applications domain and a set of IMS network enablers or other resources. Within this layer, resource access policies are applied to all requests and responses within all protocols between the different domains. This concept is illustrated in figure F.23.

F.6 Open Services Gateway Initiative (OSGi)

The OSGi service platform is a dynamic module system for the Java software development technology. It implements a complete and dynamic service model, which enables the dynamic integration and remote management of software services. Application lifecycle management is handled via APIs that allow remote downloading of management policies. A service registry allows detecting the addition of new services as well as the removal of existing services.

The OSGi specifications are being developed further by the OSGi Alliance, an open standards organization founded in March 1999 and that has formerly been known as the Open Services Gateway initiative. The organization is comprised of renowned companies such as Nokia, IBM, Oracle and Sun Microsystems. The OSGi specification is developed by the members in an open process and made available to the public free of charge under the OSGi Specification License. Several stable open-source implementations are available.

The OSGi specifications have evolved beyond the original focus of service gateways. Their applications include mobile phones as well as the open source IDE Eclipse. Other application areas range from automobiles, industrial automation and building automation to grid computing, fleet management and application servers.

The central component of the OSGi service platform is the OSGi framework, which implements a container where services can be installed and executed at runtime.

- **Bundles** are coherent units of software resources that can be independently installed and uninstalled on the OSGi framework. The resources contained in a bundle are initially invisible to other bundles in the container. In order to make some available to other bundles, the containing bundle must explicitly declare the ones that ought to be exported. Bundles, which intend on using another bundle's exported resources, must explicitly import the bundle in question.

    Technically a bundle is a Java Archive (JAR) file, which includes a manifest file, Java Class files, libraries and media files that are necessary for the implementation of its functionality. A bundle may also include further JAR files itself. The manifest file describes meta-data of the bundle such as name, libraries and dependencies.

- **Services** provide a possibility for decoupling modules on the OSGi framework. Services are available on the entire container and bundles can make use of them. An OSGi service is a Java object that is being made publicly known by an interface name. It needs to be registered with the central service registry that is available across all bundles. Bundles that need a specific service are able to query the service registry and use the service without needing to know which implementation of the service interface they are using. The OSGi service platform provides a number of standard services that must be available on every implementation.

The architecture of the OSGi framework is illustrated in figure F.24.

- **Services Layer**

    This layer specifies how bundles are connected dynamically within the framework and how they are being used as OSGi services. Services can be registered and unregistered from the framework at any given time. This dynamic behavior implies that users of a service need to deal with the possibility of its disappearance at runtime. In order to support handling of dynamic services, the specification describes three possibilities for a bundle to react to changes in the service environment: Service Listener, Service Tracker and Declarative Services.

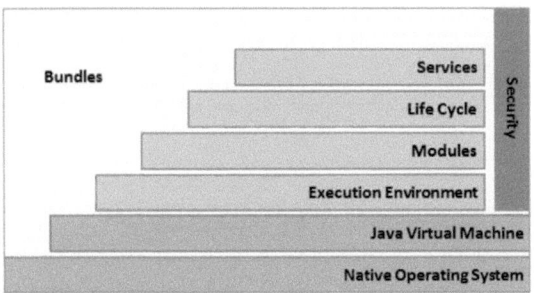

Figure F.24: OSGi Framework Layered Architecture

- **Life Cycle Layer**

  This layer defines the dynamic aspects of bundles such as the states that a bundle can be in during its life cycle, as well as the actions that cause transitions between those states.

  Manipulation of bundle states is provided by a Management Agent that implements an interface that allows external control of certain aspects of the framework. This includes features such as installing, starting, stopping, updating and uninstalling bundles during runtime without rebooting the platform or any components.

  The OSGi specification does not include the manner in which this external access is realized. Consequently different implementations of Managements Agents exist, ranging from text-based consoles to graphical web interfaces.

- **Modules Layer**

  This layer of the OSGi framework specification defines the static aspects of the underlying module concept. It defines how the framework resolves dependencies related to importing and exporting OSGi bundle code.

- **Execution Environment Layer**

  This layer provides the connection to the underlying Java software platform, the Java Virtual Machine, the file system of the host OS and the hardware beneath. It is used for defining what Java methods, Java objects, Java classes and file resources are available on the OSGi platform.

- **Security Layer** The security layer is the central part of the security concept of the OSGi service platform and enables limiting bundle functionality to predefined capabilities. The security concept is based on the Java Security Model. It expands this model to the specific requirements of the service platform and enables a configuration of security policies for each bundle separately. The support of the security layer by an OSGi implementation is optional.

F.7 Representational State Transfer (REST)

Many current Web/Internet technology-based Web Service approaches such as SOAP are complex and lead to a HTTP degradation from an application- to a transport protocol. In many cases, the Web/Internet technologies could provide the desired functionality and would be able to drive remote services themselves. The introduction of these additional layers of abstraction is often unnecessary overhead in design and implementation. Current Web/Internet technologies such as the HTTP application protocol, the Uniform Resource Identification (URI) naming standard and XML are sufficient tools to define service interfaces and messages in a standardized and efficient manner.

REST is an architectural style for distributed hypermedia systems in which requests and responses between clients and servers are built around the transfer of representations of resources. An architecture conforming to the REST architectural style is also called RESTful. The largest implementation of a RESTful architecture is the Web/Internet, which is built upon the HTTP protocol and the URI standard. REST itself is not limited to HTTP and may be based on other protocols that provide a uniform vocabulary for representational state transfer based on resources. A resource may be essentially any coherent and meaningful concept that can be addressed. A representation of a resource is typically a document that captures the current or intended state of a resource. Each resource is referenced with at least one global identifier (e.g. a URI). Manipulation of resources requires participants to communicate on a network using standardized interfaces to exchange representations of the resources.

F.7.1 REST Key Concepts

REST describes six constraints for RESTful architectures. Five of them are mandatory and any service that violates at least one of the mandatory cannot be referred to as fully RESTful. The actual implementation of the components is open to designers and developers.

Client-Server Following the well-established design principle of separation of concerns, clients are separated from servers by a uniform interface. GUI concerns are separated from data storage concerns in order to improve portability of the GUI and scalability of the server components. Decoupling of components also allows them to evolve independently, thus supporting the Web/Internet-scale requirements of multiple organizational domains.

Stateless Communication must be stateless in nature and session state is kept entirely on the client. Each request from client to server must contain all the information necessary to understand and process the request, without taking advantage of any stored context on the server. Thereby, a monitoring system does not have to look beyond a single request in order to determine the full nature of the request. This improves reliability by enabling partial fault recovery and scalability by allowing servers to free resources as quickly as possible instead of storing session state information between requests.

Cacheable Data within a response must be implicitly or explicitly labeled as cacheable or non-cacheable. Cacheable responses may be loaded from client caches for subsequent equivalent requests. Non-cacheable responses need to be labeled in order to prevent clients from reusing outdated data as response to equivalent requests. The advantages of adding cache constraints are potentially increased efficiency, scalability and user-perceived performance through partial or complete elimination of selected client-server interactions within a series of interactions.

Uniform Interface REST applies the software engineering principle of Generality to component interfaces. Implementations are decoupled from the services they provide, respectively the service interface they export. This enables multiple implementations for the same service interface and allows an independent evolution of the components as well as ensures a high maintainability and extensibility.

The guiding principles of the uniform interface:

- Identification of Resources - Individual resources can be deterministically referenced in requests by at least one globally unique identifier. For example using URIs in Web/Internet technologies-based REST systems. Servers respond to requests for resources with a conceptual representation of the requested resource.

- Manipulation of Resources through Representations - Any client that holds a representation of a resource and the appropriate permissions has enough information to modify or delete the resource on the server, including any meta-data attached.

- Self Descriptive Messages - Each message includes enough information to define how to process the message. Responses explicitly indicate their cacheability.

- Hypermedia as the Engine of Application State - Clients make state transitions only through actions that are dynamically identified within hypermedia by the server (e.g. by hyperlinks within hypertext). Except for simple fixed entry points to the application, a client does not assume that any particular actions beyond those described in representations previously received from the server are available for a given resource.

Layered System The architecture is composed of hierarchical layers. These constrain component behavior such that components cannot interact beyond the immediate layer with which they are associated. Layers can be used to encapsulate legacy services as well as to protect new services from legacy clients. Layers help to simplify components by moving infrequently used functionality to a shared intermediary. Intermediaries can also be used to enforce security policies as well as to improve system scalability by enabling load balancing across multiple networks and systems.

Code-On-Demand (optional) REST allows client functionality to be extended by downloading and executing code in the form of applets or scripts. This simplifies client development and porting by reducing the amount of functionalities and capabilities required to be implemented. Allowing functionalities to be downloaded after deployment improves the overall system's extensibility.

F.7.2 RESTful Web Services

Two main questions are answered differently by today's Web Services:

1. How does a client convey its intentions to the server? (Method Information)
2. How does a client tell the server which part of the data set to operate on? (Scoping Information)

The following summary describes how RESTful Web Services answer these questions by utilizing the HTTP vocabulary and URI naming convention for representational state transfer of resources.

A RESTful Web Service is a service implemented using HTTP and the design principles of the REST architectural style. It is a collection of resources, with four defined aspects:

- Base URI for the Web Service, e.g. http://sdp.cdtm.de/TestService
- The supported Web/Internet media types supported by the Web Service, e.g. JSON, XML
- The set of operations supported by the Web Service, using only HTTP methods (e.g. POST, GET, PUT or DELETE)
- The API must be hypertext driven.

The answers to the two descriptive questions to a Web Service can be inferred from the REST architectural principles and the above definition of a RESTful Web Service.

- **Method information:** is solely conveyed through the actual HTTP method. RPC-style Web Services, which define their own method vocabulary and convey method information within a HTTP request elsewhere, are not considered RESTful.
- **Scoping information:** is placed in the URI-path, uniquely and deterministically identifying the requested set of resources.

List of Figures

1.1	Ratio of Voice and Data Traffic and Revenue	2
1.2	Fixed and Mobile Bandwidth Evolution [150]	3
1.3	Development of Voice Traffic	4
1.4	Web/Internet Service and Application Value Chain	5
1.5	Launch Dates of Application Stores [148]	8
1.6	Thesis Research Approach	14
1.7	Relations between Chapters	15
2.1	Telecommunication Service Silos	18
2.2	SOA Triangular Model [61]	21
2.3	Service Lifecycle [251]	22
2.4	Service Interface Layer positioned between Business Process Layer and Application Layer [66]	23
2.5	The three Service Layers [66]	24
2.6	Enterprise Service Bus [251]	26
2.7	Enterprise Application Integration (EAI) across Partner Companies through Enterprise Service Buses (ESBs) [43]	27
2.8	SOA Reference Architecture [251]	28
2.9	Transformation from Telecommunication Service Silos to SDP Services	30
2.10	Device Centric vs. SDP Centric	31
2.11	Application Lifecycle	32
2.12	NGN Convergence	34
2.13	Convergence on All-IP (adapted from [226])	35
2.14	Distributed Web-Telecom Converged Services and Application	37
3.1	Web-Telecom Convergence Stakeholder	39
3.2	Distribution of mobile CSPs in Germany in August 2011 [116]	40
3.3	Longtail Business Model	42

3.4	Distribution of mobile phone OEMs and smartphone OSs in Germany in August 2011 [116]	46
3.5	Platform Adoption Criteria	50
3.6	Learning Period	52
3.7	Adoption of ASP Services	54
3.8	CSPs roles in service and application development	55
3.9	CSP - Developer Business Cooperation Models	56
4.1	Evolution of Telecommunication Service and Application Development Concepts [132]	63
4.2	Intelligent Networks [110]	64
4.3	CAMEL (adopted from[110])	65
4.4	Java API for Intelligent Networks	68
4.5	Parlay X Architecture	70
4.6	Comparison Methodology (adapted from [125])	72
4.7	Web-Telecom Convergence Platform Concepts Blueprint (adapted from [125])	74
4.8	Web-Telecom Convergence Platform Proposals Comparison [125]	76
4.9	Consolidated Mobile Platforms Comparison	82
4.10	Consolidated Mobile Development Frameworks Comparison	85
5.1	Unified Address Book as One- and Two-Level Approach	88
5.2	Social Notification Application	89
5.3	Generic Web-Telecom Converged Application Reference Architecture	91
5.4	Exemplified Technical Web-Telecom Converged Unified Address Book Application Architecture	93
6.1	Requirements derived from major Stakeholder Goals	95
6.2	Requirements derived from major Stakeholder Goals	97
6.3	Requirements derived from major Stakeholder Goals	99
7.1	From Service Delivery Platform to Application Delivery Platform	104
7.2	Web-Telecom Convergence ADP	105
7.3	Separation of Networks and Application	105
7.4	Networks and Applications Separated Scenario	106
7.5	Service Capability Manager with Policy Evaluation [28]	111
7.6	Scopes and Types of ADP Services	113
7.7	Service Execution Cycle [223]	116
7.8	Performance Evaluation of BPEL and SCXML [134]	117

List of Figures

7.9	Semi-Automatic Service Import Concept (adapted from [223])	119
7.10	General Application Store Concept	121
7.11	Logical ADP Reference Architecture	122
7.12	Technical ADP Architecture	128
8.1	Requirements Assessment	134
8.2	Prototype ADP Architecture	136
8.3	Converged Address Book Prototype Architecture	138
8.4	Semi-Automatic Service Import Prototype [223]	139
8.5	Second Iteration ADP Prototype (adapted from [74])	141
8.6	SNApp Distributed Component Architecture [74]	144
8.7	Concepts Assessment	145
B.1	Service Description Language Comparison Results [223]	156
E.1	SNApp Message Sequence [74]	163
F.1	SIP communication exchange for INVITE (call/session setup) request message using a proxy server	172
F.2	SIP communication exchange for INVITE (call/session setup) request message using a redirect server	173
F.3	3GPP Packet-Switched Multimedia Streaming Protocol Stack	177
F.4	General RTSP Message Structure	178
F.5	RTSP Request Line	178
F.6	RTSP Response Status Line	179
F.7	Streaming Sequence using RTSP, RTP and SDP	180
F.8	Real Time transport header (IP/UDP/RTP)	181
F.9	Basic Voice-over-IP PBX system	183
F.10	Fully integrated Voice-over-IP system with different locations connected via various technologies like DSL, ISDN, etc.	184
F.11	Typical Mobile Network Architecture	186
F.12	UMTS Service Architecture with IMS	188
F.13	SAE EPC Architecture [89]	192
F.14	Simplified IMS Architecture	194
F.15	IMS Identification	198
F.16	IMS Roaming	199
F.17	IMS Layers	201
F.18	IMS Enabling Services with SIP A/S	201

F.19 IMS Presence Service 202
F.20 Different SIP A/S types in an IMS SIP network 206
F.21 Servers for communications, applications and transactions 207
F.22 SCIM in an IMS Architecture [225] 208
F.23 OMA PEEM with IMS Enablers [165] 209
F.24 OSGi Framework Layered Architecture 211

List of Tables

- C.1 Mobile Platforms Comparison Details 157
- C.2 Development Frameworks Comparison 158
- F.1 GPRS Data Rates 187
- F.2 WLAN Specifications 191

Listings

8.1   Prototypical ADP SDL [223] 140
8.2   SDL Google Translate Example [223] 140
D.1   Prototype Code Generation Template 161
F.1   HTTP GET Request 166
F.2   HTTP 302 Redirect Response 167
F.3   HTTP 200 OK Response 167
F.4   RTSP SETUP Request 179
F.5   RTSP SETUP Response 180

Bibliography

[1] G. D. Abowd, A. Dey, R. Orr, and J. Brotherton, "Context Awareness in Wearable and Ubiquitous Computing," *Journal of Virtual Reality*, vol. 3, no. 3, 1998.

[2] Accenture, "Supporting Cost-Effective Service Innovation in the All-IP Era," Tech. Rep., 2010.

[3] V. Agarwal, K. Dasgupta, N. Karnik, A. Kumar, A. Kundu, S. Mittal, and B. Srivastava, "A service creation environment based on end to end composition of Web services," *Proceedings of the 14th international conference on World Wide Web - WWW '05*, p. 128, 2005. [Online]. http://portal.acm.org/citation.cfm?doid=1060745.1060768

[4] A. Al-Hezmi, F. Carvalho de Gouveia, M. Sher, O. Friedrich, and T. Magedanz, "Provisioning IMS-based seamless triple play services over different access networks," *NOMS 2008 - 2008 IEEE Network Operations and Management Symposium*, pp. 927–930, 2008. [Online]. http://ieeexplore.ieee.org/lpdocs/epic03/wrapper.htm?arnumber=4575249

[5] A. Al-Hezmi, C. Riede, and T. Magedanz, "Session and Media Signaling for IPTV via IMS," *Proceedings of the First International Conference on MOBILe Wireless MiddleWARE, Operating Systems, and Applications*, pp. 0–5, 2008. [Online]. http://eudl.eu/?id=2917

[6] Alcatel-Lucent, "Introduction to Evolved Packet Core," Alcatel-Lucent, Tech. Rep., 2009. [Online]. http://www.3g4g.co.uk/Lte/LTE_WP_0903_AlcatelLucent.pdf

[7] Alcatel-Lucent, "Service Delivery Environment (SDE)," 2010. [Online]. http://www.alcatel-lucent.com/sde

[8] Alcatel-Lucent, "Alcatel-Lucent Open API Platform and Open API Service," Alcatel-Lucent, Tech. Rep., 2011.

[9] Ali Arsanjani, Liang-Jie Zhang, Michael Ellis, Abdul Allam, and Kishore Channabasavaiah, "Design an SOA Solution using a Reference Architecture," IBM, Tech. Rep., Mar. 2007. [Online]. http://www.ibm.com/developerworks/library/ar-archtemp/

[10] N. Amram and M. Fuchs, "Detailed Research Objectives and Requirements for the Core Network Enhancements and New Entities," C-Mobile, Tech. Rep., 2006.

[11] V. Andrikopoulos, A. Bucchiarone, E. D. Nitto, R. Kazhamiakin, S. Lane, V. Mazza, and I. Richardson, "Service Engineering," in *Service Research Challenges and Solutions*. Springer, 2010, pp. 271–337.

[12] Apache Felix, "iPOJO," 2011. [Online]. http://felix.apache.org/site/apache-felix-ipojo.html

[13] Apple, "Apple App Store," 2010. [Online]. http://www.apple.com/iphone/apps-for-iphone/

[14] Apple, "iPhone OS," 2010. [Online]. http://developer.apple.com/iphone/

[15] M. Arango and C. Huitema, "Simple Gateway Control Protocol (SGCP)," 1998.

[16] H. Arnold, "Auf dem Radar - Telco Service Architecture for Web X.0," Deutsche Telekom Laboratories, Tech. Rep., 2010.

[17] A. Arsanjani, G. Booch, T. Boubez, P. C. Brown, D. Chappell, J. de Vadoss, T. Erl, N. Josuttis, D. Krafzig, M. Little, B. Loesgen, J. McKendrick, A. T. Manes, S. Ross-Talbot, S. Tilkov, C. Utschig-Utschig, and H. Wilhelmsen, "SOA Manifesto," p. 1, 2009. [Online]. http://www.soa-manifesto.org/

[18] Asterisk, "Asterisk Open Source PBX," 2007.

[19] H. Baba, N. Takaya, I. Inoue, A. Kurokawa, L. Chong Chauvot, M. Le Clec, B. Fourestie, F. Forestier Husson, and N. Edel, "Web-IMS Convergence Architecture and Prototype," in *IEEE Globecom*, 2010.

[20] A. Baravaglio, C. Licciardi, and C. Venezia, "Web Service Applicability in Telecommunication Service Platforms," in *International Conference on Next Generation Web Services Practices (NWeSP'05)*. Ieee, 2005, pp. 39–44. [Online]. http://ieeexplore.ieee.org/lpdocs/epic03/wrapper.htm?arnumber=1592404

[21] S. Baset and H. Schulzrinne, "An Analysis of the Skype Peer-to-Peer Internet Telephony Protocol," *CoRR*, vol. abs/cs/041, 2004. [Online]. http://dblp.uni-trier.de/db/journals/corr/corr0412.html#abs-cs-0412017

[22] A. Becker, "Die Architektur von Android," *Heise Mobil*, pp. 1–10, 2011.

[23] S. Bécot, I. Bedini, M. Belaunde, S. Marin, O. Rugnon, V. Hiribarren, B. Christophe, B. Molina, and G. Marton, "Empowering Telco Operator Convergence through a Common Marketplace," *IEEE*, 2010.

[24] K. Bergner, A. Rausch, M. Sihling, T. Ternité, R. Reussner, J. Mayer, J. Stafford, S. Overhage, S. Becker, and P. Schroeder, *Quality of Software Architectures and Software Quality*, ser. Lecture Notes in Computer Science, R. Reussner, J. Mayer, J. A. Stafford, S. Overhage, S. Becker, and P. J. Schroeder, Eds. Berlin, Heidelberg: Springer Berlin Heidelberg, 2005, vol. 3712. [Online]. http://www.springerlink.com/content/039c1akabt95l93y/

[25] A. Bien, *Internet Communications using SIP*. Wiley Publishing, 2006.

[26] M. Bilandzic, F. Dany, C. Menkens, and A. Schmid, "Design Research, Action Research, Qualitative and Quantitative Methods in Ubiquitous Computing," Center for Digital Technology and Management, Tech. Rep., 2010.

[27] N. Blum, I. Boldea, T. Magedanz, and T. Margaria, "Service-oriented Access to Next Generation NetworksâĂŤfrom Service Creation to Execution," *Mobile Networks and Applications*, vol. 15, no. 3, pp. 356–365, Jan. 2010. [Online]. http://www.springerlink.com/index/10.1007/s11036-010-0222-1

[28] N. Blum, I. Boldea, T. Magedanz, U. Staiger, and H. Stein, "A Service Broker Providing Real-Time Telecommunications Services for 3rd Party Services," in *2009 33rd Annual IEEE International Computer Software and Applications Conference*. Ieee, 2009, pp. 85–91. [Online]. http://ieeexplore.ieee.org/lpdocs/epic03/wrapper.htm?arnumber=5254143

[29] N. Blum, T. Magedanz, and F. Schreiner, "The Role of Service Brokers for Composed Services in an Open Service Environment," *Telekommunikation Aktuell*, no. 01, 2008.

[30] N. Blum, T. Magedanz, F. Schreiner, and S. Wahle, "A research infrastructure for SOA-based Service Delivery Frameworks," in *2009 5th International Conference on Testbeds and Research Infrastructures for the Development of Networks & Communities and Workshops*. Ieee, 2009, pp. 1-6. [Online]. http://ieeexplore.ieee.org/lpdocs/epic03/wrapper.htm?arnumber=4976202

[31] C. Bo, Z. Yang, C. Junliang, Z. Peng, and D. Hua, "Design and Implementation of Web-Telecom Hybrid Services Bus based Execution Platform over Convergence Networks," in *IEEE Globecom 2010 Workshop on Multimedia Communications and Services*, 2010.

[32] C. Bo, Z. Yang, Z. Peng, D. Hua, H. Xiaoxiao, W. Zheng, and C. Junliang, "Development of Web-Telecom based hybrid services orchestration and execution middleware over convergence networks," *Journal of Network and Computer Applications*, vol. 33, no. 5, pp. 620-630, Sept. 2010. [Online]. http://linkinghub.elsevier.com/retrieve/pii/S1084804510000603

[33] F. Bohagen and J. Binningsbo, "HSPA and LTE âĂŞ Future-proof Mobile Broadband Solutions," *Telektronikk*, vol. 2010, no. 1, pp. 1-18, 2010.

[34] BONDI, "BONDI - Open Mobile Terminal Platform," 2011. [Online]. http://bondidev.omtp.org/default.aspx

[35] I. Bose and C. Menkens, "Identifying Requirements for Mobile Distributed Applications and Service Delivery Platforms (SDP) derived from Stakeholder Goals," Center for Digital Technology and Management, Tech. Rep., 2010.

[36] G. Brown, "LTE / SAE & the Evolved Packet Core: Technology Platforms & Implementation Choices," Heavy Reading on behalf of Alcatel-Lucent, Tech. Rep. April, 2009.

[37] R. Bruns and J. Dunkel, "Event-Driven Architecture und Complex Event Processing im Überblick," in *Event-Driven Architecture*, ser. Xpert.press. Springer Berlin Heidelberg, 2010, pp. 47-82. [Online]. http://dx.doi.org/10.1007/978-3-642-02439-9_3

[38] F. Büllingen and P. Stamm, "Entwicklungstrends im Telekommunikationssektor bis 2010," Wissenschaftliches Institut für Kommunikationsdienste, Tech. Rep., 2001.

[39] E. W. Burger, S. Rajasekar, P. O'Doherty, A. Lundqvist, and T. Grönberg, "A Telecommunications Web Services Platform for Third Party Network Access and SOA-based Service Delivery," in *Proceedings of the 2007 Workshop on Middleware for next-generation converged networks and applications - MNCNA '07*. New York, New York, USA: ACM Press, 2007, pp. 1-6. [Online]. http://portal.acm.org/citation.cfm?doid=1376878.1376888

[40] P. Calhoun, J. Loughney, and E. Guttman, "RFC3588 - Diameter Base Protocol," Sept. 2003.

[41] B. Campbell, "RFC3428 - Session Initiation Protocol (SIP) Extension for Instant Messaging," 2002.

[42] D. Chakraborty, S. Goyal, S. Mittal, and S. Mukherjea, "On the Changing Face of Service Composition in Telecom," in *MNCNA*, 2007.

[43] D. Chappell, *Enterprise Service Bus: Theory in Practice*. O'Reilly Media, 2004. [Online]. http://www.citeulike.org/group/2314/article/224708?citation_format=IEEEtran#

[44] D. Chappell, "What is Application Lifecycle Management?" Chappell and Associates, Tech. Rep., 2008.

[45] Cisco, "Cisco Unified Communication Manager," 2007.

[46] A. Collins, D. Joseph, and K. Bielaczyc, "Design Research: Theoretical and Methodological Issues," *The Journal of the Learning Sciences*, vol. 13, no. 1, pp. 15–42, 2004.

[47] A. Constantinou, "Apps is the new Web: Sowing the seeds for Web 3.0," 2011. [Online]. http://www.visionmobile.com/blog

[48] R. Copeland, "Telco App Stores - Friend or Foe ?" *IEEE*, 2010.

[49] C. Cordier and I. Douplitzky, "Orange and Web 2.0," Orange, Tech. Rep., 2008.

[50] M. Cuevas, "Telcos exposing APIs," British Telecom, Tech. Rep., 2009.

[51] R. Daher and D. Tavangarian, "Resource reservation and admission control in IEEE 802.11 WLANs," in *Proceedings of the 3rd international conference on Quality of service in heterogeneous wired/wireless networks - QShine '06*. New York, New York, USA: ACM Press, Aug. 2006, p. 4. [Online]. http://dl.acm.org/citation.cfm?id=1185373.1185379

[52] V. A. Danciu, N. gentschen Felde, D. Kranzlmüller, M. Schiffers, and J. R.Watzl, "Der Cloud-Broker: dynamische Orchestrierung von Cloud-Diensten zu SmartMobile Apps," in *Smart Mobile Apps*, ser. Xpert.press, S. Verclas and C. Linnhoff-Popien, Eds. Berlin, Heidelberg: Springer Berlin Heidelberg, 2011, ch. 23. [Online]. http://www.springerlink.com/index/10.1007/978-3-642-22259-7

[53] J. Davidson and J. Peters, *Voice over IP Fundamentals*. Cisco Press, 2004.

[54] F. Deinert, A. Murarasu, A. Bachmann, and T. Magedanz, "A Base Solution for Exposing IMS Telecommunication Services to Web 2.0 Enabled Applications," in *Mobilware, LNICST 0007*, 2009, pp. 1–14.

[55] Detecon, "Future Telco Service Architecture Market Analysis," Deutsche Telekom Laboratories, Tech. Rep., 2010.

[56] Deutsche Telekom AG, "Developer Garden," 2010. [Online]. http://www.developergarden.com

[57] Deutsche Telekom Laboratories, "ISA - Towards an Integrative Service Architecture for Telcos," Tech. Rep., 2009.

[58] Deutsche Telekom Laboratories, "Connected Life and Work," Tech. Rep., 2010.

[59] P. Dornbusch, U. Sandner, P. Sties, and M. Zündt, "Fixed Mobile Convergence," Center for Digital Technology and Management, Tech. Rep., 2005.

[60] E. Drosos, "3rd Party Enabling - Integration von Telekom Services in offene Dienste- und Anwendungswelten," Deutsche Telekom AG, Tech. Rep., 2010.

[61] M. Eisele and M. Pizka, "SOA Report - State of the Art Service-Orientierter Architekturen," MSG Systems AG, Tech. Rep., 2007.

[62] M. El-Sayyad, C. Menkens, and K. Diepold, "Evaluating Cross-Platform Frameworks Based on Identified Requirements for Mobile Platforms," Center for Digital Technology and Management, Tech. Rep., 2011.

[63] S. El-Sayyad, C. Menkens, and K. Diepold, "Identifying Requirements for Service Delivery Platforms (SDP) Derived from Stakeholder Goals," Center for Digital Technology and Management, Tech. Rep., 2011.

[64] M. Ergen, "Basics of All-IP Networking," in *Mobile Broadband: Including WiMAX and LTE*. Boston, MA: Springer US, 2009, pp. 67–105. [Online]. http://www.springerlink.com/index/10.1007/978-0-387-68192-4

[65] Ericsson, "Evolved Packet Core," Tech. Rep.

[66] T. Erl, *Service-Oriented Architecture (SOA): Concepts, Technology, and Design*. Prentice Hall, 2005.

[67] T. Erl, *SOA: Principles of Service Design*, 1st ed. Upper Saddle River, NJ, USA: Prentice Hall Press, 2007.

[68] T. Erl, *SOA Design Patterns*, 1st ed. Upper Saddle River, NJ, USA: Prentice Hall PTR, 2009.

[69] P. Farley and M. Capp, "Mobile Web Services," *BT Technology Journal*, vol. 23, no. 3, pp. 202–213, July 2005. [Online]. http://www.springerlink.com/index/10.1007/s10550-005-0042-1

[70] R. T. Fielding, "Architectural Styles and the Design of Network-based Software Architectures," PhD Thesis, University of California, Irvine, 2000. [Online]. http://www.ics.uci.edu/~fielding/pubs/dissertation/top.htm

[71] R. T. Fielding, J. Gettys, J. Mogul, H. Frystyk, L. Masinter, P. Leach, and T. Berners-Lee, "RFC2616 - Hypertext Transfer Protocol - (HTTP) 1.1," Tech. Rep., 1999. [Online]. http://www.w3.org/Protocols/rfc2616/rfc2616.html

[72] France Telecom SA Orange, "Orange Partner," 2010. [Online]. http://www.orangepartner.com

[73] Fraunhofer FOKUS, "The Open Source IMS Core Project," 2011. [Online]. http://www.openimscore.org

[74] A. Friedl, C. Menkens, and M. Broy, "Design and Implementation of Cross-Plattform Compatible Web-Telecom-Converged End User Applications," Center for Digital Technology and Management, Tech. Rep., 2011.

[75] J. Garrett, "Ajax: A New Approach to Web Applications." [Online]. http://www.adaptivepath.com/ideas/e000385

[76] C. Gbaguidi, J.-P. Hubaux, M. Hamdi, and A. Tantawi, "A programmable architecture for the provision of hybrid services," *IEEE Communications Magazine*, vol. 37, no. 7, pp. 110–116, July 1999. [Online]. http://ieeexplore.ieee.org/lpdocs/epic03/wrapper.htm?arnumber=774889

[77] GigaOM, "The Apple App Store Economy," 2010. [Online]. http://gigaom.com/2010/01/12/the-apple-app-store-economy/

[78] Global System for Mobile Communication (GSMA), "High Speed Packed Access (HSPA)," 2007.

[79] Google, "Android," 2010. [Online]. http://developer.android.com/

[80] Google, "Google Apps Marketplace," 2011. [Online]. www.google.com/enterprise/marketplace/

[81] Google GmbH, TNS Infratest GmbH, Otto Group, and Trend Büro, "Smartphone Nutzung 2012," Tech. Rep., 2011.

[82] J. Graf, "Es wird keine dauerhafte Appconomy geben," pp. 2–7, 2010.

[83] P. Gutheim, R. Ermecke, C. Menkens, and A. Picot, "Evaluation of Business Enablers in the Telecommunication Industry: Applying a Software Quality Function Deployment Model," Center for Digital Technology and Management, Tech. Rep., 2009.

[84] A. Hammershoj, A. Sapuppo, and R. Tadayoni, "Challenges for Mobile Application Development," *IEEE*, 2010.

[85] H. Hannu, R. Price, and Z. Liu, "RFC3321 - Signaling Compression (SigComp) - Extended Operations," 2003.

[86] F. Hartwig, "LTE VoIP Service," Swisscom, Tech. Rep., 2009.

[87] A. R. Hevner, S. T. March, J. Park, and S. Ram, "Design Science in Information Systems Research," *MIS Quarterly*, vol. 28, no. 1, pp. 77–105, 2004.

[88] Hewlett Packard, "A new approach to value-added services," Tech. Rep., 2010.

[89] R. Hofstetter and R. Tanner, "Das Core-Netzwerk von LTE," *SEV Bulletin*, no. 21, pp. 22–25, 2008.

[90] A. Holzer and J. Ondrus, "Trends in Mobile Application Development," in *Mobilware 2009 Workshops*, 2009, pp. 55–64.

[91] P. Hoschka, "Mobile Web 2.0," W3C, Tech. Rep., 2010.

[92] D. Hunor and S. Tarkoma, "SPICE Unified Architecture," Nokia Siemens Networks, Tech. Rep., 2007.

[93] Hunor Demeter, "Mobile Service Platforms âĂŞ Architecture Whitepaper," SPICE, Tech. Rep. March, 2008.

[94] J. a. Hurtado, F. O. Martinez, O. M. Caicedo, and O. R. Rojas, "A SIP Based Next Generation Services Platform," in *International Conference on Mobile Ubiquitous Computing, Systems, Services and Technologies (UBICOMM'07)*. Ieee, Nov. 2007, pp. 160–165. [Online]. http://ieeexplore.ieee.org/lpdocs/epic03/wrapper.htm?arnumber=4402822

[95] IBM, "IBM Mashup Center," 2011. [Online]. http://www-01.ibm.com/software/info/mashup-center/

[96] Institute of Electrical and Electronics Engineers (IEEE), "802.16 (WIMAX)," 2007.

[97] International Organization for Standardization (ISO) and Open Systems Interconnection (OSI), "Basic Reference Model," International Organization for Standardization (ISO), Open Systems Interconnection (OSI), Tech. Rep., 1994.

[98] International Telecommunication Union (ITU), "Proposed Definition and Description of IPTV services for IPTV service scenario," International Telecommunication Union (ITU), Tech. Rep., 2006.

[99] International Telecommunication Union (ITU), "Confronting the CRISIS - Its Impact on the ICT Industry," Tech. Rep., 2009.

[100] International Telecommunication Union (ITU), "Very high speed digital subscriber line transceivers (VDSL)," 2010. [Online]. http://www.itu.int/rec/T-REC-G.993.1/en

[101] Internet Engineering Task Force (IETF), "RFC1889 - RTP: A Transport Protocol for Real-Time Applications," 1996.

[102] Internet Engineering Task Force (IETF), "RFC3992 - MGCP Media Gateway Control Protocol," 2005.

[103] M. A. Janson and L. D. Smith, "Prototyping For Systems Development: A Critical Appraisal," *MIS Quarterly*, vol. 9, no. 4, pp. 305–316, 1985.

[104] JBoss Mobicents, "Mobicents XML Document Management Server," 2011. [Online]. http://hudson.jboss.org/hudson/view/Mobicents

[105] G. Jie, C. Bo, C. Junliang, and Z. Lei, "A Template-Based Orchestration Framework for Hybrid Services," in *2008 Fourth Advanced International Conference on Telecommunications*. Ieee, June 2008, pp. 315–320. [Online]. http://ieeexplore.ieee.org/lpdocs/epic03/wrapper.htm?arnumber=4545547

[106] B. M. Johnson, "The Paradox of Design Research," in *Design Research: Methods and Perspectives*. MIT Press, 2003.

[107] E. Kayser, "Agile IMS Service Composition âĂŞ How to Quicker Respond to New Market Demand," in *ICIN*, 2009.

[108] M. Keen, A. Acharya, S. Bishop, A. Hopkins, S. Milinski, C. Nott, R. Robinson, J. Adams, and P. Verschueren, *Patterns : Implementing an SOA Using an Enterprise Service Bus*. IBM, 2004.

[109] W. Kellerer, "Serverarchitektur zur netzunabhängigen Dienststeuerung in heterogenen Kommunikationsnetzen," PhD Thesis, Technische Universitaet Muenchen, 2002.

[110] W. Kellerer, "Mobile Service Platforms," in *4G Technologies - Services with Initiative*. Wiley Publishing, 2008, pp. 1–36.

[111] W. Kellerer and S. Arbanowski, "Advances in Service Platform Technologies For Next-Generation Mobile Systems," *IEEE Communications Magazine*, no. August, 2006.

[112] F. Keuper, C. Oecking, and A. Degenhardt, *Application Management. Challenges - Service Creation - Strategies*. Gabler Verlag, 2011.

[113] K. Kimbler, "Moriana on SDP 2.0 Service Delivery Platforms - Definition and Evolution," 2010. [Online]. http://www.morianagroup.com/

[114] K. Kimbler, "App Store Strategies for Service Providers," *IEEE*, pp. 1–5, 2010.

[115] M. Knoll, "Handbuch der Software-Architektur," *WIRTSCHAFTSINFORMATIK*, vol. 48, no. 6, p. 454, 2006. [Online]. http://dx.doi.org/10.1007/s11576-006-0105-z

[116] S. Koebler, "Die Nutzer von Apps: Nutzertypen , Nutzungsverhalten , Usability , Zahlungsbereitschaft," Comscore, Tech. Rep., 2011.

[117] P. Kruchten, *The Rational Unified Process: An Introduction*. Addison-Wesley Professional, 2000.

[118] I. Krueger, M. Meisinger, M. Menarini, and S. Pasco, "Rapid Systems of Systems Integration - Combining an Architecture-Centric Approach with Enterprise Service Bus Infrastructure," *2006 IEEE International Conference on Information Reuse & Integration*, pp. 51–56, Sept. 2006. [Online]. http://ieeexplore.ieee.org/lpdocs/epic03/wrapper.htm?arnumber=4018464

[119] D. Krüger, "T-Labs Project Web X.0 Enabler Commercialization. The Essence of Enabling," Deutsche Telekom Laboratories, Tech. Rep., 2010.

[120] N. Kryvinska, C. Strauss, B. Collini-Nocker, and P. Zinterhof, "A Scenario of Service-Oriented Principles Adaptation to the Telecom Providers Service Delivery Platform," in *2010 Fifth International Conference on Software Engineering Advances*. Ieee, Aug. 2010, pp. 265–271. [Online]. http://ieeexplore.ieee.org/lpdocs/epic03/wrapper.htm?arnumber=5615724

[121] C. C. Le and C. Menkens, "Analyzing Development Platforms and Technologies for Mobile Applications," Center for Digital Technology and Management, Tech. Rep., 2012.

[122] H.-Y. Lee, R. Chen, and Y.-B. Lin, "An Internet-Mobile Platform for NGN/IMS Applications," in *2010 IEEE 7th International Conference on E-Business Engineering*. Ieee, Nov. 2010, pp. 364–368. [Online]. http://ieeexplore.ieee.org/lpdocs/epic03/wrapper.htm?arnumber=5704341

[123] W. Lemstra, G.-J. D. Leeuw, E. V. D. Kar, and P. Brand, "Just Another Distribution Channel?" in *Mobilware 2009 Workshops*, 2009, pp. 1–12.

[124] P. Lescuyer and T. Lucidarme, *Evolved packet system (EPS): The LTE and SAE evolution of 3G UMTS*. John Wiley and Sons, 2008. [Online]. http://books.google.com/books?id=gXAuo6c72nkC&pgis=1

[125] T. Li, C. Menkens, and M. Broy, "Comparison of Service-Oriented Architectures and existing Architectures for Telecommunication Services in an Open Telecommunication-Infrastructure," Center for Digital Technology and Management, Tech. Rep., 2009.

[126] J. Lind, "Platform X: How cross-platform tools can end the OS wars," VisionMobile, Tech. Rep., 2011.

[127] H. Lofthouse, M. J. Yates, and R. Stretch, "Parlay X Web Services," *BT Technology Journal*, vol. 22, no. 1, pp. 81–86, 2004.

[128] M.-L. Lorenz, C. Menkens, J. Suß mann, and N. Konrad, "Developer Platforms and Communities in the Telecom," Center for Digital Technology and Management, Tech. Rep., 2010.

[129] D. Lozano, L. A. Galindo, and L. García, "WIMS 2.0: Converging IMS and Web 2.0. Designing REST APIs for the Exposure of Session-Based IMS Capabilities," in *2008 The Second International Conference on Next Generation Mobile Applications, Services, and Technologies*. Ieee, 2008, pp. 18–24. [Online]. http://ieeexplore.ieee.org/lpdocs/epic03/wrapper.htm?arnumber=4756408

[130] Z. Lozinski, "IMS and the Service Delivery Platform meet Web 2 . 0," IBM, Tech. Rep., 2007.

[131] D. C. Luckham, *The Power of Events: An Introduction to Complex Event Processing in Distributed Enterprise Systems*. Boston, MA, USA: Addison-Wesley Longman Publishing Co., Inc., 2001.

[132] T. Magedanz, N. Blum, and S. Dutkowski, "Evolution of SOA Concepts in Telecommunications," *Computer*, vol. 40, no. 11, pp. 46–50, Nov. 2007. [Online]. http://ieeexplore.ieee.org/lpdocs/epic03/wrapper.htm?arnumber=4385256

[133] T. Magedanz, N. Blum, and S. Dutkowski, "Evolution of SOA Concepts in Telecommunications," *Computer*, vol. 40, no. 11, pp. 46–50, Nov. 2007. [Online]. http://ieeexplore.ieee.org/lpdocs/epic03/wrapper.htm?arnumber=4385256

[134] T. Magedanz, N. Blum, L. Lange, and A. Blotny, "Agile Dienstkomposition für einen konvergierenden Web-Telco-Markt," Fraunhofer FOKUS, Tech. Rep., 2010.

[135] T. Magedanz, E.-J. Steffens, N. Blum, L. Lange, and A. Blotny, "Platform Enabled Resource Collaboration between Service Providers," Fraunhofer FOKUS, Tech. Rep., 2010.

[136] J.-L. Marechaux, "Combining Service-Oriented Architecture and Event-Driven Architecture using an Enterprise Service Bus," IBM, Tech. Rep. April, 2006.

[137] A. Margara and G. Cugola, "Processing flows of information: from data stream to complex event processing," in *Proceedings of the 5th ACM international conference on Distributed event-based system*, ser. DEBS '11. New York, NY, USA: ACM, 2011, pp. 359–360. [Online]. http://doi.acm.org/10.1145/2002259.2002307

[138] R. Martin, *Agile Software Development - Principles, Patterns, and Practices*. Prentice Hall, 2002.

[139] F. Menge, "Enterprise Service Bus," in *Free and Open Source Conference*, 2007.

[140] D. Messerschmitt, "The convergence of telecommunications and computing: what are the implications today?" *Proceedings of the IEEE*, vol. 84, no. 8, pp. 1167–1186, 1996. [Online]. http://ieeexplore.ieee.org/lpdocs/epic03/wrapper.htm?arnumber=533962

[141] B. M. Michelson, "Event-Driven Architecture Overview - Event-Driven SOA Is Just Part of the EDA Story," Patricia Seybold Group, Tech. Rep., 2006.

[142] Microsoft, "Service Delivery Broker," Tech. Rep., 2010.

[143] Microsoft, "Windows Phone 7," 2010. [Online]. http://www.windowsphone7series.com/

[144] C. Mims, "Das Comeback des mobilen Web," *Technology Review*, 2011.

[145] MJSIP, "A Complete Java-based Implementation of a SIP Stack," 2010. [Online]. http://mjsip.org/

[146] S. Moro, S. Bouat, M.-P. Odini, and J. O. Connell, "Service Composition with Real Time Services," in *ICIN*, 2008.

[147] Motorola, "Long Term Evolution (LTE): A Technical Overview," Tech. Rep., 2007.

[148] P. Mottishaw, "Next Generation Service Delivery Platforms," Hewlett Packard, Tech. Rep. September, 2009.

[149] R. Mullins, F. Mahon, C. Kuhmuench, M. Crotty, J. Mitic, and T. Pfeifer, "Daidalos : A Platform for Facilitating Pervasive Services," in *IEEE Pervasive Computing*, vol. 207, 2006, pp. 7–10.

[150] Münchner Kreis eV, Deutsche Telekom AG, TNS Infratest GmbH, and EICT GmbH, "Zukunft & Zukunftsfähigkeit der deutschen Informations- und Kommunikationstechnologie," Tech. Rep., 2008.

[151] Münchner Kreis eV, EICT GmbH, Deutsche Telekom AG, TNS Infratest GmbH, Siemens AG, Vodafone D2 GmbH, SAP AG, Telefonica O2 Germany, and Zweites Deutsches Fernsehen, "Offen für die Zukunft âĂŞ Offen in die Zukunft. Kompetenz , Sicherheit und neue Geschäftsfelder," Tech. Rep., 2010.

[152] C. Murillo, C. Menkens, and M. Morisio, "Requirements Analysis of a New Service Delivery Platform in the Evolved Telecommunications Market," Center for Digital Technology and Management, Tech. Rep., 2011.

[153] P. Nepper and N. Konrad, "The Future of the Web and its Value Creation for Telcos," Center for Digital Technology and Management, Tech. Rep., 2009.

[154] Nicolai Josuttis, *SOA in der Praxis*. DPunkt, 2008. [Online]. http://dpunkt.de/buecher/2734.html

[155] J. Niemöller, E. Freiter, K. Vandikas, R. Quinet, R. Levenshteyn, and I. Fikouras, "Composition in Converged Service Networks: Requirements and Solutions," Ericsson Corporate Research, Tech. Rep., 2009.

[156] Nokia, "Service Delivery Platforms, Tech. Rep. 3, Mar. 2007. [Online]. http://ieeexplore.ieee.org/lpdocs/epic03/wrapper.htm?arnumber=4150578

[157] Oasis, "Web Service Business Process Execution Language," 2011. [Online]. http://www.oasis-open.org/committees/tc_home.php?wg_abbrev=wsbpel

[158] H. Ohnishi, Y. Yamato, M. Kaneko, T. Moriya, M. Hirano, and H. Sunaga, "Service Delivery Platform for Telecom-Enterprise-Internet Combined Services," in *IEEE GLOBECOM 2007-2007 IEEE Global Telecommunications Conference*. Ieee, Nov. 2007, pp. 108–112. [Online]. http://ieeexplore.ieee.org/lpdocs/epic03/wrapper.htm?arnumber=4410938

[159] OIPF, "Open IPTV Forum," 2012. [Online]. http://www.oipf.org/index.html

[160] M. Olsson, S. Sultana, S. Rommer, L. Frid, and C. Mulligan, *SAE and the Evolved Packet Core - Driving the Mobile Broadband Revolution*. Academic Press, 2009.

[161] Open Mobile Alliance (OMA), "OMA Web Services Enabler (OWSER): Core Specifications," Tech. Rep., 2006.

[162] Open Mobile Alliance (OMA), "OMA Device Management Bootstrap," Tech. Rep., 2008.

[163] Open Mobile Alliance (OMA), "OMA Service Environment (OSE)," Tech. Rep., 2008.

[164] Open Mobile Alliance (OMA), "Parlay in OSE Architecture," Tech. Rep., 2008.

[165] Open Mobile Alliance (OMA), "Policy Evaluation, Enforcement and Management Architecture," Tech. Rep., 2008.

[166] Open Mobile Alliance (OMA), "SCOMO Architecture," Tech. Rep., 2008.

[167] Open Mobile Alliance (OMA), "Client Provisioning Architecture," Tech. Rep., 2009.

[168] Open Mobile Alliance (OMA), "OMA Service Provider Environment Architecture," Tech. Rep., 2009.

[169] Open Mobile Alliance (OMA), "Converged Address Book (CAB) Specification," Tech. Rep., 2010.

[170] Open Mobile Alliance (OMA), "OMA Enabler Releases," 2010. [Online]. http://www.openmobilealliance.org/Technical/current_releases.aspx

[171] Open Mobile Alliance (OMA), "OMA Mobile Broadcast Service," 2010. [Online]. http://www.openmobilealliance.org/Technical/release_program/bcast_v1_1.aspx

[172] Open Mobile Alliance (OMA), "SACMO Architecture," Tech. Rep., 2010.

[173] Open Mobile Alliance (OMA), "Mobile Application Environment Specification," Tech. Rep., 2011.

[174] Open Mobile Alliance (OMA), "OMA Browsing," 2011. [Online]. http://www.openmobilealliance.org/Technical/release_program/browsing_v2_1.aspx

[175] Open Mobile Alliance (OMA), "OMA Global Service Architecture Overview," Tech. Rep., 2011.

[176] T. O'Reilly, "What Is Web 2.0," pp. 0–48, 2005. [Online]. http://oreilly.com/web2/archive/what-is-web-20.html

[177] OSGi Alliance, "The OSGi Service Platform," 2011. [Online]. http://www.osgi.org/Main/HomePage

[178] M. P. Papazoglou and W.-J. Heuvel, "Service oriented architectures: approaches, technologies and research issues," *The VLDB Journal*, vol. 16, no. 3, pp. 389–415, Mar. 2007. [Online]. http://www.springerlink.com/index/10.1007/s00778-007-0044-3

[179] Parlay, "Applying SOA to Telecom Service Creation and Deployment, Tech. Rep. October, 2005.

[180] C. Pautasso, F. Leymann, and O. Zimmermann, "RESTful Web Services vs. Big Web Services: Making the Right Architectural Decision," in *ACM WWW 2008 - Web Engineering - Web Service Deployment*, 2008, pp. 805–814.

[181] PJSIP, "Open Source SIP Stack and Media Stack for Presence, Instant Messaging, and Multimedia Communication," 2010. [Online]. http://www.pjsip.org/

[182] T. Pollet, G. Maas, J. Marien, and A. Wambecq, "Telecom Services Delivery in a SOA," in *20th International Conference on Advanced Information Networking and Applications - Volume 1 (AINA'06)*. Ieee, 2006, pp. 529–533. [Online]. http://ieeexplore.ieee.org/lpdocs/epic03/wrapper.htm?arnumber=1620434

[183] R. Price, C. Bormann, and H. Hannu, "RFC3320 - Signaling Compression (SigComp)," 2003.

[184] QuEST Forum, "The Telecom Quality Management System," 1998. [Online]. http://www.tl9000.org/

[185] T. Raby, "OMTP âĂŞ Who Are We and BONDI," OMTP, Tech. Rep. November, 2009.

[186] R. Riemer, "LTE-Grundlagen - LTE-Tutorial," 2009. [Online]. www.umtslink.at/content/lte-grundlagen-teil-1-278.html

[187] C. Rigney, S. Willens, and A. Rubens, "RFC2865 - Remote Authentication Dial In User Service (RADIUS)," 2000.

[188] J. Rosenberg, "RFC3856 - A Presence Event Package for the Session Initiation Protocol (SIP)," Aug. 2004.

[189] J. Rosenberg, "RFC4825 - The Extensible Markup Language (XML) Configuration Access Protocol (XCAP)," IETF, Tech. Rep., 2007.

[190] J. Rosenberg, H. Schulzrinne, G. Camarillo, A. Johnston, J. Peterson, R. Sparks, M. Handley, and E. Schooler, "RFC3261 - Session Initiation Protocol (SIP)," Tech. Rep., 2002. [Online]. http://www.ietf.org/rfc/rfc3261.txt

[191] M. Schaer, "Open Service Infrastructures," Sunrise, Tech. Rep., 2009.

[192] H. Schmidt, "Apps sind ein Übergangsphänomen," pp. 6–11, 2010.

[193] T. Schwabe, "Challenges of LTE and EPC Introduction," Telefonica O2 Germany, Tech. Rep., 2010.

[194] E. Scotto, H. Grusdt, and M. Lott, "TV-Web-Telco Integration: The Next Convergence Frontier," Nokia Siemens Networks, Tech. Rep., 2011.

[195] X. Shao, T. Y. Chai, T. K. Lee, L. H. Ngoh, L. Zhou, and M. Kirchberg, "An Integrated Telecom and IT Service Delivery Platform," in *2008 IEEE Asia-Pacific Services Computing Conference*. Ieee, Dec. 2008, pp. 391–396. [Online]. http://ieeexplore.ieee.org/lpdocs/epic03/wrapper.htm?arnumber=4780706

[196] J. Shen, Q. Tian, X. Chen, C. Ying, and K. Chen, "An Asset-Based Architecture Design Methodology for Rapid Telecom Service Delivery Platform Development," *Australian Software Engineering Conference (ASWEC'07)*, pp. 7–16, Apr. 2007. [Online]. http://ieeexplore.ieee.org/lpdocs/epic03/wrapper.htm?arnumber=4159654

[197] Siemens AG, "IMS Introduction for Developers," 2006.

[198] J. Sienel, A. L. Martín, C. B. Zorita, and B. C. Martínez, "OPUCE : A Telco-Driven Service Mash-Up Approach," *Bell Labs Technical Journal*, vol. 14, no. 1, pp. 203–218, 2009.

[199] M. Sillen and J. Nordlund, "Real-Time Audio Streaming in a Mobile Environment using J2ME," 2005.

[200] H. A. Simon, "The Sciences of the Artificial," *The MIT Press*, 1996.

[201] I. Singh, B. Stearns, and M. Johnson, *Designing Enterprise Applications with the J2EE Platform*. Addison-Wesley Longman Publishing Co., Inc., Apr. 2002.

[202] Software and Information Industry Association, "Software as a Service : Strategic Backgrounder, Tech. Rep. February, 2001.

[203] Software Engineering Standards Committee, "Standards for a Software Quality Metrics Methodology," IEEE, Tech. Rep., 2005.

[204] I. Sommerville, *Software Engineering*. Addison- Wesley Professional, 2000.

[205] G. Starke and S. Tilkov, *SOA-Expertenwissen: Methoden, Konzepte und Praxis Serviceorientierter Architekturen*. DPunkt Verlag, 2007. [Online]. http://www.amazon.com/SOA-Expertenwissen/dp/3898644375

[206] E.-J. Steffens, J. Heuer, and H. Arnold, "ISA âĂŞ Towards an Integrative Service Architecture for Telcos," *PIK - Praxis der Informationsverarbeitung und Kommunikation*, vol. 33, no. 1, pp. 3–6, Jan. 2010. [Online]. http://www.reference-global.com/doi/abs/10.1515/piko.2010.002

[207] H. Stein and N. Blum, "Service Broker for 3 Party Enabling," Deutsche Telekom Laboratories, Tech. Rep. 5, 2009.

[208] STL Partners Telco 2.0, "Voice & Messaging - A survey of operators and vendors across the Telco industry," Tech. Rep., 2008.

[209] K. Subramanian, "Microsoft Kills Yahoo Pipes Competitor," Tech. Rep., 2011.

[210] A. Sur, F. Schaffa, J. McIntyre, J. Nogima, M. Alexander, and P. Dettori, "Extending the Service Bus for Successful and Sustainable IPTV Services," *IEEE Communications Magazine*, vol. 46, no. 8, pp. 96–103, Aug. 2008. [Online]. http://ieeexplore.ieee.org/lpdocs/epic03/wrapper.htm?arnumber=4597111

[211] S. Tarkoma, J. Rovira, E. Postmann, H. Rajasekaran, and E. Kovacs, "Creating Converged Services for IMS Using the SPICE Service Platform," Nokia Siemens Networks, Tech. Rep.

[212] The 3rd Generation Partnership Project (3GPP), "Location Services (LCS) (Release 7) - 3GPP TS 22.071 V7.4.0," The 3rd Generation Partnership Project (3GPP), Tech. Rep., 2005.

[213] The 3rd Generation Partnership Project (3GPP), "IP Multimedia Subsystem (IMS) (Release 7)," Apr. 2006.

[214] The 3rd Generation Partnership Project (3GPP), "Open Service Access (OSA) Parlay X Web Services," 2008. [Online]. http://www.3gpp.org/ftp/Specs/html-info/29-series.htm

[215] The 3rd Generation Partnership Project (3GPP), "General Packet Radio Service (GPRS) - Enhanced Data Rates for GSM Evolution (EDGE)," 2010. [Online]. http://www.3gpp.org/article/gprs-edge

[216] The 3rd Generation Partnership Project (3GPP), "Universal Mobile Telecommunications System (UMTS)," 2010. [Online]. http://www.3gpp.org/article/umts

[217] The 3rd Generation Partnership Project (3GPP), "The 3rd Generation Partnership Project (3GPP)," 2011. [Online]. http://www.3gpp.org/

[218] The Linux Foundation, "Linux," 2010. [Online]. http://www.linuxfoundation.org/

[219] The Linux Foundation, "MeeGo OS," 2010. [Online]. http://meego.com/

[220] The Symbian Foundation, "Symbian OS," 2010. [Online]. http://www.symbian.org/

[221] TM Forum, "TR141 - SDF - Industry Groups Positioning Document," TM Forum, Tech. Rep., 2008.

[222] TM Forum, "TMF061 - Service Delivery Framework Reference Architecture," TM Forum, Tech. Rep., 2009.

[223] I. Todoran, C. Menkens, and H. Saikkonen, "Semi-Automatic Service Integration of Telecom and Internet Services in a Service Delivery Platform," Center for Digital Technology and Management, Tech. Rep., 2011.

[224] G. Trickey, "OneAPI : Simplifying Cross-Network Development," GSMA, Tech. Rep. November, 2009.

[225] M. Tsietsi, A. Terzoli, and G. Wells, "Towards Service Capability Interaction Management in IMS Networks," Rhodes University, Tech. Rep., 2008.

[226] K. Tutschku, "Mobile Service Evolution and Research Trends in Future Internet Chair of," Universität Wien, Tech. Rep., 2011.

[227] Ubiquity, "Applying SOA Principals In Developing Advanced Telecom Applications," Ubiquity, Tech. Rep., 2006.

[228] University of Southern California - Information Sciences Institute (USC), "RFC791 - Internet Protocol," Sept. 1981.

[229] M. Vakulenko, "The mobile services landscape: Can OEMs compete with platform vendors?" VisionMobile, Tech. Rep., 2011.

[230] K. Vandikas, E. Freiter, R. Levenshteyn, R. Quinet, J. Niemöller, and I. Fikouras, "Blending the Telecommunication Domain with Web 2.0 Services," in *IEEE*, 2010.

[231] VisionMobile, "Developer Economics 2011 - How Developers and Brands are Making Mones in the Mobile App Economy," Tech. Rep., 2011.

[232] VisionMobile, "Market Maps, Tech. Rep. April, 2011.

[233] VisionMobile, "Mobile Platforms: The Clash of Ecosystems," Tech. Rep., 2011.

[234] Vodafone RnD Labs, "Beta Vine." [Online]. http://www.betavine.net

[235] WAC, "Wholesale Applications Community," 2011. [Online]. http://www.wacapps.net

[236] J. G. Waclawsky, "IMS: A Critique Of The Grand Plan," *BUSINESS COMMUNICATIONS REVIEW*, Aug. 2005.

[237] J. G. Waclawsky, "At The Network âĂŹ s Edge," *Business Communications Review*, pp. 30–35, 2007.

[238] T. Wilde and T. Hess, "Forschungsmethoden der Wirtschaftsinformatik: Eine empirische Untersuchung," *Wirtschaftsinformatik*, vol. 49, no. 4, pp. 280–287, 2007.

[239] S. Wolak and G. Gajigas, "BetaVine - Open Beta Test Platform," Vodafone Group RnD Lab, Tech. Rep. June, 2008.

[240] World Wide Web Consortium, "Hypertext Markup Language (HTML)." [Online]. http://www.w3.org/html/wg/

[241] World Wide Web Consortium, "Simple Object Access Protocol (SOAP) Specifications," 2010. [Online]. http://www.w3.org/TR/soap/

[242] World Wide Web Consortium, "Web of Services," 2010. [Online]. http://www.w3.org/standards/webofservices/

[243] World Wide Web Consortium, "Web Service Choreography Interface," 2010. [Online]. http://www.w3.org/TR/wsci/

[244] World Wide Web Consortium, "Web Service Description Language (WSDL)," 2010. [Online]. http://www.w3.org/TR/wsdl

[245] World Wide Web Consortium, "Web Services Architecture," 2010. [Online]. http://www.w3.org/TR/ws-arch/#whatis

[246] World Wide Web Consortium, "Web Services Glossary," 2010. [Online]. http://www.w3.org/TR/ws-gloss/#defs

[247] World Wide Web Consortium, "Hypertext Markup Language (HTML) 5," 2011. [Online]. http://dev.w3.org/html5/spec/Overview.html

[248] J. Yang and H. Park, "A Design of Open Service Access Gateway for Converged Web Service," in *2008 10th International Conference on Advanced Communication Technology*. Ieee, Feb. 2008, pp. 1807–1810. [Online]. http://ieeexplore.ieee.org/lpdocs/epic03/wrapper.htm?arnumber=4494135

[249] J. Yu, B. Benatallah, F. Casati, and F. Daniel, "Understanding Mashup Development," *IEEE Internet Computing*, vol. 12, no. 5, pp. 44–52, Sept. 2008. [Online]. http://ieeexplore.ieee.org/lpdocs/epic03/wrapper.htm?arnumber=4620093

[250] L.-J. Zhang and J. M., "The Next Big Thing: Web Services Collaboration," in *Lecture Notes on Computer Science 2853*. Springer, 2003, pp. 1–10.

[251] L.-J. Zhang, J. Zhang, and H. Cai, *Services Computing*. Springer, 2007.

[252] L. Zhang, D. Estrin, S. Berson, S. Herzog, and S. Jamin, "Resource ReSerVation Protocol (RSVP)," IETF, Tech. Rep., 1997. [Online]. http://tools.ietf.org/html/rfc2205

[253] Y. C. Zhou, L. Xue, X. P. Liu, X. N. Wang, X. X. Liang, and C. H. Sun, "Service Storm: A Self-Service Telecommunication Service Delivery Platform with Platform-as-a-Service Technology," in *2010 6th World Congress on Services*. Ieee, July 2010, pp. 8–15. [Online]. http://ieeexplore.ieee.org/lpdocs/epic03/wrapper.htm?arnumber=5575613

i want morebooks!

Buy your books fast and straightforward online - at one of world's fastest growing online book stores! Environmentally sound due to Print-on-Demand technologies.

Buy your books online at

www.get-morebooks.com

Kaufen Sie Ihre Bücher schnell und unkompliziert online – auf einer der am schnellsten wachsenden Buchhandelsplattformen weltweit! Dank Print-On-Demand umwelt- und ressourcenschonend produziert.

Bücher schneller online kaufen

www.morebooks.de

VDM Verlagsservicegesellschaft mbH
Heinrich-Böcking-Str. 6-8   Telefon: +49 681 3720 174   info@vdm-vsg.de
D - 66121 Saarbrücken   Telefax: +49 681 3720 1749 www.vdm-vsg.de

Printed by Books on Demand GmbH, Norderstedt / Germany